Homicide Investigation

An Introduction

John J. Miletich

The Scarecrow Press, Inc.
Lanham, Maryland, and Oxford
2003

SCARECROW PRESS, INC.

Published in the United States of America
by Scarecrow Press, Inc.
A Member of the Rowman & Littlefield Publishing Group
4501 Forbes Boulevard, Suite 200, Lanham, MD 20706
www.scarecrowpress.com

PO Box 317
Oxford
OX2 9RU, UK

British Library Cataloguing in Publication Information Available

Library of Congress Cataloging-in-Publication Data

Miletich, John J.
  Homicide investigation : an introduction / John J. Miletich.
    p. cm.
  Includes bibliographical references (p.   ) and index.
  ISBN 0-8108-4625-X (hardcover : alk. paper)
  1. Homicide investigation. I. Title.
HV8079.H6M55 2003
363.25'9523—dc21

                                                        2002156160

∞™ The paper used in this publication meets the minimum requirements
of American National Standard for Information Sciences—Permanence of
Paper for Printed Library Materials, ANSI/NISO Z39.48-1992.
Manufactured in the United States of America.

To Robert A. Jago, a.k.a. "The Chameleon"

Contents

Acknowledgments

Like a successful homicide investigation, this book is the result of teamwork.

I gratefully acknowledge the contributions of staff at Scarecrow Press, particularly Kim Tabor, acquisitions editor; Andrew Yoder, production editor; and Cheryl Adam, copyeditor. Their professionalism provided the guidance that I needed from the beginning of this project to its successful conclusion.

I am grateful to Robert A. Jago, EPL2000, who provided the excellent photographs, including the photographs of the types of firearms used in homicides. MilArm Co. Ltd. was kind enough to provide for photographing all the firearms photographed in this book.

I would also like to acknowledge the efforts of other individuals and organizations: Teresa Bendall, Alberta Government Library, Seventh Street Plaza Site; Kevin Lindstrom, University of British Columbia Library; Lance Nordstrom, Workers' Compensation Board of British Columbia Library; and the Government Publications Department, University of Hawaii Library, Manoa.

I owe a special thank you to Rob Bateman, formerly with the Neil Crawford Provincial Center Library, and Gus and Soula Mitsoulas, Trojan Restaurant and Bar.

I apologize to anyone whose name I may have inadvertently omitted.

A Note to the Reader

References at the end of each section are provided in detailed alphabetical order in the bibliography beginning on page 255.

Chronology:
Forensic Science and
Criminal Investigation

The following timeline, spanning almost two centuries, illustrates significant developments in the evolution of modern-day homicide investigation.

1813   Mathieu Orfila published a treatise on poisons.
1835   Henry Goddard used bullet comparisons to apprehend a murderer.
1857   Detective unit established in New York.
1880   Henry Faulds discovered that powders could make fingerprints visible.
1892   Francis Galton published his book, *Fingerprints.*
1893   Hans Gross wrote a treatise on criminal investigation.
1901   Karl Landsteiner discovered four basic blood groups.
1904   Oskar and Rudolf Adler developed a presumptive test for blood based on benzidine.
1910   Edmond Locard established a police laboratory in Lyons, France.
1915   International Association for Criminal Identification established in Oakland, California.
1921   John Larson and Leonard Keeler designed a portable polygraph.
1923   Calvin Goddard helped invent a comparison microscope.
1932   Crime laboratory established for the Division of Investigation (later the Federal Bureau of Investigation, or FBI).
1933   Division of Investigation established a reference collection of firearms confiscated from individuals being investigated.

1937   Walter Specht developed the chemiluminescent reagent luminol as a presumptive test for blood.
1945   Frank Lundquist developed an acid phosphatase test for semen.
1948   First meeting of the American Academy of Forensic Sciences held in St. Louis, Missouri.
1950   American Academy of Forensic Sciences established in Chicago, Illinois.
1967   National Crime Information Center computer system established at the FBI.
1972   Computer system for management of fingerprint information established at the FBI.
1974   Detection of gunshot residue, using scanning electron microscopy with electron dispersive X-ray technology, developed at Aerospace Corporation.
1977   Masato Soba used Super Glue fuming to develop latent fingerprints.
1984   National Center for Analysis of Violent Crime established at FBI.
1985   Alec Jeffreys discovered DNA fingerprints.
1988   First DNA evidence used in United States in conviction of rapist Tommie Lee Andrews.
1991   Integrated Ballistics Identification System, used to compare marks on fired bullets and shell casings, developed by Walsh Automation, Inc.
1992   DRUGFIRE, a database for storing and linking unique markings left on bullets after a gun was fired, used at the FBI.
1996   Computerized searches of the Automated Fingerprint Identification System (AFIS) database introduced at the FBI.
1999   Database of footprints established by the Royal Canadian Mounted Police.

Acronyms

AA	Atomic absorption
ACLU	American Civil Liberties Union
ACUPIES	Automated Canadian–United States Police Information Exchange System
ADA	Assistant district attorney
AFIS	Automated Fingerprint Identification System
AIDS	Acquired immunodeficiency syndrome
AMW	*America's Most Wanted*
ASID	Automated Suspect Identification system
ATF	Bureau of Alcohol, Tobacco, and Firearms
BET	Break, enter, and theft
BSU	Behavioral science unit
CAD	Computer-aided design
CARS	Computer-assisted Robbery System
CCS	Cold case squad
CENTAC	Central tactical
CI	Criminal investigation
CIA	Central Intelligence Agency
CID	Criminal investigation division
CIS	Critical incident stress
CODIS	Combined DNA Index System
CPIC	Canadian Police Information Center
CSIRR	Crime Scene investigation, reporting, and reconstruction
DA	District attorney
DEA	Drug Enforcement Administration

DNA	Deoxyribonucleic acid
DOB	Date of birth
EDTA	Ethylenediaminetetraacetic acid
EDXA	Energy dispersive X-ray analysis
EPA	Environmental Protection Agency
FBI	Federal Bureau of Investigation
GC	Gas chromatography
GIS	Geographic information system
GSR	Gunshot primer residue
HCN	Hydrogen cyanide
HITMAN	Homicide Information Tracking and Management Automation Network
HITS	Homicide Investigation and Tracking System
HIU	Homicide investigation unit
HIV	Human immunodeficiency virus
IABPA	International Association of Bloodstain Pattern Analysts
IACP	International Association of Chiefs of Police
IBIS	Integrated Ballistics Identification System
KSA	Knowledge, skills, and ability
LAPD	Los Angeles Police Department
MAC	Military Armament Corporation
MDT	Mobile data terminal
ME	Medical examiner
MEDS	Mobile evidence drying station
MO	Modus operandi
MP	Military policeman
MPD	Metropolitan Police Department
MPD	Multiple personality disorder
MUP	Methylumbelliferyl phosphate
NAA	Neutron activation analysis
NAACP	National Association for the Advancement of Colored People
NCAVC	National Center for the Analysis of Violent Crime
NCIC	National Crime Information Center
NCIC 2000	National Crime Information Center 2000
NCMEC	National Center for Missing and Exploited Children
NIJ	National Institute of Justice
NIK	Narcotics identification kit
NLETS	National Law Enforcement Telecommunications System

NYPD	New York Police Department
NYSIIS	New York State Inquiry Identification System
NYSPIN	New York State Police Information Network
OPP	Ontario Provincial Police
OSS	Office of Strategic Services
PCR	Polymerase chain reaction
PIRS	Police information retrieval system
PML	Postmortem lividity
POI	Person of interest
PTSD	Post-traumatic stress disorder
QPP	Quebec Provincial Police
RCMP	Royal Canadian Mounted Police
RFLP	Restriction fragment length polymorphism
RNC	Radio network controller
SEM	Scanning electron microscope
SFPD	San Francisco Police Department
SLR	Single-lens reflex
SWAT	Special weapons and tactics
UCR	Uniform crime reporting
USPS	United States Postal Service
UV	Ultraviolet
VICAP	Violent Criminal Apprehension Program
ViCLAS	Violent Crime Linkage Analysis System
VIN	Vehicle identification number
WOLF	Warrant On-Line file

Introduction

"FOUR KING-TWENTY, 1-8-7
AT 7-8-2-5 EAST CHERRY LANE."

Long before the legendary adventures of Sherlock Holmes, "murder most horrid" was committed and investigated daily. Modern detectives, unlike Sherlock Holmes, are highly trained criminalists with scientific and technical expertise as well as extensive training in proven investigative techniques and procedures. Together, these multiple disciplines create a proficient weapon against unsolved crime.

Sherlock Holmes used deductive reasoning to solve the most intricate crimes. Today, modern police methods, coupled with the scientific disciplines of forensic pathology, ballistics, fingerprinting, and criminal profiling, are frequently required to solve homicides. Each of the scientific disciplines available to modern law enforcement professionals provides an additional tool used in establishing the motive, the means, and the opportunity; fixing the time and place; and developing a character profile of the perpetrator. Although the scientific tools are useful and often exacting, the art of deductive reasoning is still the most effective tool at the disposal of homicide detectives.

Homicide is an intriguing puzzle consisting of victims, perpetrators, detectives, and many other variables. Real-life homicide can be less "believable" than fictional accounts of homicide portrayed by Hollywood. The perpetrators of homicide, driven by jealousy, revenge, and greed, in a heated moment will resort to any type of weapon to achieve their goal. Victims of homicide often have an intimate knowledge of their assailant, or they may be completely unaware of their immanent danger. Although some homicides are planned and executed by professionals, most are committed at the spur of the moment and with no prior thought of concealing the act.

Guns, knives, and blunt objects are the most commonly used weapons to commit homicide. However, explosives, fire, drugs, acids, cars, and even concrete have been be used as murder weapons. The type of weapon, the method of use, the pattern of wounds, the victim reaction, and environmental factors are essential components of developing evidence from crime scene analysis. It can be said that the interaction between the victim and the perpetrator creates the crime scene.

It is essential for the first responder at a crime scene to understand the impetus of maintaining the integrity of the crime scene. The slightest scrap of paper, slip of clothing, thread, fiber, or footprint can lead to the identity of the perpetrator. Often, in public areas, onlookers can quickly contaminate a crime scene by introducing false evidence. It is essential for the investigators to maintain a systematic and methodic procedure to secure real evidence. Sketches, photos, and videotaping are all methods used in recording crime scene evidence. Delays in solving a crime result in repeated handling and storage of evidence at a police property room away from the crime scene. In addition, to further assess the evidence, analytical procedures are frequently conducted at private forensic laboratories, raising the need for a secure chain of evidence.

Investigators on a crime scene or en route to a crime scene use a form of verbal shorthand, known as "Ten Codes" and jargon, to communicate with other investigators, with ambulance crew, or with medical examiners. Ultra-high-frequency radio equipment, coupled with state-of-the-art, mobile data terminals and cellular telephones, are integral tools for effective communications during homicide investigation. Ten codes and jargon are used for more rapid deployment of personnel.

Contrary to Sherlock Holmes and his relentless character, detectives facing competing jurisdictions; lack of adequate funding; long and irregular hours; hostility from suspects, witnesses, and the victim's family; frustrations with inconsistent legal judgments, which often favor the perpetrator; and community and media pressures during high-profile cases all face high levels of stress, which may manifest as substance abuse, marital discord, and suicide.

In the 1960s, I began keeping mental notes on crime statistics, accumulating newspaper and magazine articles, and studying books about homicide. In the 1970s, I began conducting extensive database searches, and by the 1980s, I was regularly watching television true-crime programs. In the 1990s, I was able to add Internet searches.

Over the years, I have spoken at length with many police officers, including a sergeant with the New York Police Department (NYPD); a twenty-five-year veteran of the San Francisco Police Department (SFPD); a RCMP officer who told me about the murder of a young girl whose killer police knew but did not have enough evidence to convict in court; a former police officer who investigated serial murders in California; and a Calgary, Alberta, police officer who was resigning after ten years on the job. These off-the-record conversations are an important aspect of my research for this book.

This book, a print record of more than fifty years of accumulated information, will be of interest to true-crime readers and viewers of true-crime programs on televison. Some of the content presented in *Homicide Investigation* is not for the faint of heart.

"When your day ends, our day begins."

1

Types of Homicide

The ability to categorize a homicide into one or several types or classes is an effective tool used by modern-day homicide detectives. Often similarities will occur between one crime scene and another within a similar type of homicide classification. Most homicides will fall into at least one of more than a dozen types. For example, domestic homicide often stems from ongoing domestic violence and culminates in one or more partners carrying out a crime of passion. Underworld business disputes are frequently settled with homicide to send a message to other "wise guys." Victims of ritualistic homicide are abducted, often tortured, and murdered to promulgate cult doctrines. In the following chapter, we discuss twenty-two common topics of homicides.

1-8-7

It was shortly before 03:00 on Monday, June 13, 1994. Lieutenant John Rogers, Homicide Special Section, Los Angeles Police Department (LAPD) Robbery/Homicide Division, telephoned two of his detectives, Tom Lange and Phil Vannatter. Both detectives were at home and on call. Lieutenant Rogers told each detective about a "double."

A double meant a "double 1-8-7"—two homicides. These were the homicides of Nicole Brown Simpson and Ron Goldman.

Section 1-8-7 of the California Penal Code pertains to homicide. This supplementary code is commonly used in face-to-face conversations; in letters, memos, and reports; and in police radio and mobile data terminal (MDT) transmissions (Gates and Shah 1992; Henderson 1998; Lange, Vannatter, and Moldea 1997; Middleton 1994).

COOL CLOTHES

Cool clothes, clothes that many young people consider extremely fashionable, cost some young people their lives.

Cornell Mathis, twenty-one, a security guard, was at a suburban Washington, D.C., bus stop on a freezing day in January 1999. Mathis and a friend, seventeen, were both wearing Eddie Bauer jackets. Three young men approached and demanded the jackets. Mathis, who would not cooperate with the perpetrators, was shot dead. His friend was shot in the wrist.

Police began seeing this type of homicide in the late 1980s. Young people in the poor sections of New York City; Newark, New Jersey; Chicago, Illinois; Los Angeles, California; and other cities began to die and kill for expensive jackets, sneakers, and eyeglasses. Between 1994 and 1999, there were four homicides in Prince George's County, Maryland, linked to Eddie Bauer jackets ("The Cost" 1999; Darnton 1990).

DRUG-RELATED HOMICIDES

The perpetrators of drug-related homicides usually kill for revenge. The victims are more often than not young people. These individuals buy drugs on credit, then renege on the payment; steal drugs from a dealer; or sell drugs in a dealer's territory without permission, or with permission but without giving the dealer a percentage of the earnings, something normally agreed upon in advance. Sometimes a kidnapper kidnaps a drug dealer, kills the dealer, and then steals the dealer's drugs. This is known as a *tumbé*, a rip murder in the drug trade. Family members may be killed, either because they were targeted or were at the wrong place at the wrong time.

The crime scenes of most drug-related homicides contain drugs or drug-related paraphernalia such as syringes, scales for weighing, plastic bags, or substances used to "cut," that is, dilute, drugs in order to make more money by selling a larger amount of an inferior product. Police scanners and money-counting machines may also be present. The perpetrators ransack the crime scenes, looking for drugs, money, and weapons. Victims are often bound and killed execution-style—shot in the back of the head behind the ear and in the mouth. It is common to find evidence of torture on the bodies.

In 1976, in New York, Enrique Bermudez, a Puerto Rican drug dealer, sold an undercover police officer half an ounce of cocaine. Bermudez cooperated with authorities and received a five-year prison term. In 1981, after he was paroled, he apparently was afraid he might be murdered.

On Sunday, April 15, 1984, police came to 1080 Liberty Avenue in Brooklyn. The television in the living room was on. Dead people were seated in chairs. A woman had a bowl of pudding in one hand, a spoon in the other hand. There was a bullet hole in her mouth. A four-year-old boy was next to her, his arms stretched as if trying to reach her. He had been shot through the eye. There was a dead boy on the bed in the bedroom.

After investigators had finished counting all the victims, the total number was ten—two women and eight children. The children ranged in age from four to fourteen years. The victims in chairs looked as if they had been positioned to sit the way they were sitting when found by the murderers. There was one survivor of this murder, which came to be called "The Palm Sunday Massacre": a fifteen-month-old baby found under the bed.

Initial police reaction was that this murder was a drug deal gone bad and that the perpetrators were Colombians who, in order to teach a lesson, murdered an entire family. A special hotline was set up; police received 1,300 telephone calls. Detectives learned that Enrique Bermudez, the father of most of the murdered children, was dealing drugs and had done business with Christopher Thomas, another drug dealer. Thomas wanted more drugs from Bermudez, but Bermudez refused to give him the drugs because Thomas owed him $7,000. Thomas, who also had a record for burglary, was arrested, identified in a lineup, and charged with ten counts of murder. Thomas's rap sheet also included an arrest for raping and sodomizing his own mother (Axthelm and McDaniel 1984; Dannen 1991; Dietl and Gross 1988; Lange, Vannatter, and Moldea 1997; Rachlin 1995; Reavill 2000).

DUMP JOB

A person murdered in one location, transported to another location, and left there is a dump job. Dump jobs are common and frequently associated with drug cases. Killers favor rivers, woods, and parks as dump job sites.

When a body with multiple bullet holes or multiple stab wounds is found in a park and there is no blood trail or drag marks, it is highly probable that the body was transported in a vehicle and dumped in the park. There may be tire impressions in this type of crime.

When eighteen-year-old Jennifer Dawn Levin was found strangled in New York's Central Park in August 1986, her death initially appeared to investigators to be a dump job. After investigators found her underwear in another location in the park, and further analyzed the murder, they concluded she was killed in the park. Jennifer's murder, therefore, only looked like a dump job. She had been killed in the park by her date, twenty-year-old Robert Chambers, who claimed she had died during rough sex.

The body of twenty-six-year-old Laura Collins was found near an off-ramp of the Ventura Freeway in Los Angeles, California, on September 9, 1977. Her body had been dumped. She had been sexually molested and strangled. Ten other female victims of a serial killer had been dumped in Los Angeles by November 1977. Some serial killers and some hit men dump their victims, knowing that these victims will be easily found. Such serial killers dump their victims to taunt police. This taunting is part of a cat-and-mouse game in which the killers attempt to demonstrate that they are smarter than the police. Hit men who dump their victims, knowing that the victims will be easily found, send a message to anyone who might consider breaking underworld rules. Those individuals who break the rules will be murdered. On the other hand, some husbands or boyfriends dump the body of a wife or girlfriend because of ineptitude. Dumping may seem at that time to be the only option for disposing of the body.

Forensic entomology can often help investigators determine if a homicide was a dump job. Investigators note the types of insects on the body in its original position. Then investigators, at the appropriate time turn, "roll" the body over. Different types of insects underneath the body, as opposed to on top of it, very strongly suggest the victim was killed somewhere else, then dumped. This is because some insects are common in urban areas, some in rural areas. A body found in a rural area but also infested with insects common in an urban area indicates a dump job (Beil 1995; Douglas and Olshaker 1998; Gates and Shah 1992; McKenna and Harrington 1996; Stone 1986).

GOING POSTAL

On the early morning of August 20, 1986, Patrick Sherrill, forty-four, walked into the post office in Edmond, Oklahoma. Sherrill, a member of the National Guard, had a Colt .45 semiautomatic in his right hand. More than fifty postal workers were sorting mail as Sherrill, one of their fellow workers, opened fire, killing fourteen people and seriously wounding six others. He shot himself to death before SWAT team officers entered the post office. Because of the enormity of the crime, a monument called "The Yellow Ribbon" was erected in Edmond in memory of Sherrill's victims.

On October 10, 1991, in Ridgewood, New Jersey, thirty-five-year-old postal worker Joseph M. Harris was wearing a Ninja-style uniform. He broke into his supervisor's house, killed her with a Samurai sword, then shot and killed her boyfriend. Harris then killed two coworkers at the post office. Fellow workers stated Harris had been tense, sullen, and short-tempered.

On November 14, 1991, in Royal Oak, Michigan, dismissed postal employee Thomas McIlvane, thirty-one, killed four individuals, including three supervisors, at the post office. McIlvane, armed with a sawed-off semiautomatic rifle, had been involved in a seventeen-month arbitration regarding his termination.

The violent crimes committed by Sherrill, Harris, and McIlvane are three examples of many violent incidents at or associated with U.S. post offices during the years 1983–1996. During this time, the expression "going postal" became a synonym for an outburst of violence or murder.

Congressman John McHugh, Chairman, House of Representatives Subcommittee on Postal Service, worked with the United States Postal Service (USPS) to improve workplace conditions. Congressman William L. Clay, of the House of Representatives Committee on Post Office and Civil Service, headed an investigation after the murders committed by McIlvane. Of the fourteen incidents during 1983–1996 involving murder, four killers committed suicide, two were committed to mental hospitals, and five received prison sentences.

Two major reasons appeared to account for the murders. One was that the perpetrators had very serious problems with coworkers, spouses, or other family members. Two was that a variety of individuals described USPS work environments as too strictly controlled and lacking employee privacy (Lasseter 1997).

WHEN HOMICIDE IS JUSTIFIABLE

A person who kills another person commits homicide, but homicide is not necessarily a crime. A homeowner who is legally in possession of a firearm and shoots an intruder dead commits homicide. This homicide may be seen as an act of self-defense and thus may be excusable or justifiable. The homeowner may be seen as having acted within his or her legal rights in killing the intruder. Likewise, the driver of a vehicle who drives over and kills someone who runs in front of the vehicle commits homicide, even though the driver may not be at fault. Also, a mugger who with the aid of a weapon attempts to mug a victim, but is killed by the would-be victim during an ensuing struggle, is the victim of a justifiable homicide (*Encyclopedia* 1997; *Grolier* 1991; *World* 1997).

HOMICIDE AS A MESSAGE

Certain underworld homicides in which the body of the victim is easily found or is deliberately left where it can be easily discovered are messages that the victim violated one or more underworld rules.

A body with its penis stuffed into its mouth may mean the decedent had sex with someone's wife or girlfriend, or the decedent talked too much—was not discreet in talking about underworld associates or their activities. A corpse with multiple stab wounds, one of which is in the form of an X on the victim's face, may indicate the victim double-crossed someone. A body with twenty-dollar bills protruding from the mouth and anus may mean the deceased was greedy. These types of homicides also reflect the humiliation of the victim even after death.

Underworld homicides intended to send a message are difficult to solve because the perpetrator is typically a hired killer from out of town or out of state, does not have a motive, and is not a friend or business associate of the victim. A thorough investigation of the victim's life likely does not reveal a connection between the victim and perpetrator (Anastasia 1998; Cantalupo and Renner 1990; Kessler and Weston 1953; Seedman and Hellman 1974; Snyder 1959; C. G. Tedeschi, Eckert, and L. G. Tedeschi 1977).

HOMICIDE OF HOMICIDE DETECTIVES

On May 19, 1998, Hank Carr and Bernice Bowen, his girlfriend, rushed to a fire station in Tampa, Florida. With them was Joey Bennett, Bowen's four-year-old son, who had been shot in the head. Firefighters and paramedics attempted to save Joey's life, but they were unsuccessful.

Carr rushed back to the apartment where Joey was shot. There, he told police the shooting was an accident. Carr then ran away from the detectives. An officer later found him hiding in bushes a few blocks away from the apartment. The police arrested Carr and took him to their headquarters for questioning. They found out that Carr had a criminal record dating back to 1986. His past crimes included burglary, assault, and possession of cocaine.

Homicide detectives Rick Childers and Randy Bell returned Carr to the scene of the shooting, where they asked him to show them how the shooting occurred. Childers and Bell subsequently handcuffed Carr and placed the assault rifle, with which Joey was shot, in the trunk of their unmarked police vehicle. Carr was in the back seat as the detectives drove to police headquarters. He wriggled his hands free, grabbed Bell's gun, and fatally shot him. Carr then struggled with Childers, shooting him. Both detectives died in the front seat. Carr removed the assault rifle from the trunk, then carjacked a Ford Ranger.

As Carr drove north on I-275 toward Pasco County, James Crooks, a Florida Highway Patrol trooper, followed Carr. Carr, carrying the rifle, got out of the Ford Ranger and fatally shot Crooks as Crooks talked on his police radio. Other police officers pursued Carr. He shot at and hit a sheriff's helicopter, the bullet almost hitting the pilot. While attempting to escape arrest, he shot at several motorists. In Hernando County, Carr drove over a stinger, a device police placed across the highway to puncture his tires.

Carr stopped near a Shell station on State Road 50 off I-75, approximately fifty miles north of Tampa. Wounded and firing his gun at police, he ran toward the station. Inside, Carr took employee Stephanie Kramer hostage. No shots were fired during the next four-and-a-half hours. Carr assured Kramer he would release her. He telephoned Tampa radio station WFLA to give an on-air account of how Joey died, and to ask police to bring Bowen to the Shell station.

Approximately 19:30, almost ten hours after Joey was shot, Carr released Kramer. Minutes later, officers fired tear gas at the station and detonated explosive charges against the station's rear wall. SWAT (Special Weapons and Tactics) officers found Carr dead inside the station. He had apparently shot himself in the head. An assault rifle and two handguns were nearby ("Deadly" 1998; Huntley et al. 1998; Macko 2000).

HOMOSEXUAL

David Louis Schwartz was a wealthy Manhattan real estate lawyer and a partner at Cravath, Swaine and Moore. Schwartz, fifty-five, married, and a father, was found dead by a maid on November 9, 1992, at the Hutchinson-Whitestone Motel in the Bronx, a motel that rented rooms by the hour. Schwartz had checked in using the alias Lou Rothman.

Schwartz was lying on the floor. There were thirty-two stab wounds in his chest. There were condoms and lubricants nearby, and his wallet was missing. The perpetrator had tried to steal Schwartz's car, but an antitheft system prevented him from driving away.

Sergeant Ralph Barrea of the Forty-fifth Precinct showed a picture of Schwartz to a clerk in a store near the motel. The clerk stated that Schwartz was a regular customer who bought food and drinks for himself and a young companion.

A computer matched a fingerprint found in the motel room with an on-file print identifying eighteen-year-old Raymond Childs. Childs was known to police. Childs, charged with Schwartz's murder, claimed Schwartz had made certain advances toward him. Schwartz had apparently lived a double life involving homosexual sexual encounters.

The Schwartz homicide illustrated that male homosexual homicides are frequently characterized by overkill with injuries to the throat, chest, and abdomen of victims. Hustlers, who are commonly young male heterosexuals, perform fellatio on their older male homosexual customers. Hustlers do not allow customers to perform fellatio on them because hustlers usually do not see themselves as being homosexual. Sexual requests or demands of older homosexuals to allow them to perform fellatio on hustlers enrage hustlers, who attack and viciously beat these older males.

Some homosexual homicides involve sodomy. The perpetrator kills the victim to prevent the victim from identifying the perpetrator or the victim dies when the perpetrator overpowers the victim. There may be a belt or strap around the neck of the victim. For example, Warren Eling, rector of St. James the Apostle Anglican Church, in Montreal, Quebec, was found murdered in his town house on November 8, 1993. Parishioners found Eling's body in his bedroom, where the fifty-four-year-old cleric was nearly naked, his hands tied behind his head, and a leather belt tightly bound around his neck.

Eigil Vesti, a twenty-six-year-old Norwegian fashion student, was with several men at a homosexual club in Manhattan on February 22, 1985. The group left the club to go to a house in Rockland County, New York. Vesti believed they were going to a cocaine and sex party. The men, including art dealer Andrew Crispo, forty, drank wine and used cocaine at the house. Vesti was stripped, handcuffed, and sexually abused. A leather bondage mask was tightly placed on his face. He was taken outside and, while Crispo had anal sex with him, Bernard LeGeros, twenty-three, shot Vesti twice in the back of the head. The perpetrators cut a hole in Vesti's chest, collected blood into a cup, and drank the blood, vowing to keep their criminal actions a secret. A few days after police used dental records to identify Vesti, they arrested LeGeros on the basis of tips and his own calls to police. After his arrest, LeGeros admitted to police that he shot Vesti. LeGeros, who implicated Crispo in the murder, was sentenced to life in prison. Crispo was never charged in the murder. There were rumors that powerful legal and other connections helped him to avoid being charged.

There were thirty-seven documented homosexual serial killers in the United States between 1901 and 1991. Thirty-one of these killers were white, three were black, and three were Hispanic. These perpetrators, who represent thirty cases of homosexual serial murders because some killers worked together, were charged with killing approximately 280 male victims and may have murdered approximately 755 individuals.

Sadomasochistic sexual acts and male pedophilia were the most frequent motivation, with lust murders and robbery being second. Ten of the killers killed their victims in California, four in Texas. John Wayne Gacy, who strangled and tortured thirty-three mostly underage victims in Illinois between 1972 and 1978, was executed in 1994. Randy Steven Kraft, who strangled and stabbed twenty-one victims and is suspected of slaying thirty-nine in California between 1972 and 1983, perpetrated sadomasochistic thrill killings. He was sentenced to death on November 29, 1989.

"Fag workers" are individuals who either are homosexuals or may pretend to be homosexuals and who, either alone or in groups, frequent gay establishments with the intention of deceiving a "mark," or victim, through a sexual encounter in order to rob and kill the mark. Homosexual thrill killer Donald Dufour killed five individuals in 1982. Robbery and the thrill of killing were his motives.

Homophobics, individuals who have an irrational fear of homosexuals or of homosexual feelings, sometimes commit homosexual homicides. These types of homicides are referred to as gay bashing or, in street language, as fag bashing or fagicide (Came 1993; Dynes 1990; France 1999; Geberth 1996; Haden-Guest 1985; Hoffman 1968; Hogan and Hudson 1998; Miller and Humphreys 1980; Newton 2003; Stewart 1993).

HOMOSEXUAL HOMICIDE IN THE MILITARY

Airmen Terry Helvey and Charles Vins, both twenty, were in Sasebo Park in Sasebo, Japan, on October 27, 1992. It was approximately 23:30 and Helvey and Vins, both of whom had been drinking, saw twenty-two-year-old seaman Allen Schindler.

There had been rumors Schindler was gay. The rumors were true, and he was going to be discharged. Helvey and Vins, at Helvey's urging, discreetly followed Schindler. Helvey broke into a run and saw Schindler enter a washroom, where they followed him. First Helvey and then Vins attacked Schindler, who had been facing a urinal. The two airmen used their fists, but mostly their feet, during the attack, kicking Schindler in the head, left side, chest, and torso. Helvey stepped on Schindler's neck and throat before he and Vins left the washroom. Schindler was unconscious and near death.

Helvey and Vins went to the Sasebo River to wash the blood off themselves. A seaman and a petty officer saw part of the attack through a glass-block wall and went to get help.

The autopsy performed two days later at the U.S. Naval Hospital at Okinawa revealed that Schindler had eight broken ribs, a broken nose, a broken upper jaw, bruises on his brain, and a severely damaged liver. Forensic pathologist Commander Edward Kilbane stated he had never before seen a beating as severe as Schindler's.

Helvey received a life sentence, Vins a four-month sentence because he testified against Helvey (Brown 1993; Salholz et al. 1993).

INFORMANT

Songia Petite Johnson and Sonjii Yvette Johnson both lived in Monterey County, California. The first name of each of these women was pronounced "Sonya." Songia Petite knew Sonjii Yvette slightly and they lived relatively close together.

In 1989, a detective dialed a telephone number for Collier Vale, an assistant district attorney (ADA) for Monterey County. Vale wanted to tell Sonjii Yvette her life could be in danger, since she had become an informant regarding two drug-related homicides. He had offered her help before and wanted to do so again.

The woman interrupted the conversation to check on her baby. Vale realized he must have contacted the wrong person because the woman he wanted to talk to did not have children. Vale hung up. He had spoken to Songia Petite, although he had intended to talk to Sonjii Yvette. Neither Vale nor police told Sonjii Yvette about the mistaken telephone call.

This mix-up prompted Songia Petite to tell people Sonjii Yvette was an informant. This became common knowledge on the street. On August 6, 1989, two weeks after the wrong telephone number was inadvertently dialed, Sonjii Yvette drove into her driveway. Bradley "Shorty" Hardison appeared out of the shadows and fired at her six times, killing her. He was her boyfriend and the person she told police was linked to drug homicides.

The death of Sonjii Yvette, a woman who the legal system should have protected from harm but failed to do so, caused considerable controversy in Monterey County. Some local politicians and attorneys blamed Vale. This deeply troubled him. He became anxious and depressed. Colleagues and friends supported him, but it was impossible for them to convince Vale he had not caused Sonjii Yvette's death.

Russ Dubree, the chief investigator for the district attorney's office and a friend of Vale's, went to Vale's house to find out why Vale had not come to work. Dubree found Vale on the living room floor. He had put a gun in his mouth and pulled the trigger (Gabriel 1991).

MA AND PA KETTLE

Ma and Pa Kettle murders are domestic murders. The term "Ma and Pa Kettle" refers to the hillbilly characters portrayed in nine very successful low-budget comedies filmed between 1949 and 1957. Between 1965 and 1995, the number of domestic homicides dropped from approximately one out of three homicides to one out of ten of all homicides. Most domestic homicides are smoking gun homicides—homicides that are easily solved (Corwin 1997; *Halliwell's* 1995).

MASS MURDER

There does not appear to be a strict definition of "mass murderer," but generally speaking a mass murderer can be defined as a person who kills three or more individuals at one time in one location. This type of killer often dies at the crime scene. He either commits suicide or causes his own death through the action of police. When he does the latter, his death is known as suicide-by-police. He cannot or will not kill himself, but he knows police will kill him if he refuses to surrender and continues to shoot to kill them. In retrospect, family, friends, or fellow workers usually detect in him one or more signs, such as great anger, that should have been dealt with before he committed the crime.

Mass murderers can be classified as one of five types: disciple, family annihilator, pseudo-commando, disgruntled employee, or set-and-run killer. The disciple, a person under the influence of a charismatic leader, obeys the leader and kills victims who are chosen by the leader, in order to be accepted by the leader. The disciple is not likely to be from the area in which he or she commits the murder. Victims are usually strangers. The disciple does not commit suicide nor die due to police action. Leslie van Houten, a former beauty queen, was under the psychological control of Charles Manson and, for this reason committed murder at his command as his disciple.

The family annihilator is the senior male in a family. He is depressed and often abuses alcohol. This murderer kills, at one time, his entire family. He may also kill the family pet. The family annihilator is typically a lifelong resident of the community in which the murders occur. His life is one of despair and his motive is not apparent to the rest of the community.

The pseudo-commando often stockpiles assault weapons and other weapons and carefully plans his crime. His victim is society in general. His specific victims are people who are at the wrong place at the wrong time. James Huberty killed twenty-one persons and wounded nineteen at a McDonald's restaurant in San Ysidro, California, on July 18, 1984. Part of Huberty's motivation was depression over his move for economic reasons from Ohio to California.

A disgruntled employee is often a former employee who was dismissed or is on medical leave, on medication, or receiving psychological treatment. This person, believing others treated him unjustly at the workplace, returns to the workplace and looks for the persons he believes caused his problems. Postal worker Patrick Sherrill, mentioned earlier in this chapter, returned in 1986 to the post office where he had worked. As he looked for supervisors, he fired in rooms and corridors, killing and wounding numerous individuals.

The set-and-run killer usually kills for revenge. If he plants a bomb, he leaves before the bomb explodes. If he tampers with a medicine, he leaves after he places the medicine back on the shelf. He does not want to die and does not observe at the crime scene the consequences of his act. He may see later on television news coverage of his crime. The set-and-run killer does not really care that innocent people die because of what he has done. The company against whom he is trying to get revenge is his focus. Seven people died in Chicago, Illinois, and surrounding suburbs in the fall of 1982 when someone tampered with Tylenol capsules and added cyanide to them. The victims purchased the capsules in stores. The person who added the cyanide to the capsules was very likely a set-and-run killer. It is not clear, however, if revenge against a company was the killer's motive. Although there were more than 400 possible suspects, the killer was never caught. James W. Lewis, a chief suspect at one time, was convicted and jailed in 1984 for trying to extort $1 million from Johnson & Johnson, the maker of Tylenol. Lewis, who wrote a letter to Johnson & Johnson about stopping the killings, was released from jail in 1995 (Avila 2002; Bennett and Hess 2001; Holmes and Holmes 1992).

MISDEMEANOR

Misdemeanor homicides, also referred to as public service killings, refer to drug homicides. The public, including the police, have little if any interest in seeing these homicides solved because the victims and perpetrators usually are both involved in the drug trade. There are thousands of drug homicides committed annually in the largest cities. Police have other homicides they prefer to clear.

The murder in 1992 of José Yepez, a New York Upper West Side drug dealer, was a public service killing. Yepez apparently stole drugs from competitors, then sold the drugs. Even his friends were of little help to police when police attempted to apprehend his drive-by killer, who machine-gunned Yepez and three other individuals (Count 1994; Pooley 1992).

MISTAKEN IDENTITY

At 320 East 79th Street, Manhattan, there was an upscale restaurant called the Neapolitan Noodle. On August 11, 1972, a man walked into the Neapolitan Noodle with a gun in each hand and began shooting. Four men at the bar were hit. Two of them, Sheldon Epstein and Max Tekelch, were killed. Two other men were wounded.

The shooter, an underworld executioner, was there to kill mob figures supposedly having a meeting. However, the intended victims did not show up. Epstein, Tekelch, and the other two men made the mistake of sitting at the bar where the intended victims would have been sitting. The homicides of Epstein and Tekelch were not solved (Hoffman and Headley 1992; *New York Times Index* 1973).

MURDER AND MANSLAUGHTER

There are two types of murder: first-degree and second-degree. First-degree murder is characterized by malice and premeditation. The perpetrator takes some time, however brief, to plan to kill a victim then carries out the plan. Second-degree murder lacks premeditation, but it includes malice and intentional and reckless behavior. An example of first-degree murder is murder resulting from a falling-out between two business partners. One partner, believing the other partner embezzled company money and cheated him or her, plans to get revenge and does so via a carefully planned murder. An example of second-degree murder is the death of a wife by the actions of her husband who purposely operates a motorboat at a much faster speed than he should, knowing his wife is afraid of such speed. She falls out of the boat and drowns.

The difference between murder and manslaughter is the lack of malice in manslaughter. There are two types of manslaughter: voluntary and involuntary. A person who commits voluntary manslaughter may be provoked into committing this act. For example, two people become involved in an intense argument, which turns into a physical altercation. One person pushes the other one, and the person who is pushed falls against a concrete wall, accidentally injures the back of his or her head, and dies. A person commits involuntary manslaughter when this person causes a death by committing an act that is unlawful but is not a felony. The owner of a daycare center can be charged with involuntary manslaughter after a fire at the center in which children die if investigators learn that an emergency exit was not properly working (*Encyclopedia* 1997; *Grolier* 1991; *World* 1997).

MUSHROOMS

It is common for innocent people to die in shootouts between drug dealers. These individuals are often in the wrong place at the wrong time. Sometimes they die in crossfire. Sometimes they die when drug dealers shoot up a neighborhood and no one returns fire. Regardless of the exact circumstances, these victims are, in the language of the drug world, "mushrooms"—people who willingly or unwillingly "pop up" at the wrong time and pay with their lives.

In August 1988 in the Roxbury section of Boston, Massachusetts, twelve-year-old Darlene Tiffany Moore died as a mushroom. She was talking to friends when shooters from a car, apparently looking for a drug dealer, shot up the neighborhood. Two bullets struck her and she died instantly. Darlene had been living in South Carolina, where her mother believed Darlene would be safer than in Boston. Darlene had returned to Boston for a visit (Martz 1989).

PRESS CASES

Certain homicides in New York, in which victims are often middle-class individuals from Manhattan whose deaths receive extensive media coverage, are known as "press cases." The detective bureau puts extra effort into solving these cases because of continuing media attention.

The murder in the West Village in July 1990 of advertising executive John Reisenbach is an example of a press case. The stabbing death in Central Park in June 1991 of Alexis Welsh, who was walking her dogs, is another example of a press case. The shooting death, during a scuffle in March 1989, of police officer Robert Machate is a third example. Investigators are pressured by the media and by police management to quickly clear press cases. The media focuses in these cases on one or more aspects of the victim's life, such as age, sex, and socioeconomic status, which will increase public interest. The media is a powerful resource that can help investigators convey selected case information to millions of people. These people have the option of conveying tips via the media to police or directly to police. *America's Most Wanted* illustrates how television can help investigators quickly clear some homicide cases (Pooley 1992).

RITUALISTIC HOMICIDE

A cult is a group of individuals that is dedicated to, and performs rituals regarding, a specific ideal, person, or thing. One type of cult, a socially deviant destructive cult, abandons traditional ethical and religious beliefs and engages in illegal activities, including drug smuggling and murder associated with a ritual. The leader of this type of cult claims to know supernatural truths that cult members must not question. This leader prefers vulnerable young members who are searching for identity and meaning in life. The cult convincingly states that it provides the meaning new members or potential members lack. Initiated members make newcomers feel special, and new members are socialized to adopt a new identity acceptable to the cult. All members must conform without question in a communal environment, which has a siege mentality. Troublemakers are punished psychologically or physically, and they may be killed. The cult believes external forces, usually the government, may attempt to destroy them.

Another type, the satanic cult, advocates belief in the devil and attracts individuals who have psychological problems. Some of these people have a criminal background. These rebellious and angry individuals want power. They act out fantasies and sadomasochistic behavior in an environment of drug use.

Cult members or former members are often the victims of ritualistic homicides. Kidnapped individuals who have no connection to cults are also typical victims. Sometimes victims are murdered in their homes. Most victims are stabbed to death. Guns are rarely the murder weapons used in these homicides.

The perpetrator is usually a white male with above average intelligence. He is from a middle-class or upper middle class family. Often he is on drugs when he commits the homicide. The perpetrator of a satanic homicide may do the following to the body: drain the blood; cut out the heart or tongue; cut off a finger, hand, or testicle; inflict burn marks; carve a pentagram or other symbol associated with satanic worship on the body; or leave incense, urine, semen, or feces on the body.

Game wardens and park rangers often discover clandestine sites used for satanic ceremonies. Ceremonies are usually held inside a circle that is nine feet in diameter. The purpose of the circle is to protect ceremony participants against outside evil and to maintain the power of Satan. A marble slab or stone may be the altar. Black candles, a bell, a sword, cat-o-nine tails, animal masks, or an inverted cross may be present. There may also be a fire pit. Bones and teeth of victims may be in the ashes.

Investigators must be very careful when they respond to a homicide at a satanic ritual. Cult members take precautions against interruptions by outsiders, including stringing piano wire at ankle and chest height between trees. Members also place blocks of wood, which have sharp protruding nails, on the ground under leaves. Investigators can be seriously injured or killed whether or not they encounter cult members. The death in 1987 in Joplin, Missouri, of Steve Newberry was a classic ritualistic homicide. Pete Rowland, one of three perpetrators who were all members of a cult called "the Crowd," confessed to his role in the murder of Newberry. Rowland believed that Satan would appear to give him some of his power if Rowland sacrificed Newberry. Rowland, who was a drug user, engaged in self-mutilation, chanted to Satan, and tortured and killed animals. He and another satanist clubbed Newberry to death.

In 1989, fifteen victims of cult kidnappings were murdered near Matamoros, a city in Mexico across the river from Brownsville, Texas. The bodies of victims were found in shallow graves on a ranch. Most victims were killed with a machete or a hammer. Some victims were boiled alive. Mark Kilroy, a twenty-one-year-old University of Texas premed student, was one of the victims. He was in Matamoros during spring break when he disappeared. After Kilroy was dead, cult members removed his brain to give his intelligence to the leader of the cult. A bloody altar, the heads of chickens and goats, and a kettle containing blood and flesh were among the satanic ritual paraphernalia found at this crime scene. The cult was engaged in drug smuggling.

There had been rumors on the streets of Matamoros that other young men had disappeared. Some rumors were about a mysterious drug gang that had supernatural powers. In April 1989, a month after Kilroy disappeared, special anticorruption Mexican police chased a suspicious pickup truck in the Matamoros area to a clapboard building in which the police found evidence of ritualistic sacrifice. Other investigators arrived, including Oran Neck, a U.S. customs agent who had been searching for Kilroy. One of the men that police were detaining at the clapboard building confirmed that Kilroy's remains were there and that the person responsible for Kilroy's death was cult leader Adolfo de Jesus Constanzo. Police learned that Constanzo was in Mexico City. When police arrived at the apartment in which Constanzo was hiding , Constanzo ordered a loyal friend in the apartment to kill him. The friend did as told with a machine gun.

The Charles Manson crime family, a socially deviant destructive cult, was on a mission to start a race war by committing murders. On August 9, 1969, cult members murdered actress Sharon Tate and four other persons at her home in Los Angeles, California. The following day cult members, acting on orders from Manson, went to 3301 Waverly Drive in Los Angeles to murder Leno and Rosemary LaBianca. The killers stabbed Leno, forty-four, multiple times in the back and abdomen with a knife and a two-pronged fork. They wrapped his head in a pillowcase and secured it with an electrical cord. They carved the word "war" into his lower chest. The killers also stabbed Rosemary, thirty-eight, multiple times. There were twenty-two stab wounds in her upper back. The murderers covered her head with a pillowcase and tied it with a lamp cord. They wrote "Death to Pigs" in blood on the living room wall and wrote "Healter Skelter" (the misspelled title of a Beatles song, "Helter Skelter") in blood on the LaBianca refrigerator. They wrote "Rise" on the wall to the left of the front door. The Manson case is one of the best-known cases of ritualistic homicide during the twentieth century in the United States (Bennett and Hess 2001; Boyle 1995; Bugliosi and Gentry 1974; *Murder* 1991; Napolis 2000).

SMOKING GUN

A homicide in which the killer, known as a "novice," has not likely killed before, kills someone he or she knows, is easily identified, and is linked to a lot of incriminating evidence is a smoking gun case. The victim is typically a spouse, business associate, or someone else the perpetrator knows well, such as a relative. For all the reasons just described, this type of homicide is very easy to solve. The following fictional example mirrors the smoking gun homicides that are reported almost daily in the media: Neighbors call police to report another domestic disturbance. The police computer has a premise history regarding the address at which the disturbance is occurring. A premise history tells officers what has occurred before at the address and what they can likely expect to encounter when they arrive at the address. The husband has in the past punched and kicked his wife. When police arrive at the scene, the wife is lying motionless on the floor. She is covered with blood and her face is badly swollen. It appears that she has been kicked in the stomach and ribs. The husband is sitting on the floor next to an empty whiskey bottle. He is also covered with blood, especially his hands and shoes. The officers determine that the wife is dead and wait for homicide detectives and the medical examiner to arrive. They arrest the husband (Henderson 1998).

SNUFF MOVIE

In his book, *The Family: The Story of Charles Manson's Dune Buggy Attack Battalion*, Ed Sanders used the word "snuff" to refer to a movie in which there is an actual sexual murder. Three years after the publication of this book, *Snuff*, a pornographic movie, was allegedly made in 1979 in South America. *Snuff* is supposedly about the real-life torture, mutilation, and killing of a woman.

The word "snuff" has become a generic term that refers to any pornographic movie involving actual sexual murder. People throughout the world claim snuff movies exist and maintain they have seen or have access to such movies. However, snuff movies do not seem to be readily available, if in fact they exist at all. Larry Flynt, the publisher of *Hustler*, does not believe snuff movies exist. Flynt, like many other people, has seen movies that were supposedly snuff movies, but there was no proof they were this type of film.

FBI agent Ken Lanning of the National Center for the Analysis of Violent Crime (NCAVC) believes a movie must meet certain criteria to qualify as a snuff movie: the movie has to be a visual record of an actual murder, production value is the primary motive for the murder, the script indicates when the murder is to be committed, and the movie is sold commercially.

There are serious risks involved with possessing a snuff movie (Millea 1999; Russell 1998; Stine 1999; Svoray and Hughes 1997).

VICTIM-PRECIPITATED HOMICIDE

A person who consciously or unconsciously causes their own death through homicide illustrates victim-precipitated homicide. This person usually engages in a verbal altercation that escalates into a physical attack. At least one of the individuals in the altercation uses a gun, knife, or other weapon. A fist or foot is sometimes the other weapon.

As an example, a group of men went to a bar, where they drank excessively and became rowdy. A special officer asked them to leave the bar, but they remained in the bar until closing time. Later the officer physically ejected the men from the bar. One of them, Manuel, was especially angry about being ejected. He and his friends waited outside the bar, where they confronted the officer. They beat the officer with their fists, feet, and a stick. Manuel stabbed the officer twice in the back. The officer produced his gun and attempted to arrest the attackers. He fired one shot and the attackers began to flee. He again fired, seriously wounding Manuel, who a few hours later died in the hospital. Manuel's death was a victim-precipitated homicide because he started the altercation.

As another example, Joe and Bob were transients who traveled together, occasionally working as farm laborers and living in boxcars. Joe had an extensive criminal record and became violent when he drank. One day, while drinking, Joe punched and kicked Bob because he wanted him to get out of the boxcar. As Joe attacked Bob, something he had also done two days earlier, Bob managed to grab a nearby knife and stab Joe. Joe then jumped out of the boxcar and died in the railway yard as he ran to get help. Bob was later arrested and charged with involuntary manslaughter and was imprisoned for a few months (Allen 1980).

2

Homicide in the Underworld

Underworld killers, or "hitmen," participate in rigorous initiation ceremonies and kill according to clandestine contracts. Sometimes these hitmen have accomplices who provide the murder weapon or a specially equipped "getaway car." Victims with underworld ties are sometimes taken for a "one-way ride" and become "trunk music" or a "dump job." Criminals, police, and the media often assign nicknames or monikers to hitmen and other underworld figures. In this chapter, we discuss ten aspects of homicide in the underworld.

CONCRETE

When gangsters in the 1920s and 1930s wanted to kill someone, the public believed that gangsters sometimes would force their victim to stand in a washtub or other container full of fresh cement. When the cement dried, the victim would be pushed off a pier or the back of a boat in a river or lake. It was said the victim was wearing concrete overshoes. There does not appear to be any evidence confirming this practice; however, divers occasionally came across a corpse in a sunken car.

Paul Bernardo, Canadian serial rapist and killer, used concrete blocks in which he hid the body parts of Leslie Mahaffy, one of his teenage victims during the early 1990s. Bernardo dumped the concrete blocks into Lake Gibson in Ontario. Paul Bernardo and his wife Karla Homolka both received prison sentences for this and other crimes.

Many years earlier, in 1949, serial killers Martha Beck and Raymond Martinez Fernandez murdered Delphine Dowling, twenty-eight, and Rainelle Dowling, two, Delphine's daughter. Beck and Fernandez buried the bodies in the basement of the Dowling home, then poured fresh concrete over the burial site. Shortly after the murders, suspicious neighbors contacted police, who searched the house, excavated a portion of the basement floor, and discovered the bodies (Bardsley 2001; Helmer and Mattix 1998; Kelleher and Kelleher 1998; Williams 1996).

CONTRACTS

An unwritten offer by a criminal organization to virtually any person in the underworld who may be qualified to kill someone is an open contract. A contract, compared to an open contract, involves at least one killer assigned to the task and at least one victim. Regardless of the type of contract, the target is usually an underworld figure. This person may have reneged on a business deal, or he may have received a subpoena to testify in court. This person's actions make certain people in the underworld uncomfortable. The intended victim can also be a politician or investigative reporter who has repeatedly publicly criticized underworld activities, such as drug dealing, money laundering, labor racketeering, and associated them with specific groups of individuals.

The person who makes a successful hit is usually paid in cash. This perpetrator sometimes kills without charge to demonstrate his loyalty to an underworld organization. The perpetrator's status in the underworld is increased when he successfully carries out the hit, whether or not he is paid.

In early June 1976, Don Bolles, an investigative reporter for the *Arizona Republic*, left a Phoenix, Arizona, hotel, got into his car, and turned the ignition. The car blew up and Bolles, forty-seven, was seriously injured. For many years, Bolles had investigated organized crime in businesses and had received numerous death threats. He claimed the Mafia was responsible for the bombing, and before he died of his injuries, he stated John Harvey Adamson, thirty-two, was the person he had planned to meet at the hotel. Adamson plea-bargained, named alleged accomplices, and stated he was part of a murder-for-hire plot ("The Bolles" 1977; Edwards 1990; Maas 1968; "They Finally" 1976).

HITMAN

A "stone killer" is an underworld killer who kills without display-ing any emotion. This personality trait is highly desirable in a hit-man, a professional killer who helps further the ambitions of a crim-inal organization by committing murder for them. Sometimes he kills someone as a favor to another person in a criminal organiza-tion. Usually, he is obligated to kill for his employer.

The underworld, like the noncriminal world, has a division of la-bor. It requires specialists, but not everyone qualifies to be a hitman. Likewise, in the straight world, not everyone qualifies or wants to be an executioner in a state that has the death penalty. Another exam-ple is a homicide detective who views an eviscerated body at a crime scene and may later have lunch. This detective, although bothered by violence and death, learned early in homicide investigation how, for the most part, to cope with violent death.

A hitman also copes easily with bloodshed. He is an employee who is paid to kill. After killing a person, a hitman does any num-ber of things as ordinary as going to sleep or going to a wedding.

The hitman, a product of the underworld, likely has a criminal record by the time he makes his first hit in his teens or early twen-ties. He does not see anything wrong with killing as a way to earn a good living. He is confident, proud, and without remorse. He has high status in the underworld and enjoys his work.

There are hitmen who, on a contract basis, work independently, enjoying the money and lifestyle the work provides and freelancing for various criminal organizations. An independent may give a per-centage of his income to a particular crime family if he does work in that family's territory.

The following examples indicate the type of person likely to be the victim of a hitman. A person does not give a crime boss all the money stolen during the robbery of an illegal card game and some-one tells the boss. A person steals cocaine from a crime boss to sell behind the boss' back and the boss finds out. A third person, per-haps an alcoholic, talks too much, carelessly and openly, about crime family business. All three individuals are liabilities. They are a threat and can no longer be trusted.

When a crime boss decides to have someone hit, he orders a high-ranking member of his organization to ensure the job is done. This member might personally approach the hitman or might send a lower-ranking member to talk to the hitman. During a meeting, the individuals present negotiate the terms of the contract. The independent, however, can refuse a contract, depending, in part, on his moral code. He may not kill women, and a certain contract specifies that a husband and wife be killed. Another hitman may kill men and women, but not children.

A basic contract stipulates the hitman will kill a specific person for a specific amount of money by a specific date. A would-be victim has to testify in court in two months. His enemies want him dead before then. When necessary, the hitman is provided with a photograph of the intended victim, the home address, the business address, the names of associates, the names of places frequented, or other information. As much information as possible is memorized. Anything not memorized is destroyed as soon as possible. A paper trail in underworld business can be as incriminating as a smoking gun.

The hitman is paid in full before or after the hit, or he may receive an advance before the hit and be given the remaining amount after the hit. The victim's status, and whether or not he is a soft or hard target, can affect the price of the hit. A soft target is an intended victim who can, with minimal or no complications, be easily murdered. A hard target is an intended victim who cannot, for various reasons, be easily killed. Although the soft target may be naïve, the hard target may be anything but naïve. The soft target may refuse to have bodyguards, but the hard target will agree to have bodyguards.

The hitman's reputation guarantees he will do the job properly. If he does not uphold his end of the agreement, he can soon become a victim. The hitman is sometimes murdered after he carries out the hit. The reason for this is to further isolate the crime figure that authorized the hit.

Arrangements are made in this way to isolate the person who made the original decision from the hitman. For this reason, these types of homicides are extremely difficult for police to solve. In Chicago, Illinois, between 1919 and February 1, 1967, there were approximately 1,000 hits. Only thirteen resulted in a conviction.

The hitman frequents different places. The place may be a racetrack or casino. To people who do not know him, he is a person in a crowd and looks like any other customer. Places the hitman frequents are often owned by the underworld. These places are located in inner-city or upscale neighborhoods.

When initial contact is made by telephone, a code word or expression might be used to indicate a meeting place. Otherwise, the person trying to make the contact will visit places the hitman frequents.

The best way to make a near-perfect basic hit is to quietly and deliberately approach the victim from behind when he is alone, shoot him multiple times in the back of the head with a silencer-equipped .22-caliber gun held a few inches from his head, then walk away.

The hitman must be careful when he approaches the victim because, unless the hitman shoots rapidly and is on target, the victim might grab him, delaying his escape. In addition, the hitman does not want blood and brain matter splattered on his clothes. This is less likely to happen with a .22 than with a larger-caliber gun such as a .38-caliber.

A good time to make the hit is when the victim is entering or exiting a vehicle. This type of hit occurred in New York on December 16, 1985, when Gambino crime boss Paul Castellano and Thomas Bilotti, his driver, were getting out of Castellano's car in front of Sparks Steak House. Suddenly, three men appeared and shot Castellano and Bilotti in the face. The shooters fled on foot to a waiting car and escaped.

Another good opportunity for making the hit is when the victim is entering or exiting a telephone booth. This type of hit took place in San Diego, California, in February 1977. Frank Bompensiero, a hitman and FBI informer, was walking away from a telephone booth. A gunman shot him four times in the head with a silencer-equipped pistol.

A third option for making the hit is when the victim is in a restaurant. This happened at the Palace Chop House and Tavern in Newark, New Jersey, on October 23, 1935. Two men with a machine gun and sawed-off shotgun surprised and mortally wounded gangster Dutch Schultz.

With a hit, the element of surprise is crucial because, if the victim is not alone, it may be necessary to kill anyone who interferes or might be a potential witness. Usually, the hitman or hitmen have left before most people fully comprehend what has happened.

After the hitman makes the hit, he escapes according to a prearranged plan. For example, an associate in a stolen car with stolen license plates, a car stolen a few days previously and checked to ensure it will work properly during the getaway, waits for him near the crime scene. The driver and hitman then drive to a designated location, where they abandon their car and get into a second stolen car.

A variation in the escape is for the driver and hitman to split up at this location. One takes the second car, the other one continues on foot. If the hitman strongly feels someone will follow him in a car from the original crime scene, he arranges in advance for another car to smash into the pursuing car and disable it.

Other ways to escape from the crime scene, depending on overall circumstances, are to escape in a cab or blend into a crowd getting on a subway, then escape by subway.

The gun is destroyed in one of two ways. By one method, it is cut into three or four pieces, then each piece is thrown off a different bridge. The other option is to melt down the gun at a foundry where a crime family has influence.

The hitman's sole purpose is to kill the victim and leave. He is not there to negotiate with, rob, or torture the victim unless robbery and torture are included in the contract. The hit is strictly business—rarely anything else. Sometimes the victim is tersely told why he is about to die. Sometimes the person to be hit will be conned into getting into a car with people he trusts on the pretext they are going for something to eat or for drinks. A two-door vehicle is ideal because the victim will be in the backseat, from which it is difficult to escape. The individual who suddenly realizes he is about to be killed will beg the hitman not to kill him and may offer him money, cry, or make the sign of the cross.

After the victim is driven to an isolated location such as a landfill site or industrial park and is killed there, his body is disposed of in one of several ways. The body may be buried at the landfill site, compressed in a junkyard, burned in an industrial furnace, buried in a farm field, left in a construction site where concrete is to be poured, or dismembered in a butcher shop, where the body parts are placed in dark plastic bags and then thrown into a dumpster (Dietz 1983; Eppolito and Drury 1992; Joey and Fisher 1974; Maas 1997; Monaco and Bascom 1991; Shawcross 1994; Sifakis 1987).

MAKES HIS BONES

A person who murders another person to qualify for membership in certain criminal organizations "makes his bones." By murdering someone, the member-to-be proves to members that he is capable of murder and is not a police officer attempting to infiltrate the organization. If a police officer were to murder someone to become a member, he would not have any credibility as a police officer in court and, more seriously, would be charged with murder. The make-your-bones requirement lets the "right people" in and keeps the "wrong people" out (Maas 1997).

MONIKER

A moniker is a nickname that refers to a specific criminal; it can be used to identify that criminal in the underworld. This nickname is not necessarily chosen or used by the criminal to whom the nickname applies. Criminals, police, and the media assign monikers. When police know a criminal's moniker, they include it in the criminal's police file. A moniker may not be exclusive to a particular criminal. Many police departments have moniker files that cross-reference monikers with the real names of the criminals.

Some monikers are based on a single aspect of a criminal's physical appearance. Al Capone, who had a large scar on his face, was given the moniker "Scarface." Some monikers are based on a criminal's perceived state of mind. People who knew about Benjamin Siegel's bad temper used the moniker "Bugsy" when referring to him. Some monikers, based on geographical areas, identify groups of criminals. After seven inmates escaped from the Connally Unit Prison in Kenedy, Texas, in 2000, the media referred to these inmates as "The Texas 7."

When Jimmy Fratianno was growing up in Cleveland, Ohio, he would steal fruit from sidewalk stands and would be chased by police. One day Fratianno hit a police officer in the face with a rotten tomato. As the police officer chased Fratianno, a man yelled that Fratianno was a weasel. This police officer included the name "the weasel" in the police report. For the remainder of his life, Fratianno's nickname "the weasel" was in police files (Demaris 1981; King 2001; Kurland 1994).

ONE-WAY RIDE

In New York as early as 1918, a person taken for a one-way ride in an automobile was usually someone who was a member and victim of the underworld. As discussed earlier, sometimes this individual was convinced that he was going with friends for a drink or dinner, or to a business meeting, and he had no idea he would be killed. Other times, as soon as he voluntarily got into a car, he felt something was not quite right. On other occasions, the victim was forced into a car and executed inside it or at a planned destination. If he was not killed in the car and dumped into a street, he may have been forced at gunpoint out of the car, killed in the street, and left there. There were times when the victim was driven into the country, killed, and buried in a farmer's field. This type of homicide victim was a person who, knowingly or unknowingly, was a liability to certain members of the underworld.

The one-way ride is not only associated with a past era. Bodies of men and women, some of them connected to the underworld, are still found in urban and rural areas where their killer or killers left them. In New York, Umberto Pena, nineteen and a member of the Jheri Curls, a major drug gang, set out to sell crack independently. Moreta and Loren Martinez, two other members of the gang, took Pena for a ride on the Cross-Bronx Expressway. All three were in the front seat. Loren was driving. Moreta shot Pena in the head with a .22-caliber pistol. Loren opened the door then pushed Pena out onto an exit ramp (Conlon 1994; Helmer and Mattix 1998).

RODMAN

A "rod" is one of many expressions for a gun. A "rodman" is a person who supplies a group of robbers, of which he is a member, with guns. The rodman directly participates in a robbery. This individual is usually a good shot, and if necessary will kill to defend the other robbers (O'Hara and O'Hara 1994).

TRUNK MUSIC

It has been common practice in the underworld for decades to kill someone and place the body in the trunk of a car. The car is abandoned on a residential street, at an airport car park, in an industrial area, or elsewhere. It typically does not arouse suspicion until the stench of decay prompts someone to call police. Placing a body where it can be found quite easily can be an underworld message to others who deal with the underworld of the consequences of betraying certain individuals. When a person in Chicago, Illinois, is murdered and disposed of in this way, the dead person is said to have become "trunk music" (Roemer 1994).

WHEELMAN

The wheelman or driver is part of a team that commits burglaries, robberies, or murders. This person's responsibilities include obtaining a reliable car, which is usually stolen, has a powerful engine, and does not attract attention. The wheelman puts license plates from another car on the stolen vehicle. At a designated location, some distance from the scene of the crime, the criminals abandon the stolen car and then get into a "front" car, a car owned by one of the criminals.

The term "wheelman" was used as early as approximately 1919, when mobster Joe Valachi was a wheelman in New York for a burglary gang called the Minute Men. Sam Giancana, who later became head of the Chicago Outfit, was, like Valachi, a wheelman during the 1920s. Giancana worked as a wheelman and gunman for Al Capone in Chicago, Illinois. Giancana was murdered in 1975 in the basement of his home in Chicago. His murder has never been solved (Giancana and Giancana 1992; Maas 1968; O'Hara and O'Hara 1994).

WORK CAR

A "work car" is a specially modified car used in committing crimes. It has an extra powerful engine, extra shocks, hidden gun compartments, bulletproof windows, reinforced sides, and concealable license plates. This car cannot be traced easily.

Modified vans and trucks are also used as work cars. A truck with bulletproof walls and with slits in these walls through which to fire a gun was used by drug dealers in a robbery at the Dadeland Mall in Miami, Florida, on July 11, 1979 (Hiaasen and Messerschmidt 1979; Roemer 1994).

3

Serial Killers

Serial killers, both male and female, are relentless, cunning, and deceptive individuals, often described as chameleons, who live among us and feel compelled to kill until they are either apprehended by police or die. These killers thrive on stalking their victims and enjoy outwitting police. Serial killers typically leave the bodies of victims in grotesque positions that temporarily satisfy the killer's fantasy. In addition, the killer will frequently remove intimate personal belongings from the victim as trophies. In this chapter, five sections explore the motivations and criminal actions of serial killers.

FEMALE SERIAL KILLERS

Female serial killers differ from their male counterparts in a number of ways. The female serial killer generally does not torture her victims, engage in overkill, or use hands-on methods such as strangulation. Female serial killers use luring behavior and are associated with crime scenes that have combined organized and disorganized characteristics. Female serial killers tend to abuse alcohol and illegal drugs; have diagnoses of psychiatric disorders, including being manic-depressive; and usually live with other individuals.

Forensic evidence, including a .22-caliber revolver, was linked to Aileen Carol Wuornos, who, in 1990, killed middle-aged male motorists along the corridor of U.S. Interstate 75 in north-central Florida. Wuornos apparently offered her victims sexual favors in return for a ride, then robbed and killed the victims. Tyria Moore, a former lesbian lover of Wuornos, cooperated with police in the arrest of Wuornos. Wuornos was executed by lethal injection on October 9, 2002, at the Florida State Prison.

Between 1986 and 1988 in Sacramento, California, Dorothea Puente killed nine individuals, possibly as many as twenty-five. Her victims, under her care, were frail elderly persons living on fixed incomes. Dorothea Puente usually used poison. Puente killed to obtain the Social Security checks and other assets of her victims.

Some female serial killers work as a team composed of at least one other person, usually a male. A male-female team, unlike the solo female serial killer, frequently uses hands-on methods to kill, including stabbing, bludgeoning, and suffocation. These perpetrators more often than not torture their victims.

Martha Beck, a registered nurse, and Raymond Martinez Fernandez, a con man from Hawaii, murdered at least twelve and possibly as many as twenty women during the years 1947 to 1949. Beck and Fernandez, known as the "Lonely Hearts Killers," committed the murders when victims refused to enter into a love relationship with Fernandez. Beck posed as Fernandez's sister. The methods used to kill the victims included shooting, poisoning, and drowning. Beck and Fernandez wanted to bilk their victims of their assets. Both perpetrators were executed in 1951 at Sing Sing Prison.

In 1980, Carol Mary Bundy and Douglas D. Clark murdered at least six and perhaps as many as fifty people. Clark shot many of the victims in the head as he had an orgasm during oral sex with them. Bundy murdered at least two individuals. Several victims were mutilated after death. Clark was sentenced to death. Bundy received multiple consecutive prison terms (Keeney and Heide 1993; Kelleher and Kelleher 1998; Koch 2002; *Murder* 1991).

MALE SERIAL KILLER

The male serial killer is an obsessed individual, most often white and in his twenties or thirties, who kills three or more victims and has a cooling-off period between homicides.

He has a fantasy that compels him to commit murder, but the murder does not fulfill the fantasy. This leads to more fantasy, followed by more murder. The cycle is repeated until he is captured by police or dies before capture.

He does not look like anyone in particular. He is average looking and may have a job, wife, and family. His IQ has been determined to range from approximately 100 to 145. Typically, his childhood was characterized by a variety of negative experiences including sexual abuse, other physical abuse, bedwetting extending into the teen years, cruelty to animals, and arson.

Tending to be a coward, he usually chooses women as his victims. The reason is twofold: one is sexual gratification and the other is that it is easier to dominate women than men. The unmarried serial killer is unable to establish a relationship with a woman. The married serial killer is unable to maintain a continuing relationship with his wife.

He hunts like a predatory animal. He enjoys capturing, controlling, and torturing his victims. For these reasons, he will most likely strangle, stab, or beat his victims to death. This killer is not usually in a hurry to kill his prey, which he could do fast and easily with a gun. His hunting ground may cover an area the size of a city, a state, several states, or a large portion of the country.

The typical male serial killer also follows media coverage of his crimes, keeps diaries, keeps souvenirs taken from his victims, and visits victim graves or crime scenes on the anniversaries of the homicides (Kilian 1991; Methvin 1995; Ressler and Shachtman 1992).

POSING

The perpetrator of a homicide such as a serial killing engages in posing when he or she uses a victim's body, or parts of the body, as a prop to leave a message for police. Posing is associated with anger and power on the part of the perpetrator. It is a message the perpetrator is better at committing a homicide and getting away with it than the police are at solving it.

As deputies Keith O'Hara and Gail Barber entered the residence of Christina Hoyt at the University of Florida in Gainesville at 01:30 on August 27, 1990, they saw her severed head. Danny Rolling, the Gainesville Ripper, who killed four other young people that summer, had posed the head. The head was posed so that a person who opened the door would easily see the head facing him or her. Rolling pleaded guilty to the murders in February 1994 and received five death sentences three months later. He lost his second appeal on

June 27, 2002, and is currently on death row (Douglas and Olshaker 1995; "Florida" 2002; Keppel and Birnes 1997; "Murder" 2000; Ryzuk 1994).

SIGNATURE

A violent perpetrator such as a serial killer often exhibits, at a crime scene, unique behavior associated with the perpetrator's fantasies. This behavior, referred to as a "signature" or "calling card," is not necessary to commit the crime. It reflects that the perpetrator, nevertheless, has a secondary need to satisfy in addition to the first need, which is to commit the crime. The perpetrator chooses to leave, at the crime scene, a signature, which is an aspect of the perpetrator's personality. A signature, unlike a modus operandi (MO), remains a constant but is not evident at every crime scene. Sometimes an unexpected reaction from a victim interferes with a perpetrator's plans, and a signature is not left (Douglas et al. 1992).

TROPHIES

After an organized serial killer kills a victim, he often takes with him certain personal items belonging to the victim. Items such as the victim's wallet, jewelry, photographic albums, and other things are trophies to the killer.

The trophies of Jeffrey Dahmer, who killed his victims in Milwaukee, Wisconsin, included victim body parts, some of which he kept in his refrigerator. Dahmer was arrested on July 22, 1991, after one of his would-be victims escaped from his apartment in west Milwaukee and ran outside, where he flagged down a police car.

The purpose of trophies is to help the killer remember the victim later. Trophies represent, in the mind of the killer, his or her accomplishments. Many of these killers take photographs of their crimes in order to fantasize later about the crimes. Harvey Glatman, who pretended to be a photographer for a lonely hearts magazine, photographed and killed his female victims (*Murder* 1991; Newton 1998; Ressler and Shachtman 1992).

4

Police Communications and Databases

The most important tool that aids detectives during homicide investigations is accurate and complete crime scene information. Crime scene detectives collect, compile, and communicate case information over radios, cell phones, and computers. The language of the communication is often abbreviated or in the form of jargon. Case histories and suspect profiles are collected and stored in databases, which detectives can quickly access, often from the crime scene, to aid with suspect identification. In this chapter, we explore twenty-three ways in which technology is used to improve the effectiveness of police communications.

AUTOMATED CANADIAN–UNITED STATES POLICE INFORMATION EXCHANGE SYSTEM (ACUPIES)

Police in Canada can query the National Crime Information Center 2000 (NCIC 2000), located near Washington, D.C., through the Automated Canadian–United States Police Information Exchange System (ACUPIES). Information about individuals, criminal records, registered vehicles, and drivers' licenses in every state are available (Griffiths et al. 1999).

AUTOMATED SUSPECT IDENTIFICATION SYSTEM (ASID)

The Automated Suspect Identification (ASID) system and Identi-Kit 2000, both produced by Smith & Wesson, are used together when detectives want to identify a possible homicide or other suspect. Detectives at a police department that is part of a network in a specific region use a personal computer or laptop to access a digital arrest record database. This database stores images of repeat offenders and their prior arrest record information.

When a homicide is committed, detectives obtain from a witness or other person a description of a possible suspect. Then Identi-Kit 2000 software generates a facial composite based on the description obtained by detectives. ASID compares this composite to all the composites it contains. Search results are composites of individuals who resemble the original composite, and these results are ranked according to probability of likeness. Then the results are transmitted back to Identi-Kit 2000. ASID searches up to 5,000 images a minute. The entire process can take less than five minutes, depending on the type of Internet connection used. After studying all of the photos, detectives select and prepare a photo array to show a witness or other person for positive suspect identification (Smith & Wesson 2000).

CANADIAN POLICE INFORMATION CENTER (CPIC)

The Canadian Police Information Center (CPIC), established in 1972, is an online computer system that consists of nine files. The information in these files pertains to wanted persons, stolen vehicles, unidentified bodies, condensed versions of criminal records, parolees, and vehicle identification numbers (VINs). More than 60,000 law enforcement personnel from 15,000 locations coast-to-coast in Canada query CPIC. CPIC also links over 400 criminal justice agencies worldwide. Police in the United States access CPIC.

However, CPIC technology is outdated. Replacement components are very difficult to find, and the staff that kept CPIC operational are retiring. The CPIC Renewal Project was established to ensure CPIC is upgraded. The upgraded CPIC will be more versatile, secure, dependable, and user-friendly. It will transmit digital fingerprints and mug shots. The new CPIC will include customs and immigration information. Users will index and cross reference information.

Federal employees, private sector individuals, and Royal Canadian Mounted Police (RCMP) are upgrading CPIC. Tentative completion date is 2003 at a cost of $115 million (Griffiths et al. 1999; Levesque 2000).

CASEINFO

CI Technologies (CI), located in St. Augustine, Florida, develops criminal investigation software. CaseInfo, software created by CI Technologies, is used by homicide and other investigators to organize and manage case data. A CaseInfo user can display database information on a screen:

- Names of investigators and their units (e.g., domestic violence, missing persons, arson)
- Overviews of investigative units in an agency, including cases assigned to specific investigators, such as homicide, suspicious death, and fraud
- Tasks that investigators must complete to clear homicides, such as conducting interviews, submitting evidence to a crime lab, and writing final reports

Investigators search one text field or combinations of text fields and link victims, witnesses, suspects, addresses, vehicles, and businesses. Investigators use scanners, digital cameras, and image files to link photo images with other variables.

Many individuals use CaseInfo, but not every user can access all the data. Sensitive information can be made available on a need-to-know basis. CaseInfo functions as a standalone system or as part of a larger network, and is compatible with various servers, including Windows 95/98/NT, Novell Netware, and UNIX. In 1990, police used CI software to investigate the murders of students by the Gainesville Ripper in Gainesville, Florida (see chapter 3) (CaseInfo 2001).

CERTIFINDER

LEXIS-NEXIS, a major worldwide information provider, manages thousands of databases and several billion computer records, which are regularly updated.

In 1998, LEXIS-NEXIS introduced CertiFINDER, an online information service that can help homicide investigators and other law enforcement professionals locate individuals who might otherwise remain in hiding. CertiFINDER searches include corporate and limited partnership registrations, professional licenses, deed transfers, bankruptcy filings, and Social Security Administration death benefits limits. CertiFINDER also searches hundreds of daily newspapers and wire services. A person using CertiFINDER can tailor the search to fit his or her specific needs. CertiFINDER can help prosecutors locate witnesses and officers locate individuals involved in identity fraud (CertiFINDER 1999).

COMBINED DNA INDEX SYSTEM (CODIS)

CODIS is a DNA database that consists of three files. The population file contains anonymous DNA profiles and is used to statistically interpret profiles. The forensic index contains DNA profiles based on evidence associated with crimes; its DNA results are from unknown offenders. The convicted offender index has DNA profiles based on blood samples.

When this system was being developed, every state expressed interest in having its own CODIS database, containing DNA profiles of offenders convicted of crimes such as rape and murder. CODIS, a Federal Bureau of Investigation (FBI) initiative, had approximately 250,000 DNA profiles in 2000 (Bennett and Hess 2001; Fisher 2000).

COMPUTER-ASSISTED ROBBERY SYSTEM (CARS)

The Computer-assisted Robbery System (CARS) is a New York Police Department (NYPD) database that has, since the mid-1980s, compiled information about felony arrests, homicides, robberies, and sex crimes in New York City. Detectives use CARS to find information about nicknames and types of weapons, and can relate this information to potential suspects (Maple and Mitchell 1999).

GEOGRAPHIC PROFILING

The behavior of a suspect during a suspect's movement from home or workplace to where the suspect commits a crime can be analyzed in terms of geographic variables. This analysis can help investigators predict the location at which the suspect can likely be apprehended. This is the basis of geographic profiling.

Data about crimes, victims, and suspects are used to create a computer-based geographic information system (GIS). The suspect's residence, workplace, and travel routes can be indicated on a computer-generated three-dimensional map. Police foot patrol and other resources can be deployed to apprehend a suspect.

A computer program called ORION merges aerial photograph data, postal codes, census data, land use records, and other information with GIS data. ORION then calculates algorithms to create a three-dimensional map. With the aid of this map, police can strategically deploy squad cars and focus on specific areas of a city or a larger geographic area. Expensive and ineffective searches can be avoided.

Detective Inspector Kim Rossmo of the Vancouver (British Columbia) Police Department's Geographic Profiling Section helped develop ORION, which is compatible with the Violent Crime Linkage Analysis System (ViCLAS; see page 50) (Boei and Bramham 1996; Griffiths et al. 1999; Kines 1999; Ramsay 1997).

HOMICIDE INFORMATION TRACKING AND MANAGEMENT AUTOMATION NETWORK (HITMAN)

Lieutenant Edward Hocking and Sergeant Jeff Willis of the Los Angeles Police Department (LAPD) developed HITMAN (Homicide Information Tracking and Management Automation Network), a menu-driven system administered by police officers that contains records of homicides committed in Los Angeles, California, since 1985.

Hocking met with ten detectives from the Los Angeles area to get their input before HITMAN was created. He wanted the system to be comprehensive and simple. After HITMAN was successfully used in the Hollywood Division, it was expanded citywide to Los Angeles detective bureaus and homicide headquarters.

HITMAN has a freeform text field. Police officers enter text, which is then searchable. Searchers have great flexibility via personal computer to manipulate database information. Officers are not restricted to narrowly defined fields. For example, the perpetrator of one homicide drew a pentagram in blood on the body of a homicide victim. The perpetrator of another homicide put salt on the bodies of his victims, then drank their blood. It is nearly impossible to create a form with a check box for case-specific information as in these examples. Case information can be so diverse and voluminous that dealing with it in a strictly paper format can become a formidable task. HITMAN, however, electronically links database information to easily establish a variety of relationships. Police officers can then analyze the relationships between murders such as these two (Gralla 1989).

HOMICIDE INVESTIGATION
AND TRACKING SYSTEM (HITS)

The Homicide Investigation and Tracking System (HITS) is a computer system that provides investigators with information about murder, rape, and gang-related crime. HITS was established in Washington and was initially funded by the National Institute of Justice (NIJ). HITS consists of databases containing information supplied by participating jurisdictions, including jurisdictions in Washington, California, and Oregon.

Information about more than 1,300 murders committed between 1981 and 1986 in Washington formed the basis for HITS. This information was obtained from police and sheriffs' departments, medical examiners' and coroners' offices, the Washington State Department of Vital Statistics, and other agencies. Investigators then completed a multipage form containing 467 fields of information. A shorter version of the form developed after 1986 contained 250 fields.

Investigators can search for information from one field or multiple fields in any order or combination because HITS is an interactive relational-based system. For example, an investigator working a fresh homicide can query HITS to determine if it contains information similar to the information that describes the fresh homicide. If the fresh homicide is the rape and murder of a white female prostitute, the detective can determine if, during a specific time, there were other homicides with certain features common to the fresh homicide. The versatility of HITS allows investigators to identify patterns and link homicides, which before HITS may not have been linked.

HITS has other features, including the capability to identify current and former inmates convicted of murder or sexual assault and to chronologically track the activities of known murderers. When a HITS form is completed and data is entered into HITS, HITS creates a report that is sent to VICAP (Violent Criminal Apprehension Program), a national program for tracking serial killers that is administered by the FBI.

Data specific to each state that participates in HITS is also useful when each state submits information to the FBI's Uniform Crime Reporting (UCR) Program. The UCR, initiated in 1929 by the International Association of Chiefs of Police (IACP), analyzes and retains information submitted to it by local law enforcement agencies throughout the United States (Keppel and Weis 1993; United States Department of Justice—Office 1997).

MOBILE DATA TERMINALS (MDTS)

In 1983 the Los Angeles Police Department (LAPD) began using mobile data terminals (MDTs), also known as mobile digital terminals, to supplement radio communications. MDTs are small, stationary computer terminals located between the driver and front passenger seats of police vehicles. MDTs transmit and receive more information quicker than two-way radios. MDTs usually accomplish in seconds what radios accomplish in two or three minutes. Officers using MDTs bypass dispatchers who are busy doing several things at once, including communicating with cars, looking up information related to incidents, and clarifying certain information with other dispatchers. In addition, MDTs provide more privacy and safety for officers than radios. A suspect searched outside a police vehicle often hears, over the radio, what is said about him or her. It is less likely that a suspect in the backseat of a police car, let alone one standing outside the car, can read the text on an MDT, especially if the suspect is in a cage car and there is at least one officer in the front seat.

A flashing light alerts an officer that an incident to investigate has been sent to the officer's MDT. The officer types into the terminal the code identifying his or her vehicle, then hits the receive button. For example, Four-King-Twenty (4-K-20) means the vehicle is a robbery/homicide field–supervisor unit. The message received appears on the computer screen.

The incident number is first in a sequence of information displayed. This number is called the occurrence, complaint, or file number in other cities. The LAPD investigated approximately 5,500 incidents a day in 1996. The letters D-I-S, which indicate that a call was dispatched to 4-K-20, are next in the sequence. This is followed by the address of the incident: 7-8-2-5 East Cherry Lane. One-eight-seven, the code for this call, is next. This code, the California Penal Code section for homicide, means the incident is a homicide. The responding field supervisor might be dispatched "code 2"—proceed immediately, no siren.

The field supervisor then pushes the ENR button to inform the dispatcher that the status of 4-K-20 is en route to the incident. The officer obtains additional information by entering the incident number, for example, 4-8-2-0. This provides answers to: Is there a possible suspect? What type of weapon was used? Is there a criminalist on scene?

In New York, the first MDTs were installed in police cars in 1986. By 1999, 2,000 marked police vehicles in New York were equipped with MDTs. All the MDTs are connected to wireless equipment, which transmits radio waves to one of thirty-two base sites. Each site acts as an antenna and uses two frequencies: one for transmitting data, one for receiving data. Telephone lines link each base site to one of four radio network controllers (RNCs). RNCs ensure that, as patrol cars travel throughout the city, each MDT communicates with at least one base site.

New York Police Department (NYPD) officers did not initially like MDTs. These officers associated a keyboard with a secretary typing. It took approximately two years to change this attitude.

MDTs enable NYPD officers to access the New York State Police Information Network (NYSPIN) in Albany. NYSPIN receives, evaluates, and routes MDT messages to state and federal databases. The structure and content of a message determines to which database NYSPIN routes a message. A license plate check routed to the New York State Department of Motor Vehicles will tell an officer who has stopped a suspicious vehicle if a homicide suspect stole the vehicle's plates. A driver's license plate number is entered into an MDT connected to the National Crime Information Center 2000 (NCIC 2000) near Washington, D.C. NCIC 2000 can confirm if it is associated with a certain felon, regardless of where in the United States this felon may be. The National Law Enforcement Telecommunications System (NLETS), accessible via NYSPIN, allows officers access to department of motor vehicle information in any state.

MDTs were introduced as an aid to fight crime and were to be used only for official purposes. The LAPD in 1983 was to monitor MDT messages to ensure only official information was transmitted. One month of transmissions translated into a stack of printouts eleven feet high. This represented minute-by-minute chronological transmissions. Continuous staff shortages made monitoring impossible.

Although police communications technology had changed, police using newer technology in Los Angeles, New York, and elsewhere had in many ways remained essentially the same. Sports scores and other unofficial information could now be transmitted over radio and MDT occasionally when radio traffic and MDT messages were not peaking. Otherwise, the transmission of unofficial information could impede the broadcast of official information, especially high-priority information about a crime such as a bank robbery in progress (Dunn 1996; Gates and Shah 1992; Greenman 1999; Schaffter, *LAPD Codes*, 1996; Schaffter, *LAPD Crime*, 1996; Schaffter, *LAPD Unit*, 1996).

NAGRA

A Nagra is a type of tape recorder used by police in undercover work. One type of Nagra is four inches wide, six inches long, and three-quarters of an inch thick, and it uses a three-hour tape. This model can record, but does not have playback capability. The microphone, approximately the size of a pencil-tip eraser, is attached to a long wire. The Nagra can be attached to a person's back or stomach, or carried in a pocket or boot. Although it is possible to see if the tape is rolling before using this tape recorder, it is not possible to see if the tape is recording until it is played back on a playback machine. A person wearing a Nagra can record virtually anywhere. However, unlike a T-4 transmitter, whose transmissions are monitored and recorded by police, who can rush to the aid of an undercover officer if necessary, it is much less likely the officer wearing a Nagra can be reached in time if something goes wrong. A Nagra may be used when an undercover officer has numerous meetings with a criminal and when recorded evidence regarding these meetings is accumulated over a long time period. These meetings may be between an officer and a criminal who trusts the officer. The officer, although at risk, has a very high probability of leaving undetected and unharmed after each meeting (Pistone and Woodley 1987).

NATIONAL CRIME INFORMATION CENTER (NCIC)

The National Crime Information Center (NCIC) was an online real-time computer system. Managed by the FBI in Washington, D.C., the NCIC became operational on January 27, 1967. It was created in response to the need for automated sharing of crime data between agencies. Three organizations contributed to its establishment: the FBI, the Committee on Uniform Crime Records, and the IACP. Criminal justice agencies throughout the United States and Canada accessed the NCIC twenty-four hours a day, 365 days a year.

Police officers on the street radioed or phoned a dispatcher; this dispatcher accessed NCIC files via computer terminal. Officers in vehicles equipped with a mobile data terminal (MDT) directly accessed these files. The criminal history file was sometimes called the "national rap sheet." Homicide detectives used the NCIC to find information about guns, license plates, missing persons, unidentified persons, vehicles, wanted persons, and other matters.

When homicide investigators entered the name and date of birth (DOB) of a person, additional information about this person, if on file, appeared on the screen in seconds. If more than one "hit" (search result) was retrieved, investigators modified original searches by adding the sex or race of the person of interest (POI) to the investigators. When, in spite of limiting a search, several hits looked like they could be the correct hit, it was necessary to further study all the retrieved hits. Numerous hits could occur when a person with a name like "John Smith" or "Pat Jones" was queried (moreover, the name "Pat" could refer to a male or female). In general, the more specific the data entered, the more specific the data retrieved.

Initially, fifteen state, metropolitan, and federal criminal justice agencies were linked to the NCIC. Twenty years later, in 1987, the figure was sixty-seven agencies. The five original NCIC files contained fewer than 21,000 active records. By 1987, there were thirteen files and more than 18 million records.

In 1983, the Interstate Identification Index (Triple-I) became a part of the NCIC. Triple-I was accessed when an inquiring department queried NCIC for criminal record information regarding certain states. Certain states individually retained their records, rather than having them kept at the FBI in Washington. For this reason, Triple-I was called a "pointer" system. States that retained their own records responded directly to inquiring departments. Triple-I reduced query response time and reduced the amount of time the FBI spent maintaining records. In 1988, Triple-I had 11,837,835 records. The NCIC processed in June 1991 a daily average of 1,041,344 transactions involving nine files, illustrating the constant use of this resource in law enforcement ("Informational" 1991; Lyford and Wood 1983; NCIC 87-1; NCIC 1991; United 1984; Zonderman 1990).

NATIONAL CRIME INFORMATION CENTER 2000 (NCIC 2000)

The National Crime Information Center was replaced on July 11, 1999, by the National Crime Information Center 2000 (NCIC 2000). This computer system, which cost $183.2 million, is accessed by more than 80,000 criminal justice agencies throughout the United States. NCIC 2000, composed of seventeen databases, has over 39 million records and can process more than 2.4 million transactions daily. It has many more features than its predecessor. For example, NCIC 2000 can search all the derivatives of names such as "Jeff," "Geoff," and "Jeffrey." It also has mug shots and right index fingerprints and can identify images of scars, tattoos, and vehicles (National 1999).

NEW YORK STATE INQUIRY
IDENTIFICATION SYSTEM (NYSIIS)

The first time a person is arrested in New York State, this person is assigned a NYSIIS (New York State Inquiry Identification System) number. This number, which consists of seven digits followed by a letter, is issued to identify the person throughout the remainder of his or her life. An investigator who types a NYSIIS number into a computer terminal retrieves a printout containing a person's criminal history (Rachlin 1995).

POLICE INFORMATION RETRIEVAL SYSTEM (PIRS)

The Police Information Retrieval System (PIRS), administered by the Royal Canadian Mounted Police (RCMP), is a Canadian police records system. PIRS enables participating police jurisdictions to share information throughout Canada. Participants pay an annual fee to the RCMP to access PIRS (Griffiths et al. 1999).

RADIO CHANNEL ZEBRA

In San Francisco, California, between late 1973 and early 1974, black killers randomly targeted white victims during a 179-day period. When police designated a radio channel "zebra" exclusively for use regarding these murders, media in San Francisco wanted to know if the word zebra was used because of the racial nature of the murders: white victims and black perpetrators. Chief of Police Donald M. Scott denied there was any racial implication in using the word zebra. This channel was the only one available at the time for exclusive use (Howard 1979).

T-4 TRANSMITTER

The T-4 transmitter is used by police during undercover work. This transmitter is three-and-a-half inches long by two inches wide by one-quarter of an inch thick. Rather than recording conversations, the T-4 transmits to nearby police officers who monitor and record them. The T-4 has an antenna from one to two inches long, with a tiny bulb at the end that acts as the microphone. Screwing on the antenna activates the transmitter. With new batteries, the T-4 lasts approximately four hours. When a police officer is undercover, there is no way for this officer to know if the T-4 is working; only the monitoring officers know.

In a city, two blocks is the approximate broadcast range of the T-4. Because of this distance, monitoring officers can usually assist the undercover officer quickly if a problem arises. Steel structures, atmospheric conditions, and passing vehicles can interfere with transmissions. If the undercover officer goes out of broadcast range, monitoring officers do not know what is happening. If the officer wearing a T-4 is in a room where a television is on, the T-4 can broadcast through the TV the conversations it is transmitting to the monitoring officers. Everyone in the room then knows someone in the room is wearing a "wire" (Pistone and Woodley 1987).

TALK CHANNEL

When homicide detectives discuss in depth something about a homicide, a "talk channel" is an option. A talk channel is a police radio channel for conversations that are longer in duration than those on dispatch channels. Dispatch channel conversations are normally brief and require little, if any, elaboration; they are for developing incidents reported to dispatch by the public. A talk channel, unlike some dispatch channels, does not usually have numerous users competing for channel airtime. Talk channel transmissions may be scrambled. This depends on the level of sophistication of communications technology in a particular police department (Pence 1998).

TEN CODES

Ten codes are numerical expressions that begin with "10," followed by a hyphen and one or two other numbers. Sometimes a letter of the alphabet is added as a suffix. Ten codes are a part of radio and mobile data terminal (MDT) communications. Brevity, not privacy, is the purpose of these codes. The general meaning of ten codes can be easily understood from the context in which they are used.

It is easier and faster to send a message by ten code, such as "10-13" (officer requires immediate assistance), than by using words to convey the same message. This is especially true when a radio channel is heavily used. It is also easier and faster to type "10-13" and an address into an MDT than to type one or more sentences that describe the problem.

Ten codes, widely used in the United States and Canada, vary in meaning from one jurisdiction to another. In Canada, the Royal Canadian Mounted Police (RCMP) use "10-35" to indicate homicide. The Calgary (Alberta) Police Service uses "10-35" to refer to threats. In Philadelphia, Pennsylvania, however, no codes are used. According to

Willie Williams, the former chief of police in Philadelphia and Los Angeles, California, a robbery in Philadelphia is simply called a "robbery," but in Los Angeles it is called a "2-11." Some jurisdictions, including jurisdictions in Florida and Louisiana, use the word "signal" followed by one or two numbers instead of using ten codes (Alberta 1998; Lloyd and Herman 1996; McCormick 1993; Williams and Henderson 1996).

VIOLENT CRIME LINKAGE ANALYSIS SYSTEM (VICLAS)

Behavioral research and computer technology were combined by Canadian police agencies to develop a system for linking information about serial killers and other violent offenders. This system is called Violent Crime Linkage Analysis System (ViCLAS). ViCLAS contains information about homicides if they are sexual in nature, random, or apparently motiveless. A random homicide is one in which almost anyone, almost anywhere, could be the victim, and the randomness of the act can suggest the type of killer and motive. A young person, middle-aged person, and elderly person can be robbed and murdered. However, a young person, middle-aged person, and elderly person can also be murdered for no apparent reason.

ViCLAS also has information about sexual assaults, including date rapes and pedophilia crimes, and missing persons, foul play (violence), unidentified bodies, suspicious circumstances (any person or thing that does not appear to belong in a particular place or situation or belongs but contains an element that is out of context), and nonparental abductions of children.

An investigator fills out a detailed questionnaire to submit case information to ViCLAS. This questionnaire consists of 262 questions. A crime analyst analyzes each new case to determine if there are anywhere in Canada linkages with similar crimes. In one case, ViCLAS was successfully used to apprehend Francis Carl Roy, charged with the sexual assault and murder of a Toronto girl, Alison Parrott. Roy made his first court appearance regarding this murder on August 1, 1996, ten years after police began searching for Parrott's killer. Roy was sentenced in 1999 to life in prison (Griffiths et al. 1999; "Life" 1999; "New" 1996).

VIOLENT CRIMINAL APPREHENSION PROGRAM (VICAP)

Of all the homicide cases that Los Angeles police officer Pierce R. Brooks worked in 1958, two stood out because he felt that the killer in both cases had killed before. Brooks wanted to know if similar homicides had occurred in the past in Los Angeles or elsewhere. To attempt to find out, he would go to the city library, where he would look through newspapers from major cities. Basic library research was the best Brooks could do because, during the late 1950s, there was no national information center that housed information on transient killers. Brooks believed there was a way to effectively accumulate, organize, and disseminate the kind of information he needed.

In the late 1970s, he contacted the U.S. Department of Justice about his concept. Eventually, a task force of experts from over twenty law enforcement agencies studied Brooks's ideas. This task force was known as the Violent Criminal Apprehension Program (VICAP) Task Force. At the same time that the VICAP Task Force was studying Brooks's proposal, the FBI's Behavioral Science Unit (BSU) at the FBI Academy in Quantico, Virginia, was discussing the development of a National Center for the Analysis of Violent Crime (NCAVC).

The VICAP Task Force and the BSU worked together more closely. VICAP was established in 1984 after the NCAVC received a grant from the National Institute of Justice (NIJ). On May 29, 1985, Brooks entered data from the first VICAP Crime Report into the new VICAP computer system. (For more information on Brooks's career, see page 70.)

VICAP became a nationwide information center for the collection, analysis, and distribution of data pertaining to specific crimes of violence, including homicides, attempted homicides, missing persons, and unidentified bodies. Information about these crimes would be included when they involved or appeared to involve abduction or sexual motivation, or when they appeared to be random or part of a series.

VICAP includes the FBI's "mind hunters" system. FBI agents study cases, including crime scene photographs. These agents then predict certain things about a murderer, including the murderer's age, marital status, type of vehicle driven, and probable area of residence (Marriner 1991; Ressler 1986).

WARRANT ON-LINE FILE (WOLF)

The Warrant On-Line File (WOLF) is a database that detectives in New York City use to search for warrant information regarding suspects. WOLF provides the names of contacts and their addresses (Maple and Mitchell 1999).

5

Detectives

It takes years of training and experience before a uniformed officer can become a detective. Homicide detectives are specialists who only investigate murders and crimes related to homicide. The homicide detective, although in an autonomous and high-stress position, carries high status within the law enforcement community. Detectives who are often under the scrutiny of the media (particularly in celebrity cases) get little sleep when they catch a fresh homicide, and they may use gallows humor to make the best of a bad situation. In this chapter, we explore twenty-five topics about homicide detectives.

24/24 RULE

The last twenty-four hours of a victim's life and the first twenty-four hours after the victim's body is discovered are the most critical times in a homicide investigation, if the homicide is going to be solved quickly. This period is referred to as the 24/24 Rule.

Detectives want to know the routine of the victim before the victim's death. They want to know the names of individuals who saw or talked to the victim the day before the murder. Twenty-four hours after the homicide, the memories of any witnesses are still relatively fresh. Furthermore, the perpetrator may still be in the community. For this reason, many detectives do not get much sleep during the early stages of a homicide investigation (*Police Jargon* 2000).

AMERICA'S MOST WANTED (AMW)

On July 27, 1981, Reve Walsh, the wife of then–hotel developer, John Walsh, was with their six-year-old son, Adam, at a store in Hollywood, Florida. Reve allowed Adam to play video games in the toy department while she went to another department, approximately seventy-five feet away from the video games area, for a few minutes. When she returned, Adam was nowhere in sight.

Two weeks later, two citrus field workers were walking along a drainage canal near Vero Beach, Florida, approximately 150 miles away. The workers saw something in the canal, which looked like a doll's head. When they looked more closely, they realized the "doll's head" was actually a human head. A family friend subsequently identified the head as that of Adam Walsh.

John and Reve Walsh were emotionally devastated by the death of their young son. They were frustrated by the lack of coordinated effort of law enforcement in the investigation of Adam's murder, which was apparently a senseless act of random violence. Although the killer was never caught, Ottis Toole, a convicted murderer, was for a time the prime suspect in Adam's murder. Toole confessed in 1983 to having killed Adam, but he later recanted his confession. Toole died of cirrhosis of the liver on September 15, 1996, while serving a twenty-year prison term for arson. At this time, different jurisdictions in Florida did not generally cooperate adequately to share information concerning crimes in their respective jurisdictions.

John repeatedly appeared on radio and television programs across the United States, including ABC's *Good Morning America*, to generate public support for the establishment of a centralized resource for helping locate missing children. He and Reve appeared before the House Judiciary Subcommittee on Missing Children and met then-President Reagan. The Adam Walsh Child Resource Center was established with Reve's help.

The Walshes' testimony before state legislatures and Congress brought about the establishment of the Missing Children Act in 1982. This act required the Federal Bureau of Investigation (FBI) to provide computer access to information concerning missing children and unidentified dead bodies. It also allowed parents to add information for computer access when local police did not do this. The Missing Children Assistance Act was passed in 1984. It established the National Center for Missing and Exploited Children (NCMEC).

John Walsh had reservations about hosting *America's Most Wanted* when he was approached by Fox Television. He discussed with Reve the implications, including the likelihood of he and his family being targeted by certain criminals if he accepted Fox's offer. He did accept the offer, and there have been death threats against him and his family. Private investigator James Wagner, formerly a sergeant with the New York Police Department (NYPD), was Walsh's bodyguard during trips between New York and Washington, D.C.

AMW has been a very popular and successful program. The broadcast of fugitive profiles on television in the United States and Canada has resulted in the apprehension of hundreds of criminals, including numerous perpetrators of homicides (Bartley 1990; Suspected 1996; "20 Years" 2001; Wagner and Picciarelli 1999; Walsh and Schindehette 1997).

CATCHING

Catching is also known as "catching squeals." It means that during a particular shift, also known as a tour, a detective answers the squad room phones and "catches"—takes responsibility for investigating fresh homicides. Homicide detectives take turns catching. If the case the detective catches is high profile, the homicide commander may assign the best detectives to this case, even though one of them may not have caught it. This exception to the general procedure for catching may be made if a police officer or child is murdered.

The catching detective's responsibilities range from squad room paperwork to helping the district attorney's (DA's) office bring the case to trial (Ellroy 1996; McKenna and Harrington 1996; Papa 1995; Philbin 1996; Phillips 1977; Rachlin 1995; Seedman and Hellman 1974; Wolfe 1989).

CENTAC 26

Miami, Florida, was the forty-first largest city in the United States in 1980 and the nation's murder capital, with a homicide rate of 70 per 100,000 residents. The murder rates in Miami for the years 1979, 1980, and 1981 were 349, 569, and 621, respectively.

Many homicides in Miami and adjacent Dade County between 1979 and 1982 were drug-related. Some of these homicides were committed by some of the thousands of prison inmates sent by Fidel Castro from Cuba to Miami in 1980. These inmates were among the 125,000 individuals allowed to leave Cuba through the port of Mariel, an incident known as the Mariel boatlift. Some of these Cubans later participated in Miami's violent cocaine trade.

Miami and Dade County had to curb the escalating murder rate. This concern led to the formation of Centac (Central Tactical Unit) 26, a joint task force of state and federal authorities that was approved by the U.S. Justice Department and established on December 11, 1981. Raul Diaz, who wrote the operational plan for Centac 26, was appointed head of this elite team of investigators. This team, at his request, consisted of homicide and narcotics detectives. Diaz believed this expertise would increase the likelihood of solving drug-related murders.

Centac 26 had the autonomy to target particular individuals and, when necessary, work a specific case for long periods. Normally, detectives simultaneously worked numerous cases. Centac 26 detectives followed and watched targeted individuals and gave these suspects the option of cooperating or facing a long prison term.

In 1982, Centac 26, with the cooperation of the Drug Enforcement Administration (DEA), had a homicide clearance rate of 100 percent. New and old cases were cleared. This was significant because most victims and perpetrators were illegal immigrants with no fingerprints on file in the United States. Few of the weapons used in drug-related homicides were registered. It was usually impossible to obtain witness statements even when there were witnesses.

Also in 1982, Raul Diaz's star was for political reasons no longer rising. Enthusiasm and financial support for Centac 26 waned. A lieutenant who preferred deskwork rather than street work replaced Diaz. In the end, Centac 26 became a casualty of the Miami cocaine trade (Eddy, Sabogal, and Walden 1988; Gugliotta and Leen 1989).

CLEARANCE RATE

Clearance rate is an expression used by police to refer to the percentage of crimes solved during a particular time period. A homicide is cleared when a suspect is arrested or dies; when the suspect confesses to having committed the homicide and the police have a videotape of the confession or have physical evidence linking the suspect to the homicide; when the suspect knows something about the homicide known by the police but not known by the general public; or when there is physical and other evidence linking the suspect to the homicide, even if the suspect denies having committed the homicide.

A jury, however, might decide a suspect is innocent if the suspect's defense attorney is highly competent. The Nicole Simpson and Ron Goldman murders looked cleared in the eyes of the police before the O. J. Simpson criminal trial, however, the jury found Simpson innocent. There were approximately 300 homicides committed annually in New York City in the early 1950s. The NYPD's detective bureau had 3,000 investigators. Almost 90 percent of the homicides were cleared. In the 1990s, approximately 2,100 homicides were committed annually. The detective bureau had only 1,900 investigators. Consequently, approximately 60 percent of homicides were cleared.

Cases in Washington, D.C., are cleared administratively when the prime suspect dies. An example of this is the murder of Theodore Fulwood on November 19, 1992. Theodore, the brother of former police chief of Washington, D.C., Isaac Fulwood, died after leaving a convenience store. He was shot dead by two perpetrators who suddenly approached him, shooting him eleven times. Earlier, Fulwood had apparently had an altercation with one of the perpetrators. Both perpetrators died violently less than three years later. Because of this, the case was cleared even though the perpetrators were never arrested or tried (Murphy and Plate 1977; Myers 2000; Pooley 1992).

COLD CASE SQUAD (CCS)

If homicide investigators do not arrest a suspect within twenty-four to forty-eight hours of a fresh homicide, the likelihood of ever apprehending a suspect decreases daily after that. When there are witnesses, their accounts of the homicide are usually most accurate just after the homicide occurs and investigators arrive to interview them.

Some types of cases are especially difficult. Witnesses to underworld homicides are usually criminals with no desire to talk with police. Sometimes these witnesses want a deal regarding an upcoming prison sentence. When this is the situation, they want discreet contact with police. If the underworld perpetrators of a homicide learn about the actions of these witnesses, these witnesses can become the next underworld homicide victims.

Drug-related homicides and homicides committed by strangers are especially difficult to solve. It is not easy to find a motive in the latter type of homicide. Perpetrators and witnesses associated with the former type are often killed before they appear in court.

There is, however, a positive side to working a cold case, a case not worked for a year or longer and not receiving the attention it initially received because of fresh, higher priority cases, or because of no new leads. Relationships change over time. Friends become enemies— enemies become friends. Witnesses who are initially afraid to testify might change their minds over time. Some perpetrators brag about having committed a homicide. A drunken perpetrator might brag to a stranger in a bar or to a prostitute. Detectives who solve cold cases look at old information in a new way. Some detectives were patrol officers when a case was first investigated, then the case became cold. These detectives, who had since been promoted from patrol duties to homicide investigation, provide new expertise in cold case investigations. Also, detectives who originally investigated a specific case that became cold periodically review the case. They interview a witness regarding the case and sometimes obtain information that the witness did not provide when the homicide first occurred. This type of interview may help detectives solve the case. New technology, including DNA analysis, which may not have been available when a particular case became cold, may link a suspect, evidence, and victim and lead to a conviction.

In 1960, there were 9,110 recorded homicides in the United States. The figure for 1993 had risen to 24,530. Between 1989 and 1992, Dallas, Texas; San Diego, California; New Haven, Connecticut; Colorado Springs, Colorado; and Washington, D.C., were among the cities with a record number of homicides for their jurisdictions. The homicide rate would continue to increase until 1995.

Moreover, the U.S. nationwide homicide clearance rate dropped from 91 percent in 1965 to 65 percent in 1992. Washington, D.C., had an especially difficult time in 1988 solving its escalating homicides. In 1991, only 54 percent of Washington's homicides were solved during that year.

In 1992, the FBI contributed agents to the Washington Metropolitan Police Department (MPD) Cold Case Squad (CCS). This squad was later composed of MPD and FBI investigators and an assistant U.S. attorney. Investigators had considerable autonomy. They did not work shifts and did not investigate fresh homicides. The cold case concept produced definite positive results. The CCS in Washington closed 157 cold cases and several attempted homicide cases between approximately 1992 and August 1997.

Joe Hill found his father Don Hill, sixty-three, at Cobb Camp Grounds in Osceola National Forest, Florida, on November 19, 1993. The elder Hill, a retired Navy chief petty officer who had gone on a hunting trip, was dead. He had been shot with a shotgun. Lieutenant Charlie Sharman of the Baker County Sheriff's Office and a team of investigators began to investigate the Hill death.

Six days later, on November 25, Vigo Wood found his brother, Greg Wood, thirty-five, at Camp Blanding in southern Clay County, Florida. Greg, who had gone duck hunting the day before, was dead. He had also been shot in the head with a shotgun. In both cases, the families of the victims had become concerned when they did not hear from the victims within a certain time period. This prompted family members to search for the victims. Family members knew in advance the approximate location where each man would be hunting.

After killing the hunters, the killer cut and then took items from the belts of both victims. A knife and sheath were taken from Hill's belt. A .357 revolver, its holster, and a shotgun were taken from Wood's belt. The wallets of both victims were also taken.

Task Force Orion was established to solve the two murders. A nationwide toll-free telephone number for tips was set up, and hundreds of telephone calls were received. A $45,500 reward was posted. Lieutenant Jimm Redmond of the Clay County Sheriff's Office traveled to eleven states to follow up on similar murders. None of these murders, however, appeared to be related to the Florida homicides.

A year later, only occasional tips were received. Task Force Orion was disbanded. Fresher cases took precedence, but Lt. Redmond spent time every week, for the next three years, on the Hill and Wood cases.

During the summer of 1996, Detective Jon Perkins of the Glendale Police Department in Glendale, California, telephoned Lt. Redmond. Perkins was interested in producing a television episode called the "Hunter Homicides" for the program *Cold Case*. Redmond liked the idea very much. The show, televised in April 1997, helped generate new tips.

In August 1997, the Putnam County, Florida, Sheriff's Office located the .357 revolver belonging to Greg Wood and contacted Lt. Redmond. Redmond and Detective Scott Simmons bought the .357 at a pawnshop in Palatka, Florida. The gun had passed, during the previous three-and-a-half years, through the hands of more than a dozen individuals between Florida and North Carolina. Lt. Redmond traced the .357 revolver to the same person who sold a shotgun to a relative of Greg Wood's. This individual was Jimmy Ray Beagle, a thirty-nine-year-old security guard from Jacksonville, Florida.

An undercover informant wearing a wire met with Beagle, and their conversations were recorded. Voluntary interviews with Beagle on March 24, 1998, prompted him to confess to the murder and robbery of Don Hill. Although Beagle did not admit killing Greg Wood, he said he came across Wood's body and stole his guns. During the interview, Beagle was allowed to go to the washroom. When Redmond went to see why Beagle was taking a long time to return to the interview, Redmond learned firsthand that Beagle had a concealed .357 revolver. For the next nine hours, Beagle talked with Redmond and other officers, claiming robbery was his motive in the deaths of Hill and Wood. When chemical gas was used against Beagle, he fired at Special Weapons and Tactics (SWAT) officers through the washroom door. Officers returned fire. An autopsy later revealed that Beagle died from a self-inflicted .357 gunshot wound.

Cold case squads exist in large police agencies around the country. The cold case squad in Dallas, Texas, was formed in 1995. Linda Erwin, the first female homicide detective in Dallas, has worked and cleared cold as well as regular cases. In Boston, Massachusetts, cold case squad lieutenants Timothy J. Murray and Stephen A. Murphy solved the 1991 murder of thirty-three-year-old Corinne Flynn. Flynn, a multiple sclerosis patient, was raped and stabbed to death. In 1996, blood evidence was used in this case to convict Gerald C. Craffey, a carpenter and family friend, of the Flynn homicide. He received a minimum prison sentence of life.

Cold cases often remain cold until investigators receive, frequently from a family member, a hot lead. This happened in the Maylon Johnson murder. Detectives followed up the lead and cleared the case. In Newark, New Jersey, the cold case squad cleared a 1971 homicide in 1995. Susan Marie Watson, a forty-one-year-old keyboard operator, confessed to detectives that she shot to death her mother, Maylon Johnson, while Johnson lay in bed. The motive: The mother refused to do anything after Susan Marie, then a teenager, protested that the mother's boyfriend had sexually abused Susan Marie.

The best cold case investigators are those who are patient, thorough, and perseverant. Either they find a vital piece of information that original investigators missed, or they see old information in a new light. DNA evidence and the Internet are valuable investigative aids. Police departments, including the Kansas City (Missouri) Police Department and the Fort Lauderdale (Florida) Police Department, have cold case web pages. The Fort Lauderdale cold case web page lists the homicide case number, the date on which the homicide occurred, the location of the homicide, the victim's name and photograph, and the names of the detectives working the case. Police telephone numbers are also included. Anyone with potentially useful information can view the web page at home, a library, or elsewhere, and can then anonymously contact police, or can include their name and address, or name and telephone number, when they contact police (Bai 1998; "Cold-Case Unit" 1999; Flynn 1997; Fort Lauderdale 2003; Hunter 2000; *KCPD* 1999; Redmond 1998; Regini 1997; *Unsolved Homicides* 2000).

D-D-FIVE

New York Police Department (NYPD) detectives use a form known as a D-D-Five for recording progress, or lack of progress, regarding a particular case. As detectives work the case, they use a new D-D-Five to update information. D-D-Fives are kept in reverse chronological order for easy access to the most current data (Gourevitch 2000; Hirschfeld 1982).

DEATH NOTIFICATION

Death notification is difficult and stressful for police officers when officers notify a stranger that the stranger's spouse or other family member is dead as the result of an accident, homicide, or suicide. It is even more difficult when the person they notify is a family member of a police officer.

Police officers who make a death notification follow a standard procedure. When the person they have to notify is at home, they first go to a neighbor to learn something about the person to be notified. They try to determine if the person is alone, an invalid, pregnant, or emotionally disturbed. What the officers learn influences how they will deal with the person. The neighbor they initially talk to, or another neighbor who the first neighbor believes may be more capable to help, accompanies the officers.

Police officers know from experience that different people react to death notification in different ways. Some individuals remain calm, some faint, and others panic. Some people cannot believe what they are hearing and accuse the officers of lying. Certain individuals go on a rampage and attack the officers. The possibility of this is the reason why two officers should make the notification.

Officers should know as many facts as possible in order for the family member to comprehend the event. The officers should quickly, concisely, and compassionately break the news in stages. They begin by asking the family member to sit down, and then state their reason for being there—to announce bad news. Finally, the death notification is stated briefly. The next step is to offer to help the family member telephone relatives, clergy, and friends. Officers should discuss the events that led to the death as well as the current location of the body and what has to be done to have it released. Information regarding funeral arrangements should also be made available. The officers should not leave until the mood of the family member is reasonably stable. At least one officer should leave a business card because a family member often thinks of additional questions to ask after the officers have left.

In 1999, 130 police officers in the United States died in the line of duty. Forty-five officers died in shooting incidents. The total of 130 was the lowest number of officers who died in any single year since 1965. Better training and improved equipment were the two main reasons for the decrease in the number of deaths.

The line-of-duty death of a police officer deeply affects both the officer's family and the police department. Immediately after an officer's death, trained personnel should notify the officer's family in person. These individuals should also accompany the family to the hospital or morgue, and assist with all the funeral arrangements.

The department should provide continuing support for the family, including information about death benefits and the trial, if a perpetrator was the cause of the officer's death.

A supervisor should inform all the officers on duty during the incident, about the death, in person. The notification should never be broadcast over police radio, which is routinely monitored by the news media. Supervisors, in person, should also inform officers who report for later shifts. Roll call is a good time to do this. Officers who report for duty by radio after they leave their homes, and who do not go to a precinct or headquarters, should be instructed by their supervisors to telephone them as soon as possible. Supervisors can tell these officers about the death over the telephone. Officers who were at the crime scene should be debriefed. Then they should receive three to six months of psychological counseling.

Employees who were emotionally close to the officer should be promptly notified and treated with the same compassion as the family. This prevents these employees from learning of the death by telephone or from the media. The victim's partner or close coworkers should be thought of as survivors and should not be the department's primary liaison with the family. A partner or close friend at work sometimes requires stress leave until after the funeral.

The department should offer counseling to family members and officers who, during their counseling, learn to recognize the symptoms of post-traumatic stress disorder (PTSD). Recurrent memories and dreams of the event, difficulty sleeping, guilt, and difficulty concentrating are some of the symptoms of PTSD.

A thorough and professional investigation into the officer's death should be conducted, but none of the active participants should be a partner, close friend, or other person who worked daily with the deceased officer. Rumors can be avoided, or at least minimized, by keeping all staff informed about any matters regarding the death (Campbell 1987; Fewer 2000; Newland 1993; Richardson 1975).

DOG OF HOMICIDE VICTIM

Detectives routinely canvass the neighbors of a homicide victim found in a house or apartment. The detectives want to know, among other things, if any of the victim's neighbors heard the victim's dog bark during the approximate time of the murder. If the dog was at the crime scene when the perpetrator committed the crime, the dog likely smelled the perpetrator. If the dog did not bark, the dog did not react to the perpetrator as an intrusive stranger. From this, detectives can surmise the perpetrator may have been on the premises on a previous occasion or occasions. Therefore, the victim and perpetrator knew each other.

Based on this information, detectives more easily prioritize a short list of potential suspects. The names of persons known to the victim are placed at the top of the list. These individuals are investigated first. Strangers are investigated later (Hirschfeld 1982).

FLOPPED

A detective is "flopped," assigned to duty in a uniform (which ranks lower than the work of a plainclothes detective), when he or she does not carry out duties acceptable to supervising officers. When someone, for administrative reasons such as departmental cutbacks, has to be flopped, detectives are ranked according to how well they perform their duties. The detective with the least acceptable performance is most likely to be flopped (Gelb 1975; Lardner 1996).

GALLOWS HUMOR

Doctors and nurses, for professional and personal reasons, cannot allow themselves to regularly cry over terminally ill or other patients. To do so would be to jeopardize their careers and their psychological and physical health. Certain professionals, including doctors, nurses, police officers, and firefighters, cope with stress and life-and-death situations by often using what to other people appears to be insensitive behavior. This is known as "gallows humor."

Firefighters, for example, sometimes refer to burnt corpses as "crispy critters." This expression helps firefighters in distancing themselves from charred bodies. It is easier to deal with death when a corpse is thought of as nonhuman. Police officers routinely react with humor to tragedy, sickness, and irony, developing this response very early in their career. Humor helps officers deal with work-related stress. By the time an officer becomes a homicide detective, he or she is usually adept at behaving this way. Emotional involvement is counterproductive to professionally working a case.

The effect of murder scenes on homicide detectives, including body dumpsites, victims, and the families of victims, leads detectives to use gallows humor as a psychological coping mechanism. This humor involves laughing at horrible situations when most people would expect crying to be the normal response. Crying, however, would interfere with the detectives' efforts to solve homicides. A detective walks into a room in which the detective's partner is looking at a corpse lying on its back. The detective looking at the corpse turns to his partner and says, "Ed, I'd like you to meet Harry. Harry, I'd like you to meet Ed."

For public relations reasons, detectives do not use this humor at crime scenes at which the media, especially journalists with television cameras, are present (Count 1994; Delsohn 1996; Douglas and Olshaker 1995; Gates and Shah 1992; Walker 1976).

GOLDEN RULE OF HOMICIDE

"Never move, touch, or alter anything until it has been noted, sketched, and photographed" (Boyd 1979).

HOLD-BACK

Information about something specific that police withhold is a "hold-back." Detectives hold back information from the public: in other words, they do not disclose to the media all the details of a homicide, especially one that is still under investigation. If the murder weapon was a gun, detectives might not mention the caliber. If the murder weapon was a knife, the type of knife (for example, a hunting knife) might be kept from the public. If the victim was found in a house, detectives might avoid telling the media in which room the victim was found.

There are three basic reasons for withholding from the public the details of a homicide. First, disclosing only some of the details ensures that only detectives and the real perpetrator know all the details. People with serious psychological problems frequently confess to crimes they did not commit. These individuals can impede an investigation by giving police false leads and by being a nuisance. Second, a suspect might flee if the suspect believes police have sufficient evidence to make an arrest, so police often prefer to act like they don't have sufficient evidence to find him or her. Finally, detectives keep details about a homicide from the media because a confession from a suspect who knows about a homicide what only the real perpetrator knows is much more believable in court than a person with limited knowledge of the crime (Jane 2000; Kunen and Sawicki 1991; Simon 1991).

IF THEY'RE DYIN', WE'RE FLYIN'

Some police departments use expressions that are unique to that department. Such expressions help officers to informally communicate with each other and help officers to establish camaraderie.

"If they're dyin', we're flyin'" has been used by homicide detectives in Washington, D.C. This expression refers basically to the hectic pace of work for homicide detectives who respond to one homicide after another. During approximately the first quarter of 1994, Washington had seventeen homicides in nine days, three in approximately half an hour. The only homicides being solved were those at which police found the perpetrator or those in which a witness gave police the name of the perpetrator. Between 1985 and 1993, the number of homicides in Washington increased from 148 to 467 with a clearance rate of only 45 percent in 1993 (Witkin, Creighton, and Guttman, 1994).

KANSAS CITY METRO SQUAD

Clarence Kelley, a former director of the FBI, was also a former chief of police for Kansas City, Missouri. When he was in Kansas City, he knew that neighboring police agencies did not always fully cooperate to solve crimes. This lack of cooperation impeded clearing major cases. Kelly's solution to this problem was to establish a special squad of investigators to work major crimes in multiple jurisdictions. He did this in 1964, by creating the Kansas City Metro Squad. His concept was the first of its kind in North America.

Senior officials from local police agencies coordinate the metro squad and comprise a board of directors. The metro squad provides, upon request, assistance to thirty-four municipalities in the Kansas City area. The metro squad is convened within hours of the report of a major crime. An average of two dozen officers form the squad. These officers are chosen from a duty roster of several hundred personnel. Officers from different agencies comprise two-person teams. This partnership decreases the likelihood of cliques forming, which would be counterproductive to working a case.

If a squad does not clear a case within a week, the agency in whose jurisdiction the crime occurred takes over the case. In October 1996, the metro squad cleared, in five days, the homicide of Will Bonner. Bonner, twenty-three, who had apparently been involved in a methamphetamine operation, had been killed with a .25-caliber handgun. His body was found in a soybean field in Platte County, a Kansas City bedroom community (Burnside 1996).

LINKAGE BLINDNESS

Investigators may know about homicides in a specific geographical region but may not see, until a time in the future, a significant pattern common to all the homicides. The expression "linkage blindness" refers to the failure of investigators to see this pattern. They initially do not see the same modus operandi (MO) or signature associated with several or more homicides. Poor communication can cause linkage blindness, as can a huge number of links.

The police investigation that culminated in the arrest of Canadian serial rapist and killer Paul Bernardo prompted the Ontario government to issue a 400-page report critical of the way police handled the investigation. It was critical because Bernardo apparently committed his first crime that police were aware of in 1987, but he was not arrested until six years later.

In 1988, Bernardo's nineteen-year-old girlfriend told police Bernardo raped her. The rape involved anal sex, a ligature, and a verbal command by Bernardo to his girlfriend to say he is the king. These characteristics were evident in a series of rapes in Scarborough, Ontario, during the next three years. However, police did not link any of these to Bernardo.

Bernardo's bank manager called the police after he saw a sketch that was based on the comments of one of Bernardo's victims and was distributed in late May–early June 1990. Bernardo willingly cooperated with police by agreeing to have his DNA analyzed. However, two years passed before the DNA sample arrived at the lab because DNA samples from 300 other suspects also had to be tested first.

Tammy Homolka's death in late December 1990 was ruled accidental, even though Bernardo and his wife, Karla, Tammy's sister, had murdered her.

Teenage victim Leslie Mahaffy was murdered by Bernardo and Homolka in 1991. In 1992, Joan Packham witnessed the abduction from a church parking lot of teenager Kristen French. Investigators looking for French, who was murdered, searched for a cream-colored Camaro when they should have been looking for a gold-colored Nissan. This was because Packham, who had been driving around and doing errands, told Niagara Regional Police she saw what may have been kids feigning a struggle or kids actually struggling. According to Packham, a Camaro or Trans Am may have been at the scene. Police knew Bernardo had a Nissan, but he was believed to be a stalker, not an abductor: Lori Lazaruk, who was stalked by Bernardo, contacted police to tell them her stalker drove a Nissan. Police never got back to her. They were working on 40,000 tips.

Detectives asked Bernardo in May 1992 where he was when French disappeared. He was cooperative during the interview and readily admitted to detectives that he was a suspect in the Scarborough rape investigation. There was nothing in his remarks to motivate these detectives to continue pursuing this matter with Bernardo. However, they called a Scarborough detective, who told them that Bernardo was no more and no less a suspect in the Scarborough rapes than were the other suspects.

Finally, after Bernardo's eventual arrest in 1993, police failed to find hidden videotapes of torture and rape he had made in his house. Homolka received, in 1993, a twelve-year prison term for manslaughter in exchange for her testimony against Bernardo, who, in 1995, was sentenced to life in prison. Homolka may be paroled in July 2005 (Cairns 2001, 2002; Griffiths, Whitelaw, and Parent 1999; "Missed Opportunities" 1996; Williams 1996).

NOTEBOOK

A notebook is a very important aid in homicide investigation. Detectives use it to take detailed chronological notes. Some of the things they write down are the location of the victim, the apparent cause of death, the time they arrived at the crime scene, the names of individuals already there, the time these individuals arrived, the weather conditions, and the lighting conditions. Excellent notes are of great benefit in court when detectives are cross-examined by an alleged perpetrator's defense attorney. The quality of notes can make a critical difference in convicting or acquitting a defendant.

A notebook that can be easily flipped open, and whose pages cannot be removed and then replaced without any indication of this having been done, is preferable. Such removal and replacement can be done with a binder notebook, and a defense attorney can argue in court that important information may have been added or deleted. The attorney would then raise doubts about the credibility of a detective's testimony regarding statements made by witnesses at the crime scene and statements by other individuals connected to the investigation (Rachlin 1995; Simon 1991; Stroud 1987).

ONTARIO PROVINCIAL POLICE (OPP)

Ontario Provincial Police (OPP) homicide detectives work out of Orillia, Ontario, a two-hour drive north of Toronto.

These detectives use a task force approach. One detective is head of each case and is assisted when necessary by as many as one hundred support staff. Support staff team members range from a telephone receptionist to a finance manager, a victim services counselor to field detectives.

OPP homicide detectives spend considerable time in their cars because they work cases throughout the province. They are for this reason referred to as "the road dicks" ("dick" is an older expression meaning "detective"). Pentium laptops are one of their most important investigative tools: these investigators download case information, which senior officers in Orillia review. Detectives, in accordance with Canadian law, also turn over to defense attorneys cleared-case materials. This material, at a future date, will be on a CD-ROM.

OPP detectives become homicide detectives when they meet the criteria of a selection model similar to one used by the FBI. Knowledge, skills, and ability (KSA) are the basis of the selection program. Investigative skills, leadership qualities, and effectiveness in court testimony are important. It can take up to six months for a candidate to be evaluated for suitability. Peers, superiors, and subordinates are interviewed. Scores determine if the candidate will work homicide. The selection process is important because of OPP's high standards: between approximately 1994 and 1999, OPP homicide detectives cleared 92 percent of the homicides they investigated (Pron 1999).

PIERCE R. BROOKS

Pierce R. Brooks was a beat cop in Los Angeles, California, during the mid-1940s and a captain when he left the Los Angeles Police Department (LAPD) twenty-one years later. As a homicide detective, Brooks worked the "lonely hearts murders." These were the rape, torture, and murder of women in southern California by Harvey Glatman.

Glatman was an innocuous-looking man who moved to California from New York in 1957, and worked in Los Angeles as a TV repairman. He was a sadistic killer who pretended to be a photographer for a lonely hearts magazine. He conned models into believing he wanted them to pose for a photo shoot.

Each of his victims was found in the desert, bound with rope, and there was a gag in each victim's mouth. Glatman photographed the victims in various positions and various stages of undress. He kept trophies of the murders, which included articles of the victims' clothing, and used the trophies to later help him relive the murders. An examination of the expressions on the faces of Glatman's victims reveals how the expressions changed from photograph to photograph as the victims realized they were not being photographed for a magazine but were the captives of a killer who was about to kill them.

Glatman was convicted of the murders of Judy Ann Dull, Shirley Bridgeford, and Ruth Mercado, and was executed in the gas chamber in San Quentin in August 1959.

These murders convinced Pierce Brooks that police would benefit from a system that would link information about unsolved murders with similar characteristics, even though the murders may have occurred in different parts of the country. In 1982, Brooks testified before the U.S. Senate, emphasizing the need to establish the Violent Criminal Apprehension Program (VICAP). VICAP, which was discussed earlier on page 51, would retain and correlate information submitted by different jurisdictions about unsolved murders and disappearances throughout the United States. Investigators would use VICAP to look for patterns that suggest that transient serial killers are the perpetrators of certain homicides.

After Brooks left the LAPD, he became the chief of police in Springfield, Oregon. Brooks, who died in 1998, had a master's degree. He wrote a book about the mistakes made by police officers killed in the line of duty. Brooks also conducted seminars and gave lectures on police officer survival (Brooks 1975; Keppel and Birnes 1997; Michaud and Hazelwood 1998; Newton 1998).

PROP ROOM

Police use a special room, the prop room, when they interrogate a suspect. The contents of this room psychologically influence the suspect to believe police know more about the suspect's activities than may be the case. There may be crime scene photographs on a wall, file folders with the suspect's name on a table, and official-looking papers in a folder.

Detectives escort the suspect through the prop room on their way to the interrogation room. Sometimes they leave the suspect in the prop room so the suspect has time to get the impression that police have practically solved the homicide. A senior investigator may casually enter the prop room, then angrily yell out to other detectives that the suspect should not have been allowed to spend time in the prop room and should immediately be taken to the interrogation room. A prop room was used when a suspect was interrogated regarding the robbery and murder of nine people in 1991 at the Wat Promkunaram Buddhist temple west of Phoenix, Arizona ("The Buddhist" 2002).

ROBERT K. RESSLER

Robert K. Ressler, a former FBI agent who coined the term "serial killer," profiles killers of unsolved murders. Ressler, a former Viet

Nam veteran, spent twenty years with the FBI. He has interviewed
numerous serial killers, including Jeffery Dahmer and Ted Bundy; is
also an expert witness; and has lectured at Bramshill, Hampshire,
the British police training college.

He worked on the Jill Dando homicide. Dando, the popular host
of the British television program *Crimewatch UK*, the British
equivalent of *America's Most Wanted*, was shot dead in daylight in
front of her London home at 29 Gowan Avenue on April 26, 1999.
In the apartment of suspect Barry George, police found gun magazines, celebrity magazines, a gun holster, clothes matching those
of the killer, and photographs of George in violent poses. In 2001,
George was sentenced to life in prison (Brunt 2000; "Picture
Gallery" 2001).

SET

A set is a specific period during which detectives work a homicide
case. A set consists of four shifts, each shift consisting of eight or
nine hours. If detectives cannot break a case during a set, they work
another case because fresh homicides take precedence. Using a set is
understandable in scenarios such as New York in the early 1990s.
The number of homicides was soaring and the number of detectives
was dropping, so detectives had limited time to allot to each case
(Pooley 1992).

SPECIAL HOMICIDE INVESTIGATION TEAM

The Dade County Public Safety Department in Dade County,
Florida, established, in June 1979, an eighteen-man homicide task
force, the Special Homicide Investigation Team. The task force had a
mandate to investigate twenty-four drug-related homicides, which
involved Latinos and dated back to November 1978. Due to work
force shortages, the team was disbanded four weeks later. The efforts of these officers resulted in the confiscation of six pounds of cocaine, seven guns, $40,000 in cash, and one arrest for first-degree
murder (Gugliotta and Leen 1989; Hiaasen and Messerschmidt
1979).

STRESS

Homicide detectives, especially those in large urban areas, see things in their daily work that make reality-based television pale by comparison. They see, in a room, the partial remains of a baby who was viciously kicked dozens of times by a crack cocaine addict who went berserk. They may see, in the trunk of a car, a dead and mutilated underworld figure, his penis cut off and partially stuffed in his mouth. They may see the body of an elderly woman stabbed so many times that the total number of stab wounds is not determined until the body is removed and washed at the morgue.

When detectives see these types of crime scenes, they know someone close to them, family or friend, could have been the intended victim. Detectives know human lives are fragile. For this reason, detectives can be more protective of their family and friends than can most other people.

Detectives see violent death firsthand. Most other people get information about violent death secondhand or thirdhand. They hear about it on radio or from other people, see it on television, or read about it in newspapers and other publications. Their experience of violent death is neither direct nor intimate, as it is for detectives.

Images of and the smell of blood and other body fluids, as well as the grotesque facial expressions of many homicide and suicide victims, have an unsettling effect on detectives. They learn to work homicide by becoming intimately familiar with a victim's life without becoming emotionally involved in it. However, this is not easy to do. The homicide crime scene, and everything negative it reflects, is a stressor, something that causes psychological and physiological stress. Stress is the response of an organism to an influence that affects that organism. Some stress is essential for survival, but excessive stress can cause death.

When detectives arrive at a fresh homicide scene, they know that if they do not arrest a perpetrator within twenty-four hours of the crime, the likelihood of apprehending the perpetrator diminishes quite rapidly after this time. Hyperawareness of time, like at a crime scene, is another stressor. Waiting for other individuals, such as the medical examiner, to arrive is also stressful. Medical examiners are busy professionals who attend many death scenes, and they cannot always be at a particular homicide scene at the same time as detectives. Detectives may be anxious to find out if there is physical evidence under the body of the victim. However, only the medical examiner can legally move the body.

It is common for detectives to work a fresh case day and night for the first forty-eight hours, occasionally taking a few naps during this time. If the fresh case is high-profile, the media, police administrators, and victim's family will all want detectives to quickly solve the murder. As detectives work a fresh case, other cases they are responsible for are temporarily put on hold. These detectives have little, if any, time to relax. Fatigue from lack of sleep can cause case errors and concern about the cases on hold. After forty-eight hours, suspects and witnesses may have disappeared. Those who have not disappeared may be less cooperative than before. If they are cooperative, their accounts may not be as accurate as they were during the first two days.

The pager, telephone, personal computer, cell phone, mobile data terminal (MDT), and radio contribute to the pressure. All are reminders that, at any moment, this detective may have to stop doing what he or she is doing to deal with another matter. During the investigation, the detective in charge juggles communication between all the individuals involved in the investigation, the writing of reports, and communication with the media and victim's family.

Prosecutors prefer evidence beyond probable cause before they try a case. For detectives, having the satisfaction of clearing a homicide does not come quickly. Plea bargaining, encouraged by the legal system, allows perpetrators to plead guilty to lesser charges. When this happens, much of the work that detectives do ends up being a waste of time.

Dealing with the family of a victim is stressful because these individuals are often grief-stricken, angry, and frustrated. They do not understand the nuances of the criminal justice system. On the one hand, the detective has to be sensitive to the needs of the victim's family; on the other hand, the detective has to have a certain emotional distance for his or her own psychological well being. There are further complications when a family member is the prime suspect or the identified offender. Limited or inconclusive evidence means the detective has to walk a fine line in his or her relationship with this person.

Sometimes a homicide occurs in a geographical area where more than one law enforcement agency is legally responsible for solving the homicide. It is common on these occasions for different agencies to work against each other rather than to cooperate to solve the homicide. This can cause a delay in solving the homicide or the homicide may not be solved. Differences in the education, training, experience, and reputation of detectives contribute to the rivalry. Jealousy and lack of effective communication between agencies can further hinder an investigation. Social support services, such as government mental health agencies, frustrate detectives when mental health agencies prematurely release perpetrators who, upon release, commit an additional serious crime. All this can result in detectives directing their anger toward superiors, suspects, spouses, family, and friends.

Stress management for police officers begins at the police academy. Recruits are told about the necessity of developing and maintaining emotional distance in their work. Slides, videotapes, and case examples are used to impress this upon the recruits. The goal of this training is to desensitize them to what they will encounter when they graduate. New officers who express too much emotion at violent crime scenes are reprimanded. Homicide detectives are supposed to demonstrate professionalism, competence, and self-control. Even when a particular crime scene deeply bothers a detective, this detective is usually adept at hiding his or her true feelings. This investigator does not want peers to notice any sign of weakness. Gallows humor helps keep real feelings hidden. Police and underworld jargon masks certain grim realities. Someone is "whacked out" or "clipped" rather than murdered. A murder is a "1-8-7" or a "10-35."

For homicide detectives and other individuals who respond to homicide crime scenes, such as uniformed officers, paramedics, medical examiners, and prosecutors, mandatory critical incident stress (CIS) debriefing provides a regular and formal process through which to vent emotions and receive peer support without judgmental analysis. Psychologists and grief counselors, whose qualifications demonstrate that they are professionals who genuinely understand law enforcement and the traumas associated with it, can be of assistance to detectives and their families.

The homicide detective who does not produce positive results will be out of homicide in a year or two, transferred to less demanding duties. Job rotation for detectives who have been in homicide a designated maximum number of years can also help combat stress.

With job rotation, detectives are assigned to less stressful duties. Detectives exhibiting more stress than their peers are rotated more quickly. Proper diet, exercise, and positive changes in a detective's lifestyle also help manage stress (Miletich 1990; Sewell 1994; Stratton 1979).

WALKTHROUGH

As detectives arrive at the scene of a homicide, police officers already there walk with and point out to these detectives what appears to have occurred, pointing out a body, a gun, a shell casing, blood spatter, or other things that define the crime scene. This cursory look at the crime scene is the initial walkthrough.

Every person who does a walkthrough must not add anything to or remove anything from the crime scene. To discard at or remove from a crime scene a cigarette butt, match, gum wrapper, or anything else is to contaminate the scene. Some detectives prevent themselves from contaminating the crime scene by keeping their hands in their pockets during a walkthrough. Other detectives wear thin rubber gloves to prevent leaving fingerprints. Some crime scenes have so many fingerprints, some inadvertently left by police, paramedics, medical examiner's staff, or other individuals, that all these individuals are fingerprinted to eliminate them as potential suspects.

The duties of the medical examiner at the crime scene include a preliminary examination of the decedent and officially pronouncing the decedent dead. The duties of the criminalists include taking measurements, gathering and labeling evidence, and photographing and videotaping everyone and everything at the crime scene. Then detectives are allowed to remove personal effects from the victim.

After the investigation at the scene is completed, the detectives do a final walkthrough. They make certain they did everything that had to be done correctly. There can be more than one walkthrough between the initial and final walkthrough. It is common for some uniformed officers, detectives, and criminalists to spend eight to sixteen or more hours at a homicide crime scene to ensure that they investigated everything correctly (Berry-Dee and Odell 1992; Cuomo 1995; Gates and Shah 1992; Lange, Vannatter, and Moldea 1997; Rachlin 1991; Smith 1997).

6

Assessment of the Crime Scene

The crime scene, sometimes referred to as the "primary crime scene," is the place or location where a victim is found. The secondary crime scene may be a location half a block away where investigators find a victim's wallet or other evidence. The first officer to arrive at a crime scene finds the victim, confirms the victim is dead, determines if anyone else at the scene requires medical attention, covers the victim with a sheet, searches the crime scene for perpetrators, secures the scene with barrier tape, and stands by until the homicide detectives arrive. Onlookers can unintentionally contaminate a crime scene by altering, removing, or destroying evidence, such as paper, plastic wrappers, cigarette butts, or fibers. In the following chapter, we look at six things noted by the first officer on the crime scene.

BARRIER TAPE

Barrier tape, also referred to as fluorescent tape or yellow police streamers, is made of heavy yellow vinyl and is used to control crowds and restrict access to a crime scene. Unauthorized individuals are kept out of a crime scene to prevent them from contaminating it. In the United States, the most common types of barrier tape used have the following words in large letters: "Police Line—Do Not Cross," "Crime Scene—Do Not Enter," and "Sheriff Line—Do Not Cross." Barrier tape with Spanish words is also used in cities such as Los Angeles, California, which has a large Latino population.

Before barrier tape was invented, rope and wooden barricades were used to prevent unauthorized access to crime scenes. On August 12, 1962, homicide detectives in Toronto, Ontario, took a homicide investigation kit and no-entry ropes to a homicide crime scene. The homicide investigation kit, a club bag, contained items ranging from rubber gloves to measuring tapes, occurrence forms to vials. These items were used to prepare and preserve evidence. The victim, a young girl, was lying in a ditch. She had been sexually abused and shot in the heart.

A photograph of a crime scene in New York City in January 1972 depicts a homicide investigation that occurred before the use of present-day barrier tape. The scene is the sidewalk in front of the Shrimp Boat restaurant at Avenue B and East Eleventh St. in Manhattan. Black militants murdered patrolmen Gregory Foster, black and twenty-one, and Rocco Laurie, white and twenty-two. The perpetrators shot out Foster's eyes and shot Laurie six times in the groin. New York Police Commissioner Murphy stated that nine members of the Black Liberation Army were responsible for the murder of Foster and Laurie. The suspects were arrested and indicted.

The Toronto and Manhattan crime scenes reflect a time when police technology in general, and crime scene equipment in particular, were much less advanced than in 2003. The barrier tape used today is easier to see day and night than was the rope used over forty years ago. Furthermore, barrier tape is part of standard operating procedure throughout the United States and Canada (Coulson and Shannon 1999; Cuomo 1995; Eastham and McLeod 1999; Law 1999; "Murders" 1972; Webster and Aubert 1991).

COVERING THE VICTIM'S BODY

There are two basic reasons for covering the body of a homicide victim with a sheet at the crime scene. First, the body, its position, and any blood patterns present are evidence and therefore must be protected. Secondly, the body is covered to show respect for and preserve the dignity of the victim in public, especially since family and friends of the victim may be at the crime scene (Lange, Vannatter, and Moldea 1997).

CRIME SCENE

At the scene of a homicide, one of the things investigators are interested in is what the perpetrator may have left behind and the size of the area within which that something may be located. The perpetrator may have left behind a gun, shell casings, a knife, a mask, or any number of other things. This area, which is defined by where something was left behind, and regardless of size, is what investigators want to preserve for processing. For this reason, no two crime scenes are identical in size. Typically, "Crime Scene—Do Not Cross" barrier tape is used to identify the perimeters of the crime scene area.

When a homicide takes place in a house in the suburbs, it may be sufficient for investigators to designate the house and yard as the crime scene. When a homicide occurs in an apartment in a high-rise building, the apartment may constitute the crime scene.

If the victim is found in a large outdoor parking lot or a farmer's field, a distance of fifty feet in every direction from the body may be cordoned off. However, the immediate crime scene may not yield all or the best evidence. A perpetrator who used a gun, knife, or blunt instrument might, several blocks from the scene, throw the murder weapon into a dumpster, toss it under a parked vehicle, throw it onto a roof, or drop it through a sewer grating. For these reasons, crime scenes may be expanded and searched several times (Houde 1999).

DEATH AND FACIAL EXPRESSION

There is a connection between the cause of death and the type of expression on a dead person's face. If a person is shot to death, a shocked look will usually be the expression. If a person dies from blunt force trauma, a painful look will typically be on the person's face. If a person bleeds to death due to knife wounds, this person's face will have a rather relaxed look. If a person dies from a drug overdose, a smile may be present.

The eyes are an important part of the expression on a dead individual's face. The eyeballs are filled with vitreous humor, a clear and colorless transparent jelly that is enclosed by a delicate glassy membrane. When the cells in the eyes of a dead person decompose, they release potassium. The higher the level of potassium in the eyes, the longer the individual has been dead. Vitreous humor dries out completely in approximately one week. The position of the eyelid, humidity, air currents, and other factors may also affect ocular changes (O'Connor 2002; Orth 1999; United 1997).

FIRST OFFICER/FIRST RESPONDER

As the first officer, also known as the first responder, arrives at the homicide crime scene, this officer has only limited information regarding what took place, relying on what is sent to him or her by the dispatcher via radio or mobile data terminal (MDT). The dispatcher's information, although evaluated before transmitted, could be false. A caller to the police could be setting up a police officer to be a homicide victim.

When the first officer arrives, he or she determines if the perpetrator is on the premises or if anyone needs an ambulance. The crime scene can be disturbed only if a person there must be attended to by paramedics. The officer protects the scene as much as possible, not touching anything, especially physical evidence, and neither adding anything to nor removing anything from the scene. If the officer needs to use a telephone, or washroom, the officer must wait for backup. Only then can this officer temporarily leave the crime scene to use one of these somewhere else.

The first officer should also keep accurate and legible written notes, which include the names and addresses, verified with picture identification, of witnesses and other individuals at the scene. This officer should note the overall appearance of the crime scene, indicating what looks normal and what looks out of place. What the first officer observes and records could be used by police and attorneys years later. These recorded observations could help make or break a future prosecution. As this crime scene develops into a full-fledged crime scene, one officer is designated as the recorder and has a crime scene sign-in sheet. Every person at the scene must sign this sheet. The sheet records the date and time the person arrived and left the crime scene and the name of the agency or department with which the person is affiliated (Geberth 1997; Rachlin 1991).

SHARP FORCE INJURIES

The June 13, 1994, preliminary report of Los Angeles Police Department (LAPD) detectives Tom Lange and Phil Vannatter, regarding the murder of Nicole Brown Simpson and Ron Goldman, indicates both victims had sharp force injuries. Ron had these injuries in his neck, back, head, and hands. He also had a wound in his left thigh. Nicole had sharp force injuries in her neck. A knife may have produced these injuries. The word "knife," however, does not appear in the report. When objects produce sharp force injuries, it is virtually impossible to positively identify the object, unless it can be located and examined in relation to the type and size of wounds it supposedly caused.

During the criminal trial of O. J. Simpson, charged with and later acquitted of the murders, the prosecution could neither prove a knife was the murder weapon nor could the prosecution produce the murder weapon. However, there was much discussion in and out of court concerning the type of knife or other object, which inflicted the sharp force injuries. A German stiletto, military bayonet, Swiss Army knife, and Samurai sword were rumored to have been used to kill Nicole and Ron. In fact, there may have been more than one weapon (Fuhrman 1997; Kurland 1995; Lange, Vannatter, and Moldea 1997; Linedecker 1995).

7

Evidence

A victim of a homicide, "a John or Jane Doe," cannot describe the events or provide a description of the assailant, and in many cases eyewitnesses are not available or are uncooperative. At a crime scene, evidence is often the only clue to the circumstances of the crime and the identity of the perpetrator. Almost anything at the crime scene may be considered evidence. The manner in which evidence is identified, collected, and handled can make or break a successful prosecution in homicide cases. In this chapter, we illustrate twenty-one topics regarding evidence.

BAGGING THE HANDS

Actress Sharon Tate, twenty-six, and four other persons were murdered at her home in Los Angeles, California, on August 9, 1969, by members of the Charles Manson crime family. Homicide investigators put plastic bags over the hands of the victims, then securely tied the bags at the wrists.

A victim who struggles with a perpetrator might scratch the perpetrator. Traces of skin, hair, or blood might be left under the victim's fingernails. If the perpetrator is a woman with makeup, traces of makeup might be transferred during a struggle to the victim's fingernails. A fiber from the perpetrator's clothes might also be transferred to the victim and become lodged under a fingernail. Subsequent lab analysis might link some trace evidence to a perpetrator. It was routine procedure, and still is in some jurisdictions, to use plastic bags when "bagging the hands." Paper bags are now generally the first choice. Certain trace evidence in plastic bags can more easily deteriorate than in paper bags due to the condensation that forms in plastic. It is sounder practice to place a blood-soaked item of clothing in a paper rather than plastic bag. Blood can deteriorate quite rapidly, especially without a preservative such as EDTA or sodium azide. Condensation in a plastic bag can contribute to the breakdown of blood before it can be properly analyzed in a lab (Bugliosi and Gentry 1974; Danto, Bruhns, and Kutscher 1982; Geberth 1996; Noguchi and DiMona 1983).

BLOWBACK

A vacuum is created when a gun is fired and objects, including glass fragments, from a distance up to eighteen feet, instantly "blowback"—travel back toward the gun and into the muzzle. This occurs because air rushes back to fill the vacuum in the barrel and nearby debris is pulled backward.

It is common in a homicide or suicide for hair, blood, or brain matter to blow back. The victim of a homicide is usually the only object in front or behind the gun fired by a perpetrator, unless the perpetrator fires through a window, door, or wall. Blood travels further into the barrel of a high-caliber gun than into the barrel of a low-caliber gun. Blood penetrates a shorter distance into the barrel of a recoil-operated auto-loading weapon than into a gun whose barrel does not recoil. Higher-energy loads, for example .357-caliber bullets, produce greater depth of blood penetration into a barrel than does standard ammunition (Bevel and Gardner 1997; Fisher 1995; MacDonell and Brooks 1977).

BRIGHT YELLOW CHALK

Bright yellow chalk is used at crime scenes for several purposes, including marking evidence on a dark night, highlighting an area containing evidence to prevent anyone disturbing the evidence, and circling spent cartridges on concrete, asphalt, wood, or other surfaces (Fletcher 1991).

CHALK FAIRY

As police officers secure the scene at a fresh homicide, an officer not helping secure the scene sometimes draws a chalk outline around the victim, then leaves to perform duties elsewhere. This officer is known as the "chalk fairy."

The outline should not be drawn until the body is ready for removal. By this time, detectives, the medical examiner or representative, and criminalists have finished their work at the scene. When detectives first arrive, if there already is a chalk outline around the body, they do not know who contaminated the scene.

The body and evidence should be photographed and videotaped before an outline is drawn or evidence markers added. After this is done, the body, evidence, chalk outline, and evidence markers should be photographed and videotaped. The outline and evidence markers in the second set of photographs and second videotape help highlight specific features of the crime scene. The specific features can be easily referred to in court (Geberth 1996; Houde 1999; Miller 1998).

CORPUS DELICTI

The Latin expression corpus delicti means "the body of the crime." It does not mean the corpse of a victim. The body of the crime means the evidence that establishes that a crime was committed. Corpus delicti can be established with proof that the victim is dead and did not die of natural causes, even if a body cannot be produced. Corpus delicti is established regarding a murder when an injury or loss has occurred as the result of a criminal act.

Serial killers Leonard Lake and Charles Ng are associated with the kidnapping, torture, and murder of numerous individuals, including a baby. Lake and Ng began their crimes in 1984 in the San Francisco Bay area. They kept their victims in a bunker at Lake's survivalist compound at Wilseyville, California. In 1985, Lake took cyanide while being questioned by police officer Daniel Wright. After this, Lake's mother, Gloria Eberling, signed a release form and Lake, who was surviving on life support at Kaiser Permanente Hospital, died after a doctor turned off his life support system.

On November 12, 1985, at the Calaveras County Courthouse in California, the prosecution set out to establish corpus delicti and probable cause to believe that Ng committed the homicides. The prosecution inferred that twelve people died because they were the victims of a crime. Victim Brenda O'Connor was seen on videotape being threatened by the accused individuals. Victim Paul Cosner was linked to bullet holes and bloodstains in a car. Victim Harvey Dubs disappeared without picking up his last paycheck. Personal identification, a cassette recorder, a camera, and other items belonging to victims were traced to Wilseyville, where Leonard Lake and Charles Ng tortured, murdered, and buried their victims.

The intent of the prosecution was to present evidence to the court that Lake and Ng's victims did not voluntarily disappear and that their deaths were due to criminal acts and not natural causes.

Ng and his attorneys used legal maneuvering to delay his trial. For example, the attorneys argued that Ng was unlikely to receive a fair trial in Calaveras County, so the trial was moved in April 1994 from Calaveras County to Orange County. On February 24, 1999, at Santa Ana, California, Charles Ng was found guilty on eleven of twelve counts of first-degree murder and received the death penalty (Bellamy 2003; California 2000; Harrington and Burger 1999; Kurland 1994; Salottolo 1970).

DRAG MARKS

When the perpetrator of a homicide drags the body of the victim from one place to another, there may be obvious indications the body was moved. This depends on the type of surface over which the body was dragged and the type of murder weapon used.

If the body was dragged over a gravel surface, such as a road, investigators will notice the gravel was disturbed. As the body was dragged, some gravel was likely dragged with it. An obvious trail may be created depending on how fast the body is pulled. If the body was dragged across a lawn, investigators will see a trail and leaves and twigs will be out of place.

Depending on the type of murder weapon and how it was used, there may be a blood trail on a surface over which a body was dragged. Multiple stab wounds are much more likely to create a blood trail than is a carefully placed gunshot from a small-caliber gun in the back of the head.

Inside a building, the only sign of a body having been dragged may be a blood trail. If the perpetrator places the body on a sheet, blanket, quilt, or tarp, and there is only a small amount of blood when the victim is murdered, there may be no obvious indication the body was dragged. In addition, if the body is moved off whatever it was transported on, and the object used for transportation was removed from the premises by the perpetrator, no further indications of the body being dragged may be present.

On October 31, 1975, the body of Martha Moxley of Greenwich, Connecticut, was found under a pine tree a hundred feet from her home. There were drag marks in leaves and grass leading away from a pool of blood toward the pine tree where the teenager's body was found. The perpetrator, who initially beat her with a golf club, returned later to hide her body, saw she was still alive, and then stabbed her to death with the broken shaft of the golf club. Michael Skakel, cousin of Robert F. Kennedy, Jr., was tried, and in June 2002 he was convicted for Martha's murder. He was sentenced in August 2002 to twenty years to life in prison. His lawyers appealed his murder conviction a few weeks later (Fuhrman 1998; Henderson 1998; "Skakel" 2002).

EVIDENCE

The legal term "evidence" includes written material such as contracts and deeds, verbal testimony, and objects such as guns and knives, which a court allows a jury to consider in determining if something disputed in court is a fact. Direct evidence, such as an eyewitness account to a homicide, tends to prove a fact without support from other evidence, assuming the eyewitness is telling the truth. Circumstantial evidence can support a main fact. A person seen leaving a house in which a homicide took place was in the house, but is not necessarily the perpetrator of the homicide. Although direct evidence is always relevant, the court decides when circumstantial evidence is relevant.

In the O. J. Simpson criminal trial, 1,105 items of evidence were admitted (*Academic* 1998; Linedecker 1995; *New Encyclopedia* 1997; *World* 1996).

EVIDENCE MARKERS

To accurately label potential evidence at a homicide crime scene, investigators use crime scene/evidence markers. These markers are used after the scene is videotaped and photographed. After the markers are in place, the crime scene is videotaped and photographed a second time. These photographs can be used in court by the prosecution to prosecute the perpetrator.

Markers are available in two sizes: 3.5 inches by 3 inches and 3.5 inches by 5 inches. They have numbers, letters, or arrows, and when in use look like triangles from the side. Markers are either white or yellow with black numbers, letters, or arrows. At a homicide crime scene in which the perpetrator left behind five shell casings, there would be five markers, each separately numbered 1, 2, 3, 4, and 5. Each casing would also have a chalk circle around it and one marker beside it ("Crime Scene" 1999).

FIBERS

In February 1978 in East Harlem, a dead woman was found in an alley near a tenement. She had been selling church literature in nearby buildings. A very large florist's flower box and a plastic liner were near the body. Investigators sent the flower box, plastic liner, and dead female's clothing to the crime lab. First, a polarized light microscope was used to identify three types of fibers on the box and liner. All these fibers were from the dead woman's clothing.

Next the investigators examined red nylon rug fibers, blue nylon rug fibers, and rabbit hairs, which were also on the box, liner, and coat but were not present at the decedent's residence.

Then detectives heard about a man who, a day after the body was discovered, sold a rabbit hair coat to another man. Investigators obtained the coat from its new owner. Rabbit hairs from the coat were microscopically compared to rabbit hairs on the flower box liner and dead female's coat. The hairs on the flower box liner and woman's coat matched hairs on the suspect's coat.

Two nylon fiber rugs, a red one and a blue one, were in the suspect's apartment. Fibers from these rugs were compared to the questioned fibers on the decedent's clothing, flower box, and plastic liner. The known and questioned rug fibers were consistent in every way. A witness had seen the suspect carrying a large flower box a day or two before the body was discovered. Police believed the woman was killed in the suspect's apartment, placed in the flower box, taken to the roof of the building in which the suspect lived, and then thrown off the roof.

In this case, fibers were linked to people, places, and things. Textile fibers from the victim's clothes were on the liner and box. Trace fibers from the victim's clothes were on the suspect and in the suspect's apartment. Rabbit hairs from the suspect's coat were on the victim, in the alley, and on the liner. Fibers from nylon rugs in the suspect's apartment were on the victim, in the alley, on the liner, and on the box.

The defendant was tried for second-degree murder, and after two trials, he received a sentence of life in prison.

In 2001, John Eric Armstrong, twenty-eight, a former naval petty officer, went on trial in Detroit, Michigan, for the murder of five prostitutes. Armstrong may have killed as many as twenty-seven women worldwide. Fiber evidence linked him to the murder of Wendy Jordan, a thirty-nine-year-old gas station manager. Fibers from the carpet in Armstrong's Jeep Wrangler matched fibers on Jordan's tights. Minute golden flakes from Jordan's high heels were also found on the carpet on the passenger side of Armstrong's Jeep.

The importance of carefully analyzing trace evidence, such as fibers, is illustrated in the case of a homicide victim examined at the Indiana University School of Medicine Department of Pathology and reported in 1989. A red "fiber," believed to be a carpet fiber, was found on a body and analyzed. The fiber, short and coiled, was not like any known fiber. Further analysis revealed the fiber was actually the larva of a freshwater midge, a tiny two-winged fly. This type of larva, observed on bodies recovered from freshwater environments, indicated the body had been submerged in water.

Forceps, tape, and a vacuum cleaner are used to collect fibers. However, the disadvantage of using a vacuum cleaner is that it collects too much irrelevant as well as useful material. Samples from each area investigated are placed in individual containers, appropriately marked, and then sent to the crime lab for microscopic and microchemical study (Geberth 1997; Gray 2001; Hawley et al. 1989; Petraco 1986).

FOOTPRINTS IN SOFT DUST OR SNOW

A footprint left by a suspect in soft dust or snow may be used as evidence.

Normally, plaster of paris, a powder, would be mixed with water and the mixture gently poured into the indentation. The mixture would solidify and swell in approximately twenty minutes. The swelling would enable the plaster to record even minute details of impressions. However, plaster of paris cannot be used to preserve a footprint in soft dust or snow. Instead, a mist of cellulose acetate dissolved in acetone is sprayed over the footprint. The acetone vaporizes as the mist settles on the surface of the footprint. This produces a fine molded skin of acetate, which can be used as the basis of a conventional cast (Kind and Overman 1972).

FORENSIC

The word "forensic" is derived from the Latin word *forensis*, which means forum. Forensic evidence is evidence for the forum, or courtroom (Dowling and Iscan 1982).

GUNPOWDER RESIDUE

Powders burn inside a firearm. Smokeless powder, which became available in the 1880s, is used in modern ammunition. Black powder or Pyrodex (a substitute for black powder) is used in antique weapons and replicas of these weapons. Modern ammunition does not contain black powder for two main reasons: one, black powder produces a large amount of smoke, and two, it decreases projectile velocity. Smokeless powder burns very quickly and black powder burns slowly. Escaping gases under high pressure—not an explosion in the firearm—create the loud bang heard when a firearm is discharged.

After a person pulls the trigger of a gun, a bullet and other substances, including soot (unburned grains of powder), burned grains of powder, and a metallic spray of primer are expelled from the barrel. Barium and antimony, two metallic elements present in primer mixing components, are detectable in gunshot primer residue (GSR).

They are detectable when most center-fire ammunition is discharged. Neutron activation analysis (NAA) or atomic absorption spectroscopy (AA) can determine the amount of barium and antimony present on swabs used on the suspected shooter's hands. Another method involves the use of adhesive disks to pick up microscopic particles of GSR from the hands. A scanning electron microscope (SEM) conducts energy dispersive X-ray analysis (EDXA) and can detect barium and antimony. SEM-EDXA produces a visual image of particle size and shape where barium and antimony are detected.

GSR testing can associate an individual with a firearm, but this does not identify this person as the shooter. Any person near a recently fired gun may possibly have GSR on his or her clothes. Gases containing the soot, however, travel only a few inches because they are extremely light. Unburned powder grains travel only one or two feet. Trace elements, including powder, are blown back on to the shooter. Trace elements can remain on the shooter for a number of hours. For this reason, investigators should determine as soon as possible if a suspect fired a particular gun. The suspect can easily remove trace elements by washing his or her hands.

A criminalist can test a suspect at the scene of a crime for gunshot residue. The criminalist sprays a solution of nitric acid on to the hands of the suspect, then uses a cotton tipped applicator to dab the palm and back of each hand. The swab is sealed in a test tube for analysis at the lab. A variation of the procedure is to roll a small aluminum roller covered with sticky cellophane tape over the suspect's hands. The tape is then pulled off and preserved as evidence (Aaron 1991; Davis 1994; Noguchi and DiMona 1983; United 1997).

HAIR

Clean tweezers should be used to remove hairs found at a homicide crime scene. These hairs should be carefully placed in a clean pillbox, folded into a piece of clean paper, or kept in another secure container. Regardless of where a hair sample is placed, the entire sample should be placed into its container. No part of the sample should be crushed or in any way exposed from the pillbox, folded piece of paper, or other container.

Analysis can reveal if the hair is from a person or from an animal. Animal hair can be further identified as being from a particular type of animal, for example, a dog or cow. Analysis of human hair can, within limits, reveal a number of things, including the race of the individual, the part of the body from which the hair originated, if the hair was forcibly removed, and if the hair contains a chemical dye. It is possible to determine if a hair is from a man or a woman only when the root is attached. A single hair root can be identified in a DNA test.

Hair collected from a homicide victim should be collected from a number of different areas of the body, including the crown of the head, eyebrows, arms, underarms, chest, pubic area, and leg areas. Approximately forty hairs should be collected from each area. Separate samples should be packaged separately.

Hair samples should be pulled from both victims and suspects. Samples obtained by cutting should be cut as close as possible to the skin. A new comb or clean tweezers should be used for each individual to avoid contamination.

Dog hairs on the bodies of child homicide victims in Atlanta, Georgia, matched hairs in the home and car of Wayne Williams. Williams, a talent scout, was sentenced in 1982 to life in prison (Fisher 1995; *Murder* 1991; O'Maley 1994).

JOHN DOE/JANE DOE

A dead body that cannot be identified is designated as "John Doe" or "Jane Doe," depending on the sex. Once the body is designated, the body is assigned a number. Numbers are assigned in sequential order. Usually, tattoos, dental work, a missing persons report, or other methods of identification are useful in identifying the body (Blanche and Schreiber 1998; Gilmore 1998; Henderson 1998; Howard 1979).

LINT PICKUP ROLLER

A lint pickup roller can effectively collect trace evidence due to its large area of sticky tape. The topmost layer of debris, such as hairs, sticks to the tape. A "tape lift" is, in this context, tape that has collected something of interest and potential value to crime scene investigators.

The trace evidence a perpetrator may leave at a crime scene, such as a hair in the living room of a residence, may be on top of, or slightly below, the surface of a rug. Investigators might be able to link a hair to a suspect. A household vacuum cleaner, on the other hand, recovers too much debris, but a vacuum cleaner with a special filter overcomes this problem: Only the trace evidence on top of or slightly below the surface of the rug is drawn into the vacuum cleaner (Houde 1999).

LIVIDITY

When a person's heart stops pumping blood, gravity causes the blood to accumulate in the lowest portions of the body. Within half an hour to two hours after death, the body turns a reddish-purple to purplish color, similar to the color of a bruise or a port wine stain. This change of color within a relatively short time after death is known as lividity, postmortem lividity (PML), or livor mortis.

Eight to twelve hours after death, lividity is fixed, meaning that discoloration will remain in place even though the body may be moved. Before this time, livor will shift when a body is moved.

If a body is lying on its back, lividity will be evident in the small of the back, posterior part of the neck, and posterior parts of the thighs. There is no PML on any part of the body where its weight squeezes the blood out. If the contact between a body and the surface on which the body is located is firm, blood cannot pool in this area and PML is not found there.

Homicide detectives who examine a body lying on its stomach and note fixed lividity on the back of the body know that the body was moved. Detectives use this information to determine if anyone who was near the body is telling them the truth regarding how they found the body or whether or not they moved it (Cyriax 1993; Rachlin 1995; Simon 1991; Stroud 1987; Williams 1997).

RAT HOLES

When a shotgun loaded with a buckshot cartridge is fired at a person from a distance of eight inches or less, the resulting wound is almost circular in shape, as if a huge single bullet rather than scattering shot was fired. If a perpetrator places a shotgun loaded with this ammunition so that the barrel touches the victim's head, and the perpetrator pulls the trigger, this can decapitate the victim.

In August 1989, police went to 722 North Elm Drive in Beverly Hills, California, in response to a 911 call. Officers discovered the bodies of José and Kitty Menendez in the television room of their mansion. The millionaire video executive and his wife had been shot-gunned to death. José's brains were blown out. Kitty had received a blast in the face. Both victims also had other shotgun wounds. Police stated the bodies did not look human because of the severity of the damage done to them. Lyle and Erik Menendez, sons of the victims, were convicted of these murders and sentenced in 1996 to life in prison without parole.

Powerful explosive impacts produce gaping wounds. Police sometimes refer to these gaping wounds as "rat holes." "Pumpkin balls," large and heavy single slugs fired from a twelve-gauge shotgun, can cause that type of damage. These slugs can easily blast holes through a car's body.

When a victim is examined for gunshot wounds, a small wound generally suggests an entrance wound; an example of a small caliber gun is the .22-caliber. A large wound generally suggests an exit wound. Weapons that can produce these two different types of wounds include .38- and .357-caliber guns. This is not necessarily true of 12-gauge shotgun wounds. A 12-gauge at close range can produce entrance wounds that look like exit wounds. A rookie detective's testimony in court may be jeopardized by a defendant's attorney during cross-examination if the attorney knows this fact about 12-gauge shotgun entrance wounds and the detective is not as knowledgeable as the attorney (Davis 1994; Lawrence et al. 1989; "Menendez Brothers" 1996; Simon 1991).

RIGOR MORTIS

Chemical changes in the muscle tissues of a corpse cause rigor mortis, a hardening of the muscles. It first begins in small muscles and is evident in upper parts of the body, then becomes noticeable in lower parts of the body. Rigor mortis appears within two to four hours after death, becoming fully established within six to twelve hours. If a body's arms are extended while rigor mortis is in effect, the arms will remain extended if the body is lifted. Small and large muscles relax again within thirty-six hours of death, and rigor mortis begins to decrease as a body begins to decompose (Simon 1991; Sweetman and Sweetman 1997; Williams 1997).

TAPE LIFT

A piece of transparent tape three inches long can be used to remove certain potential evidence from a crime scene. A crime scene technician might see a tiny fiber on the back seat of a car in which a victim was murdered. In such a scenario, the technician would place the tape over the fiber to remove it from the back seat. The tape, sticky side down, would be placed over a petri dish and the dish covered with a glass lid. The dish would be placed under a microscope and the properties of the fiber would be studied. At a future date, it might be possible to link the fiber with a homicide suspect (Henderson 1998).

TRACE EVIDENCE

Very small amounts of fiber, hair, soil, and other substances, which can often link a perpetrator to a homicide victim, are trace evidence. If investigators found a body in a farmer's field and there are traces of soil on the body that are not found in the immediate area, the body was most likely transported from another location and dumped in the field. Investigators later may have a suspect who lives many miles from where the victim was dumped. The suspect has a van, which is examined for trace evidence. Samples of the soil found on the victim are found in the van. This does not conclusively prove the suspect is the perpetrator, but it enables investigators to build a stronger case against the suspect.

The importance of a single hair as trace evidence was seen in the case of twelve-year-old Polly Klaas. She was abducted on October 1, 1993, from her home in Petaluma, California. A single hair found in Polly's bedroom was subsequently linked to her abductor and killer, Richard Allen Davis, who was convicted of murder and sentenced to death. He is currently on death row in San Quentin State Prison in San Quentin, California (Barthel 1989; Fisher 1995; Smith 1994).

WRISTS

Detectives and criminalists at a homicide crime scene examine the wrists of a victim to determine if, at some point in time, the wrists were bound. Wrists may be bound with a belt, rope, necktie, wire, or strips of cloth, but not always, and injury to the skin is not always obvious. If there is evidence of hair loss on the wrists, the wrists may have been bound with tape. Tape would have removed some hair when a perpetrator removed the tape, leaving for detectives and criminalists a partial absence of wrist hair as a clue to how the perpetrator treated the victim (Henderson 1998).

8

Wounds and Injuries

The wounds and injuries to a possible homicide victim or victims reveal many of the events in a homicide. Death may be from natural causes, accidental encounters, victim-perpetrated suicide, or homicide. The cause of death is not always obvious and often leads to further examination by a medical examiner. In this chapter, we examine fourteen types of wounds and injuries.

AUTOEROTIC ASPHYXIA

A person can constrict the carotid arteries in the neck, decrease the flow of blood to the brain, and during masturbation experience heightened sexual pleasure while in a temporary state of asphyxia, a decrease in the amount of oxygen in living tissues and an increase of carbon dioxide.

This practice is also known as "sexual asphyxia" and "ritual masturbation." It used to be called "practicing rock climbing" and "practicing tying of knots," when individuals engaging in this activity accidentally died.

The indoor setting for autoerotic asphyxia is usually the bedroom, bathroom, closet, or storage room of a residence. Sometimes it is practiced indoors at work. The outdoor setting is usually under a tree. Indoors, the person suspends himself by the neck with a rope, belt, electrical cord, or dog leash from a hook in the ceiling or from a beam. Outdoors, he usually suspends himself from a tree.

The person is usually a male, a depressed loner between twenty and forty years of age. A towel or other protective padding around the neck separates the neck from the ligature. This helps prevent accidental hanging, reduces pain from the ligature, and prevents the formation of ligature marks—things people would question. This person may have a knife in his hands with which to cut himself down if he begins to pass out. A stool or chair is nearby for stepping onto or off, depending on whether or not he wants to increase or decrease the pressure on his neck as he hangs.

If this person increases the pressure on his neck to the point at which he begins to pass out, he may not have time to step on a chair or stool in order to decrease the pressure. He may not have time to use the knife to cut himself down. He may not regain complete consciousness and may die.

The individual who practices autoerotic asphyxia is frequently a transvestite who, at times, ties or in some other way constricts his genitalia. He also sometimes ties his hands in front of him or behind his back. It is common for him to have erotic books and photographs nearby. A handkerchief or tissues with which to wipe semen may be present. Although some men blindfold themselves or wear a hood, others arrange mirrors to view the act. Still others set up a camera with a delayed time shutter release in order to photograph themselves. Other men use a video camera.

Forensic psychiatrist Park Dietz reported about autoerotic deaths involving the hydraulics of heavy machinery. One report was about a forty-two-year-old Asian man who was found by his father hanging by the neck and suspended by a rope attached to the raised shovel of a backhoe. This man had referred to the tractor as "Stone" and had written about it in a newsletter to friends. Another report was about a sixty-two-year-old white man found by a neighbor. The decedent was under the front bucket of a tractor in his barn. He was nude except for high-heel shoes and nylon stockings. His body was inverted in such a way that completely raising the hydraulic bucket would cause his body to be suspended by his ankles.

Death from autoerotic asphyxia can be an accident, suicide, or homicide. When an accidental hanging or strangulation occurs and an autopsy is performed, pulmonary edema, petechial hemorrhages, and fractures of the thyroid cartilage are noted. In New York, during the period 1964–1965, there were 106 deaths by hanging, two of which were classified as accidental autoerotic asphyxia. In Los Angeles County, during the period 1958–1970, there were twenty-five deaths by autoerotic asphyxia.

It could be a homicide if two individuals participated, one actively and one passively. The active participant dies; the passive participant survives. The passive individual may be waiting to engage in autoerotic asphyxia when the former individual accidentally hangs himself, but one person could hang another person under these circumstances and claim the death was an accident. Investigators must determine the precise role of the survivor in the death of the decedent.

When Dr. Thomas Noguchi was the chief medical examiner of Los Angeles County, he received a telephone call from a detective, who reported the suicide of Albert Dekker. Dekker was a character actor who portrayed diverse rolls, including suave Europeans and mad scientists. Dekker had apparently committed suicide and when Noguchi arrived at Dekker's home, Noguchi saw that Dekker had hanged himself in the bathroom. A rope from a beam suspended Dekker. The rope was also wound around his throat and wrists. There was a towel beneath the part of the rope around his throat. Dekker could easily remove his hands from the rope. The pulley arrangement he set up would allow him to regulate the amount of pressure to his throat.

The autopsy revealed Dekker had hanged himself. His death, however, was not a suicide, but rather an accidental suffocation. This was Noguchi's conclusion based on past deaths that he had investigated and on a psychological autopsy of Dekker (a psychological autopsy is a thorough and retrospective investigation of a person's behavior leading up to their death). Dekker had been engaging in autoerotic asphyxia (Cooper 1973; Noguchi and DiMona 1983; O'Halloran and Dietz 1993; Walsh 1977).

BITE MARKS

No two sets of human teeth are exactly alike. This becomes evident when sets of teeth are compared regarding size, shape, wear, restorations, breakage, and other factors. A person's occupation can have a bearing on the condition of his or her teeth. A tailor holding pins between his or her teeth alters the condition of the teeth.

Relatively few individuals have their fingerprints on file. Criminals and certain government employees are a few of these people. More people, however, have a dental record accessible to forensic odontologists and police. The perpetrator of a homicide or other crime such as rape or child abuse may bite the victim during or after the crime. The bite creates a tooth mark pattern on the victim's skin. Lips, tongue, and cheeks play a role when the bite mark is inflicted. The psychological state of the perpetrator is also an important variable.

A forensic odontologist bears in mind all of the above. This expert also takes into account crime scene photographs of the victim, statements from investigators, whether the bite was inflicted before or after death, and the position of the body when it was discovered. The latter is very important because a change in the position of the body can change the appearance of a bite mark. The value of bite mark evidence is that it can link a perpetrator to a crime or clear an innocent person.

Bite marks are found in both heterosexual and homosexual homicides, involving voluntary and forced sexual activity. A sexually oriented homicide will most often have bite marks characterized by an abrasion pattern, which radiates in a linear fashion and surrounds the bite marks. The homicide of a child who is battered typically has bite marks that look like tooth marks. The back, shoulders, face, and scrotum are the usual locations of bite marks in homosexual homicide victims. The breasts and thighs are the typical locations of bite marks in heterosexual homicide victims. Furthermore, it is impossible to inflict a bite mark without leaving a trace of saliva. A serologist can sometimes link the saliva to a particular person.

In 1970, in Connecticut, a high school senior allegedly murdered his mother, brother, sister, and grandmother. There was no indication of forced entry or of a struggle at the family residence. There were no fingerprints on the murder weapons, which belonged to the family. However, a reddish-blue mark on the left breast of the sister was used to link the accused brother to the murder of the other family members. The state forensic odontologist linked the bite mark to the suspect, who confessed to the murders. He was found not guilty by reason of insanity ("Fatal Compulsion" 2000; Levine 1977; Luntz 1973; Medland 1991).

COLOMBIAN NECKLACE/COLOMBIAN NECKTIE

Sukru Boztepe, a computer hardware repairman and resident of Brentwood in Los Angeles, California, and his wife, Bettina Rasmussen, both in their twenties, were out late on the night of Sunday, June 12, 1994. They had taken charge of a restless Akita from their neighbor, screenwriter Steven Schwab. While walking his own dog earlier, Schwab had encountered the barking Akita. Its paws and some of its fur were bloody, but it did not appear to have any apparent injuries. He did not know the dog's owner and there was no fast way to identify the dog. The Boztepes offered to help Schwab. Perhaps the agitated Akita would lead them to its home. It did—875 South Bundy Drive.

The Akita stopped at an open gate. Sukru and Bettina saw, because of moonlight, a walkway extending beyond the Akita. Blood was trickling down the walkway tiles. At the bottom of the steps of a condominium was the body of a woman. She was in a fetal position in a pool of blood. Her name was Nicole Brown Simpson, age thirty-five.

The Boztepes ran across the street to pound on the door of a house, hoping to use a telephone inside to call police. The woman in the house, believing someone was trying to break in, dialed 911. Los Angeles Police Department (LAPD) Officer Robert Riske, the first officer on the scene, arrived shortly after midnight at South Bundy. Sukru and Bettina told Riske where to find the body. Riske noted that Nicole, wearing a ripped and bloodied cocktail dress, was almost decapitated, her neck cut from ear to ear.

There was a second body, that of twenty-five-year-old Ronald Lyle Goldman, a waiter and friend of Nicole's. Goldman was sprawled in bushes approximately ten feet from Nicole. There were slashes on both sides of his neck. His left jugular vein had been severed.

At the trial of defendant O. J. Simpson, attorney Johnnie L. Cochran, Jr., contended that underworld figures, not O. J., were likely the real killers. These individuals, Cochran maintained, killed Nicole and Ron as a warning to a female friend of Nicole's. This friend, a cocaine abuser, had been a temporary resident at the condominium. She left on June 8 to enter a drug treatment center.

Cochran wanted to know if the slit throats signified Colombian necklaces, murders in which the throats of victims are cut ear-to-ear.

Colombian necklaces, attributed to the Colombian underworld, are punishment for people who double cross drug cartels. A Colombian necktie is another type of revenge murder. A victim's throat is cut vertically, then the tongue is pulled through the slit and left hanging like a necktie on a shirt. Criminals have used "necktie killings" on men, women, and children. These victims are at times found seated in rows of chairs.

LAPD robbery and homicide detective Tom Lange, forty-nine, who arrived at the homicide crime scene at approximately 04:30 on June 13, was questioned by Cochran about the slit throats. Lange joined the LAPD in 1967. By 1994, he had been involved in the investigation of more than 250 homicides. He maintained the deaths of Nicole Simpson and Ron Goldman were rage killings, not drug hits because there was overkill in the way that the victims were murdered. A preponderance of evidence indicated O. J. Simpson was the killer (Bosco 1996; Bugliosi 1996; Darden 1996; Edwards 1991; Jonnes 1996; Lange, Vannatter, and Moldea 1997; Linedecker 1995).

CONTACT HEAD WOUND

A contact entrance wound to the forehead is a gunshot wound from a gun whose barrel is either in direct contact with a victim's skin or within a few inches of the skin when the perpetrator shoots the victim. In a hard-contact wound, the muzzle of the gun is pressed into the skin, indenting it. The muzzle is held lightly against the skin in a loose-contact wound. There is soot around the entrance of both wounds. Soot is embedded in the seared skin of the hard-contact wound. Washing cannot completely remove this soot. Soot present in a loose-contact wound can be easily wiped away. Scorched skin and shriveled hairs surround this type of jagged and gaping wound. The bullet bursts through the skull and scalp, exiting through the back of the head, creating a very large jagged exit wound. The bullet blows tissue and blood outwardly through the exit wound.

When Andrew Cunanan killed Italian fashion designer Gianni Versace in Miami, Florida, on July 15, 1997, he used a .40-caliber Taurus semiautomatic. Cunanan approached Versace from behind, pointed the gun behind the left ear, and pulled the trigger. The gun was so close to Versace's skin the gun produced a tattoo of burned gunpowder on his neck. The tattoo, the size of a half-dollar, is called a "stippling effect." When Cunanan shot Versace a second time, the bullet penetrated the right side of Versace's face next to his nose. After the shooting, Andrew Cunanan calmly walked away (DiMaio 1999; Helpern and Knight 1977; Orth 1999).

CUT THROAT IN HOMICIDE

The cut throat of homicide victims does not have the precision seen in suicidal persons who cut their own throat. Victims and perpetrators struggle and change their positions in relation to each other. For this reason, the perpetrator may inflict cuts from different directions. As the victim attempts with his or her hands to ward off the knife, the knife makes defense cuts on the palms of the victim's hands or between the victim's fingers (Hall 1976).

CUT THROAT IN SUICIDE

The cut throat of suicidal persons has a generally careful and clean appearance. Before cutting, these persons usually extend their heads. This results in the line of wounds frequently being transverse. The carotid arteries move back and are not cut, and loss of blood is reduced.

Right-handed individuals cut their throat from left to right. There may be a few hesitation cuts on the throat before the lethal cut is made. As the cut is being made, pressure on the knife is considerable, initially making the wound deep, then shallow, as the knife cuts across the throat, sloping slightly up toward the chin (Hall 1976).

DEFENSE WOUNDS

Defense wounds, also known as defense cuts, are seen in victims who are attacked with a sharp instrument, typically a knife. As a perpetrator slashes with a knife at a victim, the victim raises his or her hands to defend against the knife. The defense wounds are parallel cuts in the victim's fingertips, palms, and forearms.

In June 1994, when Nicole Brown Simpson and Ron Goldman were murdered in Los Angeles, California, both victims attempted to fight off the killer. Both Nicole and Ron had defense wounds on their hands (Lange, Vannatter, and Moldea 1997; Stroud 1987; Sweetman and Sweetman 1997).

HANGED OR GARROTED

Investigators see a victim in a room. The victim may be lying on the floor, sitting on a sofa, or be in some other position. Marks on the victim's neck are of special interest to investigators. If the direction of the marks is straight upward, the victim was hanged and the body was moved. If the direction of the marks is backward, the victim was garroted and the body may have been moved. An autopsy would reveal the official cause of death and the extent to which hanging or garroting contributed to death (Hirschfeld 1982; Mims 1998).

PATTERN INJURIES

A perpetrator who strikes a victim with a blunt object and leaves an imprint of the object's shape on the victim's skin inflicts a pattern injury. For example, different types of hammers produce different types of pattern injuries. A hammer with a round head produces circular contusions (bruises) and lacerations (tears). The claw of a claw hammer produces paired injuries. Contusions and lacerations are the most common blunt force injuries. A belt produces more than one type of pattern injury: It produces a linear contusion when the edge of the belt contacts the skin, there may be a wider contusion produced when a belt strikes on its side, and a woven belt imprints an image of the belt's weave on the skin.

As a perpetrator strikes a victim with a linear blunt object such as a baseball bat, the object displaces the blood directly underneath the point of contact. The object, which contacts the skin, produces two parallel lines that border the area of impact.

A person may have a pattern contusion deep within the epithelium and not visible to the naked eye. Ultraviolet or infrared light may reveal this type of contusion. Forensic odontologists use these light sources when they examine barely visible or old bite marks.

A pattern abrasion is a rubbing away of the topmost layers of the epidermis. Fingernail scratches, imprints of carpet fabric, and ligature marks around the neck are pattern abrasions. The flat portion of a hot iron or a hot liquid produces thermal pattern injuries. An immersion burn is characterized by a line of demarcation between burned and unburned tissue. A splash burn is characterized by an irregular line and blotches of burned skin over an isolated area of thermal injury. This area is usually round or oval. Pattern injuries are also seen in vehicular homicide. The force of impact may leave an impression of the victim's clothing on the bumper of the offending vehicle because dye from the clothing may be transferred to the bumper (Geberth 1996; Parks and Kim 2000; Smock 2000).

PUGILISTIC ATTITUDE

Some individuals who die in a fire are found by fire and arson investigators in what appears to be a defensive boxing pose or fetal position known as the pugilistic attitude or pugilistic stance. This condition occurs when a person is exposed to intense heat over an extended period. Large muscles in the arms and legs contract and pull the limbs toward the torso. The fingers are gradually drawn toward the palms and the hands may be cupped.

Sometimes a body will be exposed to intense heat, but will not have a pugilistic attitude. This may be because the body was dead and in rigor mortis before the fire. Heat and cold affect the onset of rigor, rigor disappearing more rapidly in a warm than in a cool environment.

A burned body that is not in a pugilistic stance, but is on its side with its hands stretched behind its back, is a homicide victim when there are remnants of burned duct tape on the body's wrists and forearms. The remnants of burned tape indicate the decedent was tied to something such as a chair consumed by the fire. A lack of obvious indications of torture, gunshot wounds, or stab wounds may mean that the fire destroyed signs of this type of trauma. An autopsy and X-rays may help locate signs of trauma (Crowley 1999; Red-sicker and O'Connor 1997).

STAB WOUNDS IN HOMICIDE

Homicide victims stabbed to death with a knife may have multiple random wounds. There may be wounds in areas of the body not accessible to the victim. There will be torn wounds due to a struggle between the victim and perpetrator, and defense cuts on one or both of the victim's hands. The chest and stomach are typical areas for knife wounds in these victims. Wounds are sharp at both ends when a double-edged knife is used. Wounds are rounded at one end and sharp at the other when a single-edged knife is used. Homicidal stab wounds penetrate clothing (Hall 1976).

STAB WOUNDS IN SUICIDE

Individuals who commit suicide with a knife usually concentrate on stabbing themselves in the area of the heart. This area is often the epigastric region, where there are no ribs or other obstacles that can impede a knife thrust. Furthermore, most people can feel their heart beat quite strongly in this area. Suicidal persons sometimes lift their clothes to make it easier to successfully stab themselves. Usually, a single, clean wound is found in the bodies of these individuals. There will not be any indication of attempts at stabbing and no defense cuts on the hands (Hall 1976; Rho 1978).

STRANGULATION

When a person's neck is compressed to the point of strangulation and blood is prevented from reaching the brain, this individual rapidly loses consciousness and dies.

Trauma to semirigid structures in the neck can cause this type of death. The hyoid, a U-shaped bone at the base of the tongue, is one of these structures. It can fracture when its two ends are pressed together. The thyroid cartilage, another structure, can break easily when calcified and pressed together. Both the thyroid cartilage and the hyoid bone are above the cricoid cartilage, and in this part of the neck a thin layer of muscle, connective tissue, and skin protect the carotid arteries through which blood flows to the brain.

Cerebral ischemia (obstruction of the flow of blood to the brain) and hypoxia (deficiency of oxygen in the tissues) result when structures in the neck, including blood vessels, are compressed. Arterial circulation is occluded, there is loss of consciousness, and the body goes limp.

Tiny pinpoint hemorrhages caused by burst capillaries in the whites of the eyes are the ocular indicator of strangulation. These hemorrhages, referred to as petechial hemorrhages, are not always obvious to the observer. They are sometimes located under the eyelids.

Women and children are the usual victims of strangulation asphyxia because they are more easily overpowered than are healthy men. An examination of the causes of death over a ten-year period in New Jersey did not yield any healthy unimpaired adult males who died in this way. Scratches and cuts in a victim of strangulation asphyxia usually indicate that the victim struggled with the perpetrator before death. If there are no indications of struggle in some victims, it is reasonable to assume that drugs or alcohol impaired these victims when they were strangled.

Thirteen women were murdered, apparently at random, between June 14, 1962, and January 4, 1964, in Boston, Massachusetts, and the suburbs of Lynn, Cambridge, Salem, and Lawrence. The victims ranged in age from nineteen to eighty-five years. Seven victims were white; six were black. One victim was stabbed to death; twelve were strangled. Some were raped; others were brutalized with objects. Although some women were strangled with a ligature, others were manually strangled.

On January 4, 1964, Pam Parker, eighteen, and Pat Delmore, nineteen, left work and went home to the apartment they shared with their new roommate, nineteen-year-old Mary Sullivan. Pam and Pat found Mary in the bedroom. She was propped up on the bed. Her eyes were closed, her head leaning against her right shoulder. The handle of a broomstick protruded from her vagina. She had been strangled with two scarves and a nylon stocking.

Mary Sullivan was the last victim of the Boston Strangler.

More than a year after her death, attorney F. Lee Bailey contacted Boston police and told them he might know the identity of the strangler. The man was Albert DeSalvo, thirty-three, known to police because of numerous sexual assaults and breaking and entering charges. DeSalvo had apparently pretended to be a talent agent who gained the confidence of his victims by stating he wanted to measure them for modeling assignments.

DeSalvo confessed to the murders, was tried in January 1967, and was sentenced to life in prison, where he was stabbed to death in 1973. Three convicts were charged with his murder, but no one was ever convicted.

In Boston, in May 2000, family members of Mary Sullivan and Albert DeSalvo held a press conference, demanding the case be reopened in order for all the facts of the Boston Strangler case to be known. Police supposedly misplaced physical evidence during the original investigation. Swabs of the killer's semen were among the misplaced evidence. Furthermore, DeSalvo's behavior did not adequately fit the behavior of serial killers as they are known today. Serial killers do not surrender to police as did DeSalvo. They kill until they are apprehended or until they die.

George Nassar, a convicted murderer who was in prison with DeSalvo, knew him well. Nassar, still in prison, may be the real Boston Strangler or may have committed some of the murders attributed to DeSalvo. However, according to John Donovan, who was head of homicide at the Boston Police Department when the murders were committed, DeSalvo was the Boston Strangler because he had detailed information about every crime scene, and police kept crime scene information very confidential. DeSalvo confessed in detail to each murder.

Six-year-old JonBenet Ramsey was found dead by her father, John Ramsey, in the basement of her parents' home in Boulder, Colorado, on December 26, 1996. There was a ligature around her neck and a ligature around her right wrist. Ligature strangulation usually indicates homicide. Dr. John E. Meyer, Boulder County coroner, issued JonBenet's autopsy report on August 13, 1997. Asphyxia by strangulation and craniocerebral trauma were the cause of death. There were petechial hemorrhages in her eyes. No alcohol and no drugs were detected in her body (Baden and Hennessee 1989; Berry-Dee and Odell 1992; Blank-Reid 1999; Bruno 1993; Frank 1966; Posner 2000; Ubelaker 1992; Wecht and Bosworth, Jr. 1998; Wolfe 1989).

TAUNTING WOUNDS

Some perpetrators who use a knife as a murder weapon torture their victims by inflicting taunting wounds before killing the victim. These wounds are nonfatal cuts and punctures caused by sticking and cutting motions. Taunting wounds penetrate the skin and cause considerable pain.

Nicole Brown Simpson's body did not have any apparent taunting wounds when she was murdered in Los Angeles, California, in June 1994. She died quickly from a vicious attack in which she was almost decapitated. Ron Goldman's body, found at the same crime scene, had a number of taunting wounds. There was a nonfatal cut across his neck and five nonfatal puncture wounds on his cheek. Even after Goldman was clinically dead, the killer inflicted postmortem wounds (Lange, Vannatter, and Moldea 1997).

9

Fingerprints
and Fingerprinting

Fingerprints are one of the quickest ways of establishing the identity of a person, and are perhaps the second best way after DNA analysis. The arrangement and relationship of ridges on each print makes every person's fingerprints unique. Fingerprint-developing techniques use powders, iodine, fumes, and Super Glue to make an otherwise invisible fingerprint visible. Once a fingerprint is lifted, it is entered into the Automated Fingerprint Identification System (AFIS), where it is compared with fingerprints of known felons. In this chapter, we explore ten aspects about fingerprints.

AUTOMATED FINGERPRINT
IDENTIFICATION SYSTEM (AFIS)

Police have two options for entering a suspect's fingerprints into an Automated Fingerprint Identification System (AFIS). The first option is to use the traditional ink method. This involves stamping and rolling the fingers on a ten-print card. The card is then scanned into a computer. This method is not always efficient. Repeated smudges necessitate the procedure to be redone multiple times.

The second option is to use a live-scan machine. This entails placing a suspect's fingers on the glass surface of a scanner. This procedure captures an image of the fingers, then displays them to ensure the image is of a sufficiently high quality. If the computer rejects the image, the procedure must be repeated. The computer stores in its database the accepted image. Hard copies of fingerprints can be printed when necessary.

AFIS creates a geometric "map" of finger ridge patterns and fingerprint minutiae, then translates the information into binary digital code. The code is entered into the computer's memory. A new record is created when a suspect's fingerprints do not match prints already in the system.

The computer uses a mathematical algorithm to search a fingerprint file. In minutes, the fingerprint being searched is compared to fingerprints in the file. A scoring system, which assigns points to criteria used by technicians when they manually match prints, finds possible matches. The number of matches retrieved is a number that a fingerprint expert can reasonably examine in a few hours.

The San Francisco Police Department (SFPD) implemented AFIS in 1984. Using AFIS, the SFPD ran 13,425 latent print searches between 1984 and 1988. This produced 2,752 identifications, which is approximately 20 percent of all searches. Furthermore, AFIS helped solve ninety-eight homicides.

AFIS became operational at the California Department of Justice in Sacramento, California, in the fall of 1985. A day later, the AFIS latent print database matched, in three minutes, a latent print from an automobile linked to the "Night Stalker" serial killer to a print of twenty-five-year-old Richard Ramirez. He was charged two days later with one of fifteen murders. According to Los Angeles police, it would have taken a technician sixty-seven years to match the fingerprints manually by examining cards (Burzinski 1999; Fincher 1989; Zonderman 1990).

DEVELOPING FINGERPRINTS WITH POWDERS

Powder is the preferred substance to use for developing latent, that is, hidden fingerprints on hard, dry, and smooth surfaces. The powder used should easily cling to fingerprint ridges and should contrast well with the background on which the powder is applied.

A white or gray powder should be used on a dark surface, black powder on a light-colored surface. Anthracene, a fluorescent powder, is used on a multicolored background. An ultraviolet light causes the powder to fluoresce, making background colors faintly visible.

A brush with a three-inch handle and one-and-a-half-inch soft hairs should be used. A separate brush should be used with each type of powder to avoid mixing powders. When the handle of a brush and a container of powder are the same color, this helps to avoid, or at least minimize, the likelihood of mixing powders.

A small amount of powder is placed on a piece of paper. A brush is used to pick up the powder and distribute it lightly across the area containing a fingerprint until outlines of the ridge are visible. Powder is added as required. Surplus powder is tapped from the brush when maximum development is completed. A brushing motion makes the print more visible. Brushing in the same direction as the direction of the ridges can also remove surplus powder (O'Hara and O'Hara 1994).

DISFIGUREMENT OF FINGERPRINTS

Criminals have attempted to destroy their fingerprints with a variety of methods, including sandpaper, acid, and surgery.

During the early 1930s, Public Enemy Number One, John Dillinger, had surgery to remove his fingerprints. Dillinger paid a surgeon $5,000 for the surgery and $25 a day to stay at his house. The surgery produced scars that obscured the ridges in the center of each finger above the first joint. However, the ridges outside the center section remained intact. There was still more than enough skin on the fingers from which to take Dillinger's prints and make a match.

In 1990, fingerprint experts noticed that a suspect arrested in a drug case in Miami, Florida, had fingerprints with disfigured ridges. The suspect had cut his fingerprints into small pieces then transplanted the pieces onto other fingers, producing broken ridge patterns. However, Tommy Moorefield, a latent print specialist, used cut photographs of the prints to fit together ridge patterns. It was then possible to compare and match the prints with other prints and to convict the suspect (Fisher 1995).

FINGERPRINT LIFT CARDS

A crime scene technician spreads fingerprint powder over an object that might have latent fingerprints, then brushes away the excess powder. If the powder reveals a print, which can be used to compare to prints on file, the technician carefully places over the print a pre-measured piece of transparent tape. After the tape is firmly affixed to a print, the technician slowly "lifts" the tape and with it a fingerprint. The technician then carefully affixes the tape to a three-inch by five-inch lift card. A white card is used for a print lifted from a light surface, a black card for a print removed from a dark-colored surface.

Cards are photographed and the prints are enlarged to five times their original size, then compared to prints in AFIS (Simon 1991).

FINGERPRINTS

Located on the pads of a person's fingers are ridges, slightly raised areas of skin. The arrangement and relationship of one ridge to another forms a pattern. This arrangement and relationship makes every person's fingerprints unique. This is true even for identical twins. Arches, loops, and whorls are fingerprint patterns. One or more patterns or variations of patterns are, with few exceptions, on the fingertips of every person. A person may have only loops, or only arches and whorls, on all ten fingers. A basic pattern recognizable in many people is known as a class characteristic. A "core" is the approximate center of the fingerprint's pattern area. A "delta" is the first "fork," separation, nearest the center of divergence. The "point of divergence" is the place where a line changes direction. A core, a delta, and a varying number of ridges between the core and delta are found in individuals who have loop patterns. The core, delta, and number of ridges are class characteristics because these characteristics may apply to more than one person. Ridge endings and "bifurcations," areas that branch out or separate, are called points or minutiae. They are also class characteristics. A "termination" is a ridge that is not continuous. A "trifurcation" is the point at which a ridge separates or divides into three ridges. A "minutiae point" is the place on a fingertip where each ridge ends and divides (Fisher 1995; Geberth 1997; Ragle 1995).

FINGERPRINTS AND RIGOR MORTIS

Rigor mortis must be absent to fingerprint a deceased person. Usually, however, bending the fingers can extend them forward. Pressing on the finger just above the knuckle can extend each finger, and the palm can be straightened until it is flat by pressing on the wrist. It is sometimes necessary to print different areas of the palm separately to get an overall impression of the palm. Cutting the tendons, which make the hand curl, is necessary when pressing inward on the hand cannot eliminate rigor mortis. The joints at the base of the fingers and wrist are cut.

Stretching the skin of the fingers and palms usually eliminates the deep wrinkling or creasing in these two areas. When the skin is still flexible, most wrinkles can often be removed by grasping the skin on the back of the finger and pinching. If the tendons in the palm have not been cut, bending the fingers backward can usually eliminate wrinkles in the palm. Small areas of the palm can be flattened by stretching the skin with one hand and inking and printing with the other one.

Tissue builder, whether water or viscous material, injected into several different parts of a finger or palm can remove deep wrinkles. Good fingerprints can then be taken.

When fingerprints cannot be taken using standard methods, the fingers or hand have to be severed. Each severed finger should be correctly labeled and kept separately in a preservative in its own vial. On rare occasions, skin is separated completely from the hand and kept moist in a preservative until the skin can be printed (Cowger 1983).

HEALTH ASPECTS OF FINGERPRINT POWDERS

Fingerprint powders are carbon-based fine-grained dust produced from lampblack, graphite, or willow charcoal. Filler added to the powder prevents them from becoming a compact mass, which would make dusting for prints more difficult.

Fingerprint powders have positive and negative aspects. The positive thing about these powders is that they stick to the salt in perspiration that produces a fingerprint. The negative thing is that they also stick to the hands and arms of police officers and settle in officers' nasal passages. This has affected officers differently. Some have developed allergies. Others have had fingerprint powders accumulate in their lungs. Still others have had their nasal passages thoroughly congested. Although some officers have worn masks, masks have not been of much help.

However, there are newer methods of raising fingerprints. Chemical sprays containing ninhydrin can be applied to paper, cardboard, and certain wood surfaces. Ninhydrin, rather than reacting to salt in perspiration, reacts to amino acids in skin. Sprays, however, are toxic and must be kept out of eyes and lungs. For this reason, it is preferable not to spray an object at a crime scene. Whenever possible, the object should be taken to a crime lab and sprayed in a well-ventilated area. Ninhydrin, unfortunately, is not the solution to the shortcomings of powders (McArdle and McArdle 1988).

IODINE FUMING

Iodine fuming is a procedure used to develop latent fingerprints on paper and cardboard. When the fumes are over paper, they darken latent prints. An iodine print is called "fugitive" because it can disappear soon after it is developed. For this reason, the print should be photographed as soon as it is clearly visible.

In a lab, iodine crystals in a crucible are heated in a glass case and fumes are produced. The fumes drift upward and darken latent prints on paper suspended at the top of the glass case. Paper and greasy surfaces at a crime scene can be treated with a portable iodine-fuming device. The device consists of an open-ended glass tube, which contains iodine crystals separated from calcium chloride by glass wool. The warm breath of the person using the portable device increases sublimation of the crystals. The portability of the device makes it easy for the person using it to direct the stream of resulting vapor in virtually any direction (O'Hara and O'Hara 1994; Salottolo 1970).

SUPER GLUE

In the late 1970s, the Japanese National Police invented a fuming method for developing fingerprints. This method, simple and effective, is the cyanoacrylate method, also known as the Super Glue method. Approximately 98 percent of the commercially available product Super Glue is cyanoacrylate ester. Moreover, in the late 1970s Super Glue was a source of cyanoacrylate ester used for developing fingerprints. The Super Glue method effectively develops fingerprints on nonporous surfaces such as metal, wax paper, and plastic bags.

An airtight glass or plastic container, called a fuming tank, is an essential part of the Super Glue method. If an item to be processed is sufficiently light, the item is suspended from the top of the container. Otherwise, the item is placed inside the container so all sides are exposed to vapor. Adding glue to cotton dipped in a sodium hydroxide solution accelerates fuming. A safe heat source, such as a large lightbulb placed next to one side of the tank, also accelerates fuming.

After the cotton is dry, it is placed in the container. Several drops of Super Glue are placed on the cotton. Glue vapor sticks to friction ridges and a gray or white image appears within an hour.

The fingerprint is photographed when it is completely visible. The glue has hardened the impression. The print can be lifted several times without concern that the print will be smeared or destroyed in some other way (O'Hara and O'Hara 1994; Redsicker et al. 1994).

TYPES OF FINGERPRINTS

When a person touches an object, perspiration or a substance the person touched, such as dirt or blood, is transferred from the ridges of the fingers to the touched object. This leaves an impression. An impression visible to the naked eye is called a patent or visible print. An impression not visible to the naked eye is called a latent print. An impression depressed below the original surface of a soft substance like butter or putty is called a plastic print.

Objects with clean, smooth surfaces, such as glass, paper, and enamel, have surfaces on which it is relatively easy to leave a fingerprint. These surfaces usually retain a print without spreading it. A fingerprint must be deposited with a certain amount of pressure. Too much pressure will spread the print. Moving the finger will smear the print.

Finally, it can be difficult to get a print off human skin (Fisher 1995; Geberth 1997; McArdle and McArdle 1988; O'Hara and O'Hara 1994).

10

Firearms, Poisons, and Uncommon Weapons

In the heat of the moment, anything can be used as a murder weapon. Many underworld killers and disgruntled spouses use small-caliber handguns to commit homicides. Although less frequently used, acids, poisons, and dynamite are just as deadly. In this chapter, we examine twenty-one topics about murder weapons.

.22-CALIBER GUN

On June 19, 1975, in the suburb of Oak Park outside of Chicago, Illinois, Sam Giancana, head of the Chicago Outfit, was in the basement of his bungalow, frying sausages. It was after 22:00. A man whom Giancana apparently knew entered the bungalow through the basement steel door and, in a moment, as Giancana continued frying the sausages, shot him once with a silencer-equipped gun in the back of the head. As Giancana lay face up on the floor, the killer placed the gun barrel into Giancana's open mouth and fired one more shot. Then he stuck the gun under Giancana's chin and fired upward five times.

On June 5, 1968, Senator Robert F. Kennedy, the Democratic candidate for the U.S. presidency, was making a speech in the Ambassador Hotel in downtown Los Angeles, California. After Kennedy finished the speech, he and his entourage began taking a prearranged shortcut through the hotel's kitchen. Kitchen staff and a Jordanian by the name of Sirhan Sirhan were part of the crowd. As Kennedy and his entourage continued moving through the kitchen,

Sirhan moved to within a short distance of Kennedy and fired eight shots, four of them striking the presidential hopeful. A Walker's H-acid test, conducted later, indicated Sirhan's gun was between one and six inches from Kennedy's coat when Sirhan opened fire.

The death of Tamara Rand, fifty-five, of San Diego, California, looked like a professional hit. There was no indication of forced entry into her house. Robbery did not appear to be the motive. Her husband found her body on November 9, 1975, when he arrived home from work. She was in the kitchen and had been shot with a silencer-equipped gun five times in the head. Rand had had controversial business dealings in Las Vegas, Nevada. She had claimed she was a partner in the Stardust Hotel. In spite of a police investigation, the case was not solved.

What do these murders have in common? A .22-caliber weapon was used to kill Giancana, Kennedy, and Rand. Sirhan Sirhan, for example, used an 8-shot Iver Johnson Cadet Model .22 revolver with a 2.5-inch barrel.

A J. C. Higgins Model 80 .22-caliber, and a High Standard Model 101 .22, have been associated with murders committed in California and Nevada by the Zodiac killer. The Zodiac shot or stabbed his victims. His first known gunshot victim was Betty Lou Jensen who was shot on December 20, 1968, in Vallejo, California. To date, the Zodiac killer has not been apprehended.

The Office of Strategic Services (OSS) used the High Standard HD Military .22 caliber pistol, equipped with a silencer, during World War II. Street gangs call the .22-caliber gun a deuce-deuce or double deuce. Its predecessors can be traced back approximately 150 years. The Smith & Wesson Model 1 revolver and the .22-caliber cartridge were both introduced in 1857. Two years later, in 1859, Colt manufactured the Colt No. 4 Model pistol derringer, which fired a .22 cartridge.

Sturm, Ruger and Company in Southport, Connecticut, began manufacturing .22s in 1949. Thirty years later, this company produced the one-millionth Ruger .22 auto pistol.

For decades, professional killers have preferred a .22-caliber pistol, silencer-equipped, for hitting a victim at close range. One reason is the gun's size. Many models are easily concealed. The Lorcin-1 .22, Sterling 302, and Wilkinson Sherry are a few examples. The size of such weapons makes it easier for killers not to draw attention to themselves. Professional killers, however, do not necessarily favor these three models. There are many more from which to choose.

A bullet fired from a .22, held a few inches from the victim's head, will enter the head and ricochet inside the skull, causing massive internal damage, but will not likely exit the skull because of the bullet's relatively low velocity.

Without an exit wound, investigators cannot plot the trajectory of the shot fired. Any amount of useful information that is missing in a homicide case understandably can make it more difficult for detectives to solve the case. Other reasons why professional killers prefer to use a .22 are because it is relatively quiet, has virtually no recoil, and produces little splatter of blood and brain tissue.

The shooting of patrolman Frank Serpico on the night of February 3, 1971, illustrates that a bullet from a .22-caliber gun does not always penetrate the human skull. Serpico was on a narcotics raid at 778 Driggs Street in Brooklyn, New York, when someone shot him in the head. The bullet went through Serpico's left maxillary sinus, the cavity on the left side of his nose. The bullet then traveled down and to the right, breaking into fragments in the back of his jawbone. Rather than shattering the jawbone, the bullet tore through facial nerves. This caused localized paralysis, but no major veins were damaged. A bullet fragment stopped half a centimeter from the big carotid artery on the side of his neck, through which blood flows to the brain. Had the fragment traveled a bit further, he would have rapidly bled to death at 778 Driggs Street (Corwin 1997; Cuomo 1995; Edwards 1990; Findley 1998; Giancana and Giancana 1992; Graysmith 1986; Maas 1973; Melanson 1991; Murano and Hoffer 1990; Noguchi and DiMona 1983; Paulson 1993; Pence 1998; Peters 1999; Pileggi 1995; Roemer 1994; Sachs 1997; Sasser 1998; Simon 1991; Tanner 1977; Wilkinson 1979).

AK-47

The AK-47 is an assault weapon designed in the former Soviet Union. This weapon, used by armed forces worldwide, is compatible with magazines that contain from five to forty rounds. It can also be equipped with a seventy-five-round drum.

The AK-47 can cause a large number of casualties in a short time period. On January 17, 1989, in Stockton, California, Patrick Purdy, twenty-six, a drifter armed with an AK-47-style rifle and a 9-mm pistol, opened fire at an elementary school. Purdy killed five children and wounded thirty other people. Then he shot himself. Also in 1989, this time on September 14, Joseph Wesbecker, forty-seven, armed with an AK-47, entered the Standard Gravure printing plant in Louisville, Kentucky. Wesbecker, a former Standard Gravure employee who was on disability leave due to personal and work problems, spent half an hour in the plant. After he killed or wounded twenty people, he fatally shot himself. Wesbecker had been on Prozac for depression.

The Bounty Hunters, a Los Angeles, California, drug gang, has also used the AK-47, one of several assault weapons used in drug-related shootings.

It is easy to illegally purchase weapons, even in Canada, where gun control laws are much stricter than in the United States. A woman in her mid-twenties was arrested near the University of Alberta in Edmonton, Alberta, on July 21, 2000. She had an AK-47 stuffed down her pants and asked passersby if they wanted to buy the gun (Church 1989; Cornwell 1996; Katz 1997; "This Street Vendor" 2000).

ARSENIC

Arsenic can exist in a number of forms: a steel-gray brittle metal, an oily liquid, a crystalline solid, and a gas. Arsenic as a white powder is water soluble, almost tasteless, and virtually odorless. However, the breath of the victim of arsenic poisoning can have a garlicky odor, which can tip off investigators. The acute lethal dose of the crystalline form is 200 mg. Ant poison, weed killers, and paints are a few of the sources of arsenic.

The perpetrator of arsenic poisoning often administers arsenic to the victim's food or drink. Symptoms appear within hours or days after ingestion. Acute symptoms appear within half an hour to two hours. Vomiting, severe abdominal pain, and a metallic taste are among the initial symptoms. Jaundice and kidney failure are among the subsequent symptoms. The victim dies within twenty-four hours to four days from circulatory failure. Diarrhea, edema of the face, sore throat, salivation, and hair loss are some of the symptoms of chronic arsenic poisoning. This type of poisoning occurs over a prolonged time period. Generally speaking, the smaller the amount of arsenic that enters a person's body, the longer the person will survive. This person, however, will exhibit symptoms of being poisoned. Chronic arsenic poisoning is sometimes confused with gastroenteritis or neurological disease.

Atomic absorption (AA) can be used to detect arsenic in hair, food, blood, nails, and urine. The toxic level in blood is 0.6 to 9.3mg/liter (United 1997).

BEHAVIOR OF BULLETS

When a person pulls the trigger of a gun and a bullet begins to travel down the barrel, no one can predict with 100 percent accuracy the bullet's final destination.

There is no guarantee a .357 magnum, a powerful gun compared to a .22-caliber, will kill a person every time, even when the .357 magnum is placed against the back of someone's head and the trigger is pulled. The bullet, instead of entering the skull, may knock the person unconscious, travel erratically, and exit from the forehead without causing permanent brain damage.

On the other hand, a person may be shot in the wrist with a .22-caliber gun. The bullet enters a vein, travels upward through the vein up the arm and into the heart, and kills the person.

Although Capone-era killer Baby Face Nelson was struck multiple times with buckshot and .45-caliber bullets, he killed two FBI agents and stole their car. Fifteen .45-caliber bullets hit Pretty Boy Floyd, another killer from this era. He purportedly lived for another fifteen minutes and swore at the FBI agents who shot him.

A large-caliber gun is no more a guarantee of instantaneous death than is a small-caliber gun a guarantee that death might not occur. John Hinckley fired six times when he attempted to assassinate President Reagan in 1981. Four individuals were hit. The fifth bullet hit a window of Reagan's limousine. The sixth bullet was, at first, difficult to find. Then two FBI agents found it across the street, where it had hit a second-story window and shattered.

When a bullet strikes an object such as a human bone, the bullet changes direction and often its path cannot be traced. However, investigators can determine a bullet's trajectory by lining up the holes in two different surfaces through which the bullet passed. Traditionally this has been done by placing a dowel through a hole and using protractors, a carpenter's level, and a plumb line to determine the angle of penetration. The high-tech method is to aim a laser beam through the holes and see where the beam leads.

When a bullet strikes certain objects, the shape of the bullet is altered. The change in shape causes the bullet to deflect at a different angle. In other words, the angle at which a bullet strikes an object, the angle of incidence, does not equal the angle of rebound (Fisher 1995; Sherrill 1973).

CYANIDE

Cyanide is available in liquid form as hydrogen cyanide (HCN), also known as prussic acid. A mineral acid mixed with cyanide salts can produce pure hydrogen cyanide gas.

The sodium, potassium, and calcium salts of cyanide are crystalline materials. The sodium and potassium salts of cyanide are white, smell like almonds, have a bitter taste, and are easily dissolved in aqueous liquids. Fumigants, rodenticides, and electroplating solutions are a few of the sources of cyanide.

The acute lethal dose of cyanide is 270 ppm in air or 50 mg of HCN. It can be detected in beverages, blood, and autopsy organ specimens. The toxic levels are 12.4 mg/liter in blood and 0.1 mg/liter in urine. Metabolic asphyxiation results when cyanide prevents respiration at the cellular level, in particular depriving the brain and heart of oxygen.

The perpetrator of cyanide poisoning administers cyanide to the victim through food or drink. Symptoms can appear in as short a time as thirty seconds after the ingestion of cyanide. The symptoms of acute poisoning include headache, vomiting, confusion, seizures, and cardiovascular collapse. Cyanide poisoning can be confused with heart attack or acute asthmatic attack (United 1997).

DRUGFIRE

A computer system developed by the FBI and Mnemonic Systems, Inc., provides information about ballistics to participating crime labs in the United States. The name "DRUGFIRE" was chosen for this system because the words "drug" and "fire" are associated with drug-related violence involving guns.

After police obtain a gun suspected of being used in a shooting, the gun is test-fired in a crime lab. The casing is mounted under a video camera, which is attached to a computer. The video camera captures a digital image of the targeted part of the casing. For comparison purposes, the firing pin impression is of particular interest. After the computer identifies the distinctive characteristics of the image, the computer digitizes the image. The computer then compares the digitized image to images stored in a database. There is a match or hit when casing data entered is similar to data in the database.

DRUGFIRE can simultaneously display up to twenty-four images. They can be magnified, displayed side by side, and overlaid. DRUGFIRE can exchange images of cartridge cases, bullets, ejector marks, extractor marks, and chamber marks between crime labs using high-speed telephone connections. Before the advent of DRUGFIRE, it would be nearly impossible for firearm examiners in New York to link a single gun to multiple shootings in a city as far away as Los Angeles, California. As of October 1999, there were more than 225,000 stored images.

Although DRUGFIRE is a valuable tool, the opinions of firearm examiners carry more weight, regarding the degree of similarity of cartridge cases, bullets, and guns ("The FBI's" 2001; Fisher 2000; Houde 1999; Saferstein 2001).

DUM DUM BULLET

In the 1890s, the British in India initially used ineffective bullets against attacking tribesmen. These bullets did not have enough stopping power. For this reason, an expanding bullet was developed at Dum Dum, the British arsenal in suburban Calcutta. The metal jacket of a standard bullet was left open at its tip. This bullet, the dumdum, flattened upon impact with living tissue, causing considerably more internal damage than an ordinary bullet. Most bullets of the day made a clean perforation, but did not necessarily cause death. After dumdum bullets were used in 1898 at the Battle of Omduran in the Sudan, there was international outrage. A year later, the Hague Conference outlawed the use of dumdum bullets in war. Great Britain was accused of using these types of bullets again between 1899 and 1902, during the Boer War.

During Eliot Ness's law enforcement career in the 1930s and 1940s, a killer by the name of Picchi, who intended to shoot Ness, was arrested by him during a violent struggle moments before Picchi could shoot him. Ness examined Picchi's gun and saw that each bullet in the cylinder was a dumdum. A cross was cut into the lead nose of each bullet so the bullet would flatten out upon impact. Ness had seen dumdum bullet holes in bodies. Each hole was the size of a silver dollar.

On the evening of May 16, 1957, Ness died at age fifty-four at his home of a massive heart attack. For a man who had seen a lot of violence, this was an ironic way to die (*Academic* 1998; *Columbia* 1993; DeSola 1988; *Encyclopedia* 2000; Ness and Fraley 1957; Nickel 1990; Owen 1975).

DYNAMITE

Alfred Nobel, Swedish chemist and inventor, invented dynamite in 1867. He combined nitroglycerine with kieselguhr, a soft, white, porous substance. Kieselguhr consists of the skeletons of diatoms, minute aquatic plants found worldwide. Nobel noticed that nitroglycerine in dynamite had a lower explosive capacity than liquid nitroglycerine, yet nitroglycerine in dynamite could be more easily detonated. Dynamite then and now, unlike liquid nitroglycerine, is less sensitive to shock and much easier to handle and transport.

Today, diatomaceous earth, wood pulp, or sawdust absorb the nitroglycerine in dynamite, stabilizing the otherwise volatile nature of nitroglycerine. Present-day dynamite, which also contains sodium nitrate or ammonium nitrate in addition to nitroglycerine, is packed in waxed paper or plastic cylinders called cartridges. Cartridges range from approximately one to eight inches in diameter and from four to thirty inches in length. A detonating cap or blasting cap is inserted into one end of the cartridge, and a fuse or electric current is used to detonate the dynamite.

Nathan Allen lived next door to his married uncle, James McFillin, who believed his wife was in love with Nathan. Nathan, who worked at Bethlehem Steel in Baltimore, Maryland, got into his truck at work one day in 1979, turned the ignition, and died in the ensuing explosion. A passenger was injured.

Federal agents investigated the explosion and linked the dynamite to McFillin, who was convicted and sent to federal prison. The agents had found taggants at the crime scene. Taggants were developed in 1977, in response to terrorist bombings. Taggants are tiny markers combined with the ingredients of dynamite when it is manufactured. The taggants in the dynamite James purchased contained color-coded particles, the size of flakes of pepper, visible under a microscope. The colors in a taggant identify the manufacturer and batch number of the dynamite. Sales and distribution records can be a paper trail to the purchaser of dynamite. Agents who studied the taggants determined the exploded dynamite was manufactured in West Virginia in December 1978. James purchased two sticks of this dynamite.

Glen Fischer, the owner of Fischer Apiaries, was in his pickup truck near the town of Gorman in southern California on the morning of June 10, 1983. Fischer was on his way to meet at 08:30 a park ranger who was going to help him find a remote canyon in which to store 120 beehives.

He met the ranger and got into her truck. After they stopped in Caswell Canyon and Fischer had walked approximately one hundred yards, he smelled something unpleasant, and then came across a dead body.

The body was that of a man, and part of the head was missing. The remaining part faced west. His feet faced east, the right foot crossed over the left foot. The left arm rested against a bush and pointed skyward. His right arm extended southwest. The decedent was wearing a three-piece suit. His shirt was partially open. The front and back pockets of his pants were pulled out. He was not wearing a wristwatch. Approximately seven feet from the body was part of a jawbone containing several teeth.

Sheriff's homicide detectives Willi Ahn and Carlos Avila caught the case. They checked Los Angeles Police Department (LAPD) computer records for information about missing persons. Twenty-eight days earlier, on the evening of May 13, 1983, Roy Alexander Radin had disappeared. His assistant had filed a missing person's report with police in West Hollywood.

Radin, a New York theatrical producer, was last seen getting into a limousine in front of the Regency Hotel in Los Angeles. He was going to have dinner in Beverly Hills with Laney Jacobs, a cocaine dealer from Miami, Florida. Radin, Jacobs, and movie producer Robert Evans had been working on becoming business partners, regarding several proposed movies.

Radin had been avoiding Jacobs because Jacobs believed he was involved in the theft of cocaine from her house. Radin denied any involvement. They were going to discuss the matter over dinner. Radin, however, was suspicious of Jacobs's motives and arranged to have Demond Wilson, who had starred in the television series *Sanford and Son*, to tail the limo. Wilson lost the limo in traffic.

There were five people in the limo: Radin, Jacobs, Alex Marti, Bill Mentzer, and Robert Lowe. Lowe was the driver. Marti and Mentzer were hired by Jacobs to kill Radin. Marti and Mentzer prevented Radin from getting out of the limo when Jacobs jumped out. Lowe then drove to Caswell Canyon where Fischer would, five weeks later, come across Radin's body. Marti had shot Radin twenty-seven times in the head, then removed Radin's Rolex watch and a ring. Mentzer had shot Radin once in the head. Dynamite was then ignited in Radin's mouth.

Marti and Mentzer told Bill Rider, head of security for Larry Flynt in Los Angeles, about the murder because Rider hired Marti, Mentzer, and Lowe to be bodyguards for Flynt, the publisher of *Hustler*. Rider talked to police. Detective Avila learned at the LAPD that Bill Mentzer was a suspect in a recent contract murder.

Between the time of the murder and the time investigators removed Radin's remains from the crime scene, there were only seventy pounds of remains left to remove. Mentzer, Marti, Lowe, and Jacobs were convicted on July 10, 1991: Mentzer and Marti were convicted of first-degree murder and kidnapping with intent to murder, and Lowe and Jacobs were convicted of second-degree murder and kidnapping with intent to murder. All four appealed their convictions.

On November 1, 1955, Daisie Walker King and Jack Gilbert Graham, her son, were at Stapleton Airport in Denver, Colorado, where she asked him to purchase three insurance policies from a coin machine. There was a different beneficiary for each policy; the total value of the policies was to be $6,250. Graham, however, mistakenly purchased in his name a policy for $37,500.

His mother, who was about to leave for Alaska to visit a relative, had excess luggage weight of thirty-seven pounds. Jack assured her she would need all her luggage. After United Airlines flight 629 departed with Daisie King and forty-three other individuals on board, Jack Graham, while having dinner at the airport restaurant with his wife and child, left the table and went to the washroom, where he vomited. Eleven minutes after taking off, the four-engine United Airlines flight exploded and crashed. All on board died.

On November 10, Graham told a stranger how flight 629 had blown up. On November 13, the FBI questioned him, he confessed, and he was arrested. Twenty-three-year-old Jack Gilbert Graham had placed a time bomb in his mother's luggage. The bomb consisted of a timer, hotshot battery, blasting caps, and twenty-five sticks of dynamite. He was convicted and sent to the gas chamber at the Colorado State Penitentiary on January 11, 1957.

During his childhood, Graham exhibited cruelty to animals and once set fire to a garage. In 1951, he forged over forty checks. Later that year, he spent sixty days in prison for bootlegging and carrying a concealed weapon. By 1955, he had held forty-five jobs since leaving school. He lied on projective psychological tests. Psychiatrists described him as sane, but a sociopath. All of this information can be used to argue that, from a very early age, it was inevitable that Graham would eventually commit murder (*Academic* 1998; Brown 1998; *Collier's* 1996; Ellroy 1996; *Encyclopedia* 2000; Nash 1980; Wick 1990; Witkin 1996; Wolfgang 1967; *World* 1998).

FIREARMS AND HOMICIDE STATISTICS

The six states, in 1997, from highest percentage to lowest percentage, in which firearms were used in homicides were the District of Columbia (80 percent), Mississippi (79 percent), Louisiana (78 percent), Maryland (78 percent), West Virginia (76 percent), and Tennessee (76 percent).

The six states, in 1997, from lowest percentage to highest percentage, in which firearms were used in homicides were North Dakota (17 percent), Delaware (31 percent), Iowa (31 percent), Hawaii (33 percent), Wisconsin (42 percent), and Nebraska (48 percent) ("America's" 1999).

FIREARMS IDENTIFICATION

Grooves, which are in front of the chamber in a gun, spiral toward the muzzle and enable a bullet to rotate as it travels down the barrel.

The rotation allows the bullet to move in a relatively straight line. Most guns have between two and twenty-two grooves. This is not true of smooth bore weapons, such as shotguns.

"Lands" are the higher areas between the grooves. "Rifling" refers to all the lands and grooves. The lands become the grooves on the bullet, and the grooves become the lands, as a bullet travels down the barrel.

A tool, which varies from one manufacturer to another, creates rifling when a barrel is manufactured. Each tool has imperfections, which remain in the barrel. The imperfections are used to identify a gun. The imperfections also appear on a bullet as it moves down the barrel because the bullet is softer than the barrel. Bullets fired from a particular gun are unique in appearance because of barrel imperfections.

Six characteristics help in the classification of a fired bullet. The characteristics are caliber, number of lands and grooves, direction of twist, width of lands and grooves, depth of groove, and weight. Caliber is the diameter of the bore in a weapon, and is expressed in one hundredths of an inch in the United States, for example, .22 and .32. The number of lands and grooves can usually be counted without requiring magnification. The lands and grooves on a bullet slant either right or left, showing the direction of the twist. A micrometer or toolmaker's microscope can measure the width of lands and grooves. The depth of a groove is approximately .005 inches. Although the weight of a bullet should be noted, the weight does not always play an important role in classifying a fired bullet unless a gun of the same make is available for comparison.

A bullet can be linked to a particular type of gun without the gun being present because most firearms manufacturers maintain very high quality control standards. Different manufacturers place serial numbers in different locations. Some serial numbers include letter prefixes or suffixes. Other serial numbers have been removed, but can be restored. Some guns never had a serial number.

Barrel length, number of bullets fired, and type of finish on the metal can be taken into account when tracing a gun to the person who possessed it at a particular time. When investigators have a gun they believe is a murder weapon, a firearms identification expert fires the gun, such as a .25, into a box of cotton. The box is made of wood or metal and is approximately six feet long, one foot high, and one foot wide. The cotton prevents the bullet, which is later retrieved, from losing any of its markings. Investigators know if they have the murder weapon when the recovered bullet is compared to a bullet from a homicide victim and both bullets are identical from the viewpoint of ballistics.

Large-caliber firearms, such as a .45, are fired into a tank of water because the markings may be polished off if these weapons are fired into cotton. The tank may be similar in shape and size to the box containing cotton. However, the tank may be positioned vertically so the firearm specialist fires down from a footstool or ladder rather than horizontally. Test samples are retrieved and marked as being test samples in order not to confuse the samples with bullets retrieved from victims. The latter bullets are evidence.

A forensic comparison microscope is used to compare two spent bullets at a time. If the rifling in both bullets is identical or virtually identical, then both bullets were very likely fired from the same gun (Graysmith 1991; Salottolo 1970; Scanlon 1978; Sullivan and Aronson 1981).

HOMICIDAL POISONING

Homicidal poisoning is murder when poison, in sufficiently harmful dosage, is deliberately administered to one person by another person with the intention of causing death. A poison can be inorganic or organic. An organic poison may be destroyed in the body during a person's life, the process possibly continuing after death until no poison remains. An inorganic poison remains in the body, where it is changed into a relatively nontoxic compound. An excessive amount of a substance that is normally in the body, sodium chloride for example, can cause death, just as a small amount of a highly toxic poison, such as ricin, can bring about a person's death.

One way for a poison to enter the tissues of the body is through intact skin. This can also cause accidental deaths through poisoning. When an arsenical compound was deliberately applied to a vagina to treat an infection, the person died from arsenic poisoning because the arsenic was rapidly absorbed from the compound into her bloodstream. Cyanide solutions, splashed into the eyes and rapidly absorbed, have also caused death.

The second way for a poison to enter the tissues of the body is through broken skin. A hypodermic syringe can be used to inject a poison intramuscularly or intravenously. The third way for a poison to enter a person's body is orally through food or drink.

Arsenic remains in the body, where it can be found in hair and nails years after death. Yellow phosphorus, possibly poisonous when ingested, is converted into phosphates. It would be impossible to distinguish these phosphates from the phosphates normally present in the body.

Murder through homicidal poisoning has usually occurred in family settings. A spouse, usually the wife, would over time poison her husband. However, homicidal poisoning is an extremely rare form of murder. There were in the United States, between 1980 and 1985, 114,305 homicides committed that could be classified. This constituted an average of 19,050 homicides annually. Homicidal poisoning comprised less than 0.5 percent of violent deaths.

Deaths classified as poisoning do not include narcotics even though narcotics, like poisons, are chemicals. Cocaine absorbed through the lining of the nose has caused death, but narcotics are used in medical treatment and recreationally to make a person feel better. Poisons, on the other hand, are viewed as generally destructive in and of themselves. A person who used arsenic recreationally would be thought of as mentally ill (Adelson 1987; Holden 1966).

INTEGRATED BALLISTICS IDENTIFICATION SYSTEM (IBIS)

Forensic Technology, Inc. (FTI), an engineering firm in Montreal, Quebec, developed the Integrated Ballistics Identification System (IBIS), a computerized system that matches spent bullets and cartridges found at crime scenes.

The origins of IBIS go back to approximately 1990. At that time, Michael Barrett, a former ballistics expert at the Royal Canadian Mounted Police (RCMP), approached the Walsh Group, the parent company of FTI. Barrett was interested in combining computer vision applications with bullet identification. Barrett's efforts helped IBIS become a reality in 1993.

A firing pin, ejector, and gun barrel are three parts of a gun that leave distinct deformations, or "signatures," on a bullet as it is fired and leaves the barrel. IBIS repeatedly scans the deformations with a laser-guided microscope, digital camera, and specimen manipulators. This creates a 360-degree photograph that is accurate to 1/4,000th of a centimeter. Operating on a server, IBIS compares the photograph to signatures of the same caliber of gun previously acquired. IBIS searches its own records as well as networked databases. This takes less than one hour. Then a list is generated of potential bullets most likely fired from the same gun.

Police in New York, New York; New Orleans, Louisiana; San José, California; and Cape Town and Pretoria, South Africa, are examples of cities in which police use IBIS. A firearms examiner who manually matches crime scene bullets would have to compare these bullets with every bullet of the same type in storage. This procedure would take four hours.

IBIS was successfully used in 1998 after two individuals were arrested in San José, following a police chase. A semiautomatic pistol was thrown from a Honda Accord during the chase. The pistol was recovered and test-fired, then its signature was entered into IBIS. IBIS connected the pistol to spent shell casings at three different shootings. The individuals in the Honda were charged with several offenses, including attempted murder (Hornyak 1999).

MAC-10

In 1979 the Bureau of Alcohol, Tobacco, and Firearms (ATF) made a decision regarding the MAC-10 machine pistol. The ATF unintentionally designated the MAC-10 as semiautomatic, a weapon relatively easy to purchase. Criminals, or someone acting on their behalf, could purchase a MAC-10 and face only minimal red tape. The MAC-10 semiautomatic could then be easily converted into an illegal automatic. For a semiautomatic weapon to fire, its trigger is pulled once for each bullet fired. For an automatic weapon to fire, its trigger is pulled back and a continuous barrage of bullets is fired until either finger pressure on the trigger is released or the magazine is empty.

If the MAC-10 had been designated automatic, it would have been more difficult to purchase. The purchaser would have had to fill out forms for local and federal authorities; would have had to have fingerprints taken; and would have had to pay a tax. A person who possesses an improperly registered automatic weapon can receive a prison sentence and at least one fine, perhaps multiple, fines.

The MAC-10 and MAC-11, its cousin, were created and perfected by Gordon Ingram, who learned during World War II about the practical aspects of weapons. Ingram furthered his experience in 1949, while working for a newly established firm in Los Angeles, California, the Police Ordnance Company. After leaving Police Ordnance in 1952, Ingram worked on a submachine gun in Thailand. One year after he joined Sionics, Inc., located near Atlanta, Georgia, Sionics management established a separate company in 1970, the Military Armament Corp. (MAC). Then the MAC-10 and MAC-11 were developed, many with silencers. The main difference between the models was caliber: MAC-10 was .45 or 9 mm and MAC-11 was .380. MAC Corp. closed after production stopped, due to company politics, in 1973, and it filed for bankruptcy in 1975. A new company continued to produce the weapons in 1976.

The MAC-10 and MAC-11 each weigh an average of 8.4 pounds, measure approximately 10.5 inches overall, have a thirty-round magazine, and can be concealed in the glove compartment of a large car or in a shoulder holster. Each fires between 700 and 1,145 rounds per minute, depending on the date of manufacture of the particular weapon.

By the time the MAC-10 was reclassified, in 1982, as an automatic weapon, thousands had been sold as a semiautomatic and some fell into criminals' hands. The murderer of Alan Berg, an outspoken talk show host, used a MAC-10 to kill Berg in Denver, Colorado, on June 18, 1984. A drug dealer used an automatic MAC-10, in August 1985, to outgun four police officers in a shootout at the Doral Hotel in Miami Beach, Florida (Cormack 1979; Larson 1994; Leo 1993; Newton 1990; Stengel, Diederich, and van Voorst 1985).

SATURDAY NIGHT SPECIAL

On September 22, 1989, in St. Jacob, Illinois, Kathy Gaultney walked up to her drunken husband, Keith, who was asleep in their bedroom, and shot him twice in the head with a .22-caliber gun. She dumped the contents of drawers on top of her husband to make the murder look robbery-related, then she called police. The murder of Keith Gaultney was the culmination of arguments between Kathy and Keith over his alcoholism and unemployment, her involvement in drug dealing to earn money for basic needs, and especially his threats to tell police about her involvement in drug trafficking. Rachel, Kathy's teenaged daughter, told police three weeks later what really happened. Kathy was arrested, tried, convicted, and sentenced to prison.

This type of homicide is frequently committed with a Saturday Night Special, an inexpensive, mass-produced, easily concealed handgun. This type of gun is small-caliber, readily available, and legal. It is typically associated with domestic disturbances and robberies of small businesses such as liquor and convenience stores. The purchase price of one in 1999 was approximately $50. Kathy Gaultney purchased her .22-caliber Saturday Night Special at a gun shop in Collinsville, Illinois, and then took shooting lessons at a shooting range (Barkas 1978; Clarkson 1998; Landre, Miller, and Porter 1997; Middleton 1994; Sasser 1990; Simon 1991; Symonds, Woellert, and Garland 1999).

SILENCERS

A silencer is a device attached to the end of a gun to muffle the noise of the gun when the gun is fired. Silencers are usually tubular in shape and range in length from one inch to two feet. The outside diameter ranges from half an inch to three inches.

Different materials have been used to make illegal silencers, including plastic bottles, lawnmower mufflers, and motorcycle mufflers. Metal or rubber baffles (disks), steel wool, or fiberglass is placed inside the silencer. Some silencers filter out soot and powder normally expelled from the barrel. Silencers not made to screw into the end of a gun barrel are welded or soldered to the barrel. A threaded connection allows for a gas-tight seal. Some crudely made silencers are attached to the muzzle of a gun with tape.

Gases are released when a gun is fired. The gases in a silencer-equipped gun are contained at first, then gradually dissipated. A silencer that reduces the sound of a gunshot by twelve decibels reduces the audible sound by 75 percent.

In 1984, a high-caliber automatic weapon equipped with a silencer (a MAC-10; see pages 212–213) was used to kill Alan Berg, a controversial radio talk show host in Denver, Colorado. This gun made approximately 10 percent of its normal sound.

In the United States, silencers have been subject to control by Federal Law since 1934. They were manufactured commercially until 1976. Only soldiers and police officers under certain conditions are permitted to legally possess a silencer (DiMaio 1999; Fisher 1995; Scroggie 1977).

SMOOTHBORE FIREARMS

The inside of the barrels of smoothbore firearms, such as shotguns, are completely smooth, lacking rifling, or grooves inside the barrel, which stabilize the spin of a bullet as it travels through the barrel, exits the barrel, then travels toward its target.

Pistols, revolvers, and rifles are rifled firearms. They fire bullets—single, solid projectiles. Shotguns, smoothbore firearms, fire shells that contain multiple pellets. Shotguns, however, can also fire "slugs," which are solid projectiles. Rifled firearms, after being fired, eject shell casings. Smoothbore firearms eject shell husks.

Shotguns, when compared to other types of firearms and especially handguns, such as .357 revolvers and .38 revolvers, have not been very popular with criminals. Criminals have generally preferred to use well-made, easily concealable, large-caliber handguns.

The FBI's Supplemental Homicide Reports show that, in 1993, shotguns were used to commit 5 percent of all murders. Between 1982 and 1993, 687 law enforcement officers were killed, 7.4 percent with shotguns. In 1994, shotguns represented 9.7 percent of all the guns traced by the National Tracing Center of the Bureau of Alcohol, Tobacco, and Firearms (ATF). In 1995, however, 17 percent of all stolen gun information in the FBI's stolen gun file was about shotguns (Randall 1997; Zawitz 1995).

STRYCHNINE

Pure strychnine alkaloid, derived from the tree *Strychnos nux-vomica*, is a white powder. The powder is crystalline, extremely bitter, soluble in aqueous solutions, and without a characteristic odor. Strychnine is found in rodenticides. The acute lethal dose taken orally is 30 mg to 100 mg. It kills by arresting respiration.

The perpetrator of strychnine poisoning administers strychnine to food, beverages, or medication. When strychnine is administered orally, symptoms appear within fifteen to thirty minutes. The symptoms of acute strychnine poisoning include muscle stiffness and painful cramps. The face may exhibit a sardonic grin. The symptoms of strychnine poisoning can be confused with grand mal epileptic seizures or tetanus.

Strychnine can be detected in food, medications, urine, and autopsy organ specimens. It can be detected with ultraviolet (UV) spectrophotometry or gas chromatography (GC). The toxic level in blood is 21 mcg/ml; in urine, 9.1 mcg/ml (United 1997).

SULFURIC ACID

John George Haigh lived at the Onslow Court Hotel in London, England. By all appearances, he looked affluent, but he was deeply in debt; he had gambling debts and had not paid his hotel bill.

On the afternoon of February 18, 1949, Haigh was at his workshop with Olive Durand Deacon, an elderly resident of the Onslow. They had discussed a business matter four days earlier about manufacturing disposable stick-on fingernails. He told her he might be able to help her. As she looked at some material on a bench, Haigh aimed a .38 Enfield revolver at the back of her head and squeezed the trigger.

He immediately drove to the workplace of a contact he owed money, promised to pay back the loan, and, before too long, returned to the workshop. Haigh had made certain he had an alibi.

He removed Deacon's Persian lamb coat, rings, necklace, watch, earrings, and, from her handbag, anything he believed would be of value to him. Then he stuffed her body into a forty-gallon steel oil drum treated to withstand the corrosive effects of acid.

After he took off his clothes and put on rubber clothes, including a rubber apron and a gas mask, he pumped sulfuric acid into the oil drum. Sulfuric acid is a viscous oily liquid, which is highly corrosive and dissolves most metals. When sulfuric acid is exposed to living tissue, it removes water from cells, killing them. Sulfuric acid, however, does not dissolve body fat quickly.

Deacon's body disintegrated slowly and sank beneath the pink-colored bubbling liquid.

At 18:30, Haigh left to have a snack, which he paid for with money he took from Deacon's handbag. After returning to the workshop, he completed his work, placed a lid on the drum, and left, taking with him the Persian lamb coat and jewelry. He went to the George Hotel and had dinner.

Haigh had used acid in the past when he committed murder. In 1944, he killed an old acquaintance, William Donald McSwann, dissolved the body in acid, and then poured what was left of the body down the drain in an apartment. Haigh, who had conned William's parents into believing William was alive but in hiding to avoid military service, enticed them to his apartment, where he shot them, then used acid to dispose of their bodies. Haigh successfully posed as their son and inherited their estate.

In 1947, he murdered at his workshop a Dr. and Mrs. Henderson and used acid to dispose of their bodies. Haigh sold their assets.

When a woman who was a close friend of Deacon expressed concern about Deacon's disappearance, Haigh, at his own request, drove the woman to the Chelsea Police Station. Haigh and Deacon's friend spoke to a female detective, Sergeant Lambourne. Something about Haigh bothered Lambourne. Lambourne spoke to the manager of the Onslow, who told her Haigh recently paid his long-standing hotel bill. She also checked to see if Haigh had a criminal record.

Detective Inspectors Shelley Symes and Albert Webb questioned Haigh about Deacon's disappearance. His workshop was searched. Haigh had hid his gun and incriminating papers in a box in the trunk of his car, but after the search he moved them to the back of his workshop. Detective Sergeant Pat Heslin returned to the workshop, where he found the box and a receipt for a Persian lamb coat, which had been cleaned. Pathologist Keith Simpson found at the crime scene human gallstones, small bones, an acrylic denture, and part of a plastic handbag.

Haigh was arrested at the Onslow Court Hotel on February 28 and after extensive questioning admitted killing Olive Durand Deacon. Hoping he would be declared insane and not receive the death penalty, Haigh claimed he cut the necks of his victims and drank their blood.

His trial began on July 18 and ended on the following day. There were thirty-three witnesses for the prosecution, one for the defense. The court was not convinced Haigh was insane. The jury deliberated for seventeen minutes before it reached a decision. Haigh was found guilty and appealed unsuccessfully. He was executed at the age of forty on August 10, 1949 (Gale 1996; Van 1995; Waddell 1993).

TEC-9

The Tec-9, manufactured by Intratec U.S.A. of Miami, Florida, is a handgun with a thirty-six-round magazine. Silencers and barrel extensions can be added to models that have threaded barrels. This weapon can be easily concealed under a coat, and its finish resists fingerprints.

Students Eric Harris, eighteen, and Dylan Klebold, seventeen, used a Tec-DC9 handgun and three other weapons during a shooting rampage at Columbine High School in Littleton, Colorado, on April 20, 1999. These shooters killed twelve students and a teacher. Harris and Klebold wounded twenty-three others, then fatally shot themselves in the school library (Angell 1999; Church 1989; "United States" 1996).

UZI

Major Uziel Gal designed the Uzi, a 9-mm submachine gun. It can be fired as either a fully automatic or a semiautomatic weapon. The rate of fire of this 8.2-pound gun is 550 to 600 rounds per minute, using a ten-shot or twenty-five-shot magazine.

The Uzi, manufactured by Israel Military Industries, is imported into the United States by Action Arms of Philadelphia, Pennsylvania. The U.S. Secret Service uses a compact version of this gun. In 1986, 41,482 Uzi 9-mm guns were manufactured; in 1997, 67,844. In 1986, 24,781 Uzi 9-mm guns were exported; in 1997, 20,857.

In Los Angeles, California, on August 10, 1999, Buford O. Furrow, Jr., thirty-seven, a white supremacist, armed with an Uzi semiautomatic and a Glock 9-mm handgun, opened fire at a Jewish community center. Furrow wounded three children, a teenager, and one adult. He later shot and killed a postal worker. In 2001, Furrow received two life sentences plus an additional 110 years in prison without possibility of parole ("America's" 1999; Angell 1999; Buford 2001; Church 1989; Moyer 1983).

WOOD CHIPPER

Pan-Am flight attendant Helle Crafts, thirty-nine, left Kennedy Airport in New York with friends, who dropped her off at her home in Newtown, Connecticut, at approximately 19:00 on November 18, 1986.

Six weeks earlier, on October 7, Dianne Andersen, Helle's divorce lawyer, received a report from private investigator Keith Mayo. His report confirmed that Helle's husband, Eastern Airlines pilot Richard Crafts, forty-nine, was having an extramarital affair. Helle decided to have Richard served with a divorce writ on November 14, when their children would be away. Dianne became concerned about Helle when Helle had not contacted her by Thanksgiving. Helle had told Dianne that if anything happened to her, it would not be as the result of an accident. After unsuccessfully attempting to get in touch with Helle, Dianne called Keith.

When Helle's friends phoned her at home, Richard told them Helle had left on short notice for Denmark because her mother was seriously ill. However, Helle's friends and Keith were suspicious and did not believe Richard. They knew about Helle and Richard's marital problems. Keith had surveillance photographs of Richard and Nancy Dodd, a woman from New Jersey with whom Richard was having an affair.

Richard had worked for the CIA's (Central Intelligence Agency) Air America in Asia, but quit in 1966. He carried a gun and kept numerous weapons in the basement of his and Helle's home. Richard was also a volunteer police officer.

On November 17, Richard had paid cash for a 183-pound freezer and transported it in his Toyota pickup to his home. Credit card receipts examined by police confirmed that on the same day Helle disappeared, November 18, Richard rented a Brush Bandit 100 wood chipper from Darien Rentals. This wood chipper, weighing 4,220 pounds and operating at 1,200 rpm, had two twelve-inch blades and a wheel that was two inches thick and weighed 900 pounds. The hopper could accommodate objects up to one foot in width. The objects placed in the hopper and in contact with the wheel would be cut into chip-size pieces.

A newspaper article published on December 17 described Helle as a missing person. On December 26, police with a search warrant entered the Crafts home at 5 Newfield Lane in Newtown. In the bedroom, Sue Lausten, a friend of Helle's, helped police recreate the bedroom to make it appear the way it was when Helle lived in the house.

Dr. Henry Lee, chief of the Meriden forensic laboratory, combined tolidine, ethanol, glacial acidic acid, and distilled water to produce orthotolidine solution, which is used as a presumptive test for blood. Lee placed the solution on spots he found with a magnifying glass on the mattress. The spots turned a bright blue color, indicating the spots were probably blood. Lee believed the droplets on the mattress landed with medium velocity and that, if Helle was murdered in the room at the time the blood struck the mattress, she was not lying down. She was possibly standing near the bed. The materials covering the mattress, including the sheets, were pulled back because the blood fell directly on the mattress. Unwashed washcloths and newly laundered towels in the bathroom both tested positive for blood.

Joseph Hine, a roads department driver who was clearing snow from River Road after midnight on November 18, saw a wood chipper. He also saw the wood chipper at 05:30 near Silver Bridge and noticed small piles of wood chips in a number of locations along River Road.

Investigators sorted through leaves and wood chips near the river. Anything that was not a leaf or wood chip was set aside. Different objects were placed into separate bottles. Hairs were recovered from wood chips and compared with hairs from a hairbrush Helle had at home. A human tooth was found, compared with Helle's dental chart, and identified as being her tooth. The tip of a fingernail was also found.

Divers near the Silver Bridge found a chainsaw, which they sent to Leers Laboratory. Analysis revealed tiny fragments of bleached and dyed human hairs belonging to Helle. Blue-green fibers from Helle's nightclothes, and flesh and blood, were also present in the chain saw. The blood type was the same as Helle's blood type. Although the chainsaw's serial number was eroded, it was chemically restored in the lab. The number "E5921616" was traced to a dealership. The purchaser was Richard Crafts.

Richard Crafts was arrested for murder on January 13, 1987. His first trial in 1988 ended in a mistrial. During his second trial, he was found guilty of first-degree murder and sentenced on January 8, 1990, to fifty years in prison.

When Richard murdered Helle and disposed of her body, he had walked up behind her in the bedroom and struck her twice with a blunt object, possibly a flashlight. Then he wrapped her body in a sheet. Being careful not to wake up the children, he carried the body out of the house, leaving through the back door. The freezer in the Toyota pickup was already plugged in and switched on. He placed the body into the freezer and returned to the house to clean up the bedroom. When the body was frozen, he drove to a wooded area, dismembered the body with a chainsaw, and packaged the body parts in dark plastic bags. At the Silver Bridge, he placed the bags into the wood chipper. Virtually all the body "chips" ended up in the river, except for debris deposited in several locations along River Road. At some point, he threw the chainsaw into the river.

Only six ounces of Helle's remains were ever recovered ("Bodies" 2000; Borman 2000; Herzog 1990).

Ritualistic Homicide: Posed Victim.

Photo By R.A. Jago

Domestic Homicide: Blood Splatter and Defense Wounds.

Robbery Homicide: Blunt Object Trauma.

The Body Is Evidence.   Photo By R.A. Jago

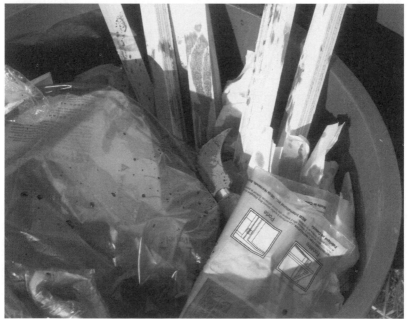

Discarded Weapon in Trashcan.   Photo By R.A. Jago

Robbery Homicide: Single-Entry Head Wound (Small Caliber).

Photo By R.A. Jago

Robbery Homicide: Powder Burns.　　　　　　　　　　　*Photo By R.A. Jago*

Norinco M-93 .22 Caliber and Walther P.P. .32 ACP.　　　*Photo By R.A. Jago*

Israel Military Industries UZI Model B 9 mm.   *Photo By R.A. Jago*

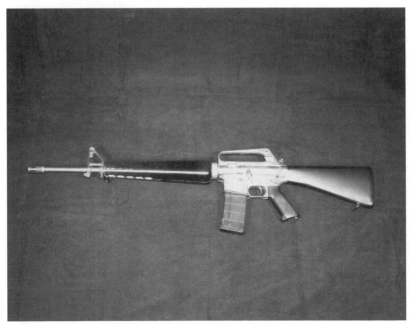

Colt AR-15 SP-1 .223 Caliber.   *Photo By R.A. Jago*

Bullet Holes in Windshield (.22 Caliber).   *Photo By R.A. Jago*

Vehicle Interior: Trajectory Angle (.22 Caliber).   *Photo By R.A. Jago*

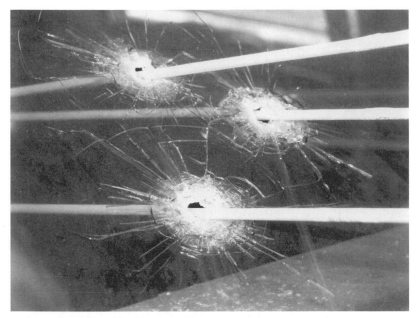

Bullet Holes in Windshield (.22 Caliber).   *Photo By R.A. Jago*

Multiple Shooting.   *Photo By R.A. Jago*

Photo By R.A. Jago

Suspicious Vehicle Abandoned in a Remote Location.

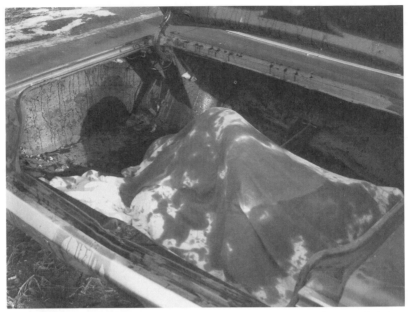

Underworld Homicide: "Trunk Music."　　　　　　　　*Photo By R.A. Jago*

Underworld Homicide: Blood Evidence.　　　　　　　　*Photo By R.A. Jago*

Photo By R.A. Jago

Victim Removed, Trunk to Be Processed for Evidence.

Random Homicide: Evidence Markers.   *Photo By R.A. Jago*

A Bloody Knife.   *Photo By R.A. Jago*

A Bloody Hatchet Found Near the Victim.   *Photo By R.A. Jago*

A Bloody Rag in the Underbrush.   *Photo By R.A. Jago*

A Shoe Print in Loose Soil.   Photo By R.A. Jago

A Tire Impression in Loose Soil.   Photo By R.A. Jago

11

Integrity of Evidence

Crime scene investigators wear special clothing and take special precautions in collecting, handling, and storing evidence. Often evidence collected from the crime scene is removed and stored in a secure location away from the crime scene pending assessment and analysis. The movement of evidence from the crime scene through to the display of evidence in the courtroom must be carefully documented. This is known as the chain of evidence. A broken chain results in inadmissible evidence. In this chapter, we examine nine tools used by crime scene investigators to maintain the integrity of crime scene evidence.

BUNNY SUITS

Some police departments require forensic personnel, such as photographers and fingerprint experts, to wear latex surgical gloves and "bunny suits" at a homicide crime scene. Bunny suits are disposable white-hooded coveralls. The gloves and suits help prevent forensic staff from inadvertently contaminating the crime scene with anything that could be misconstrued as genuine trace evidence. A hair, button, or thread from one of these individuals could contaminate the scene.

If investigators do not wear bunny suits, investigators should at least wear latex gloves and identical shoes that have a unique mark on the heel and sole. An X could be the unique mark. This will help the crime scene photographer distinguish between investigator and suspect shoe prints.

Edmond Locard, the French criminologist, is associated with the premise that every person who commits a crime leaves something at the crime scene and takes something away. This is the underlying reason for the use of the gloves and bunny suits (Barrett 1994; Douglas 1992).

CANVASS THE NEIGHBORHOOD

A canvass, an attempt by police to obtain information of interest to them regarding a specific matter, can be conducted in several ways. Knocking on doors and talking to the person who answers is one way. Asking questions at a roadblock is another way. Interviewing persons in the street or at a mall are other ways.

The main reason detectives do a canvass is to locate potential witnesses or anyone else who may know something about a crime. These detectives should write down the name and address of each person they interview. Photo identification is preferable. Locations where no one is at home or where some individuals are temporarily absent should be recanvassed. There are times when multiple canvasses are necessary. Some people may not be willing to speak openly and honestly until a third or fourth visit by detectives.

It is preferable to conduct a canvass at a reasonable time. A middle-of-the-night canvass should, if possible, be avoided. Disturbing people who are sleeping, and who have to go to work in the morning, is likely to be counterproductive. It is also preferable that homicide detectives, not patrol officers, conduct a canvass. Homicide detectives are specialists and are more experienced in interview techniques than are patrol officers, who are generalists (Geberth 1996; Seedman and Hellman 1974; Simon 1991).

CHAIN OF EVIDENCE

The chain of evidence, also called the "chain of custody," is a record indicating the location of evidence from the time it is discovered, at the homicide crime scene, until it is presented in court. The record should include the name of each person who handled evidence. Record entries should be accurate and consistent, providing the correct sequence for evidence transferred from one person to another.

The month, day, time of day, and year, noted beside the name of each person who possessed evidence for a specific period, helps maintain the chain of custody.

The chain is broken if, at any time, there is a gap in the record. This is when neither a person nor place can be located that accounts for the gap.

When there is a gap, a defense attorney can argue the evidence was not properly handled, was tampered with, and therefore should not be admitted in court. This argument, if accepted by the court, could completely undermine the prosecution's case against the defendant. An unbroken chain of evidence is essential to effective prosecution (O'Maley 1994; Philbin 1996).

CRIME SCENE CLEANUP

After a homicide or suicide victim is removed from a public area, such as a parking lot, firefighters or sanitation workers are the individuals who usually clean up the area after the police and the medical examiner have left. However, when a homicide or suicide takes place in a private residence, the property owner, not the municipality, is responsible for the cleanup. The cleanup is an extremely painful task for the family of the deceased, especially when the death occurs in a private residence. In addition to the emotional trauma family members experience, they also risk contracting AIDS, hepatitis, or meningitis if they do the cleanup.

There are, coast-to-coast throughout the United States, companies that specialize in cleaning up a room or other area in which a homicide or suicide occurred. These companies, many of which are members of the American Bio-Recovery Association, are in numerous cities, including Los Angeles, California; Phoenix, Arizona; Baltimore, Maryland; and New York, New York (Willing 1999).

CRIME SCENE INVESTIGATION, REPORTING, AND RECONSTRUCTION (CSIRR)

Crime Scene Investigation, Reporting, and Reconstruction (CSIRR), developed by Graphic Data Systems of Englewood, Colorado, is a computer-based system used for recording information required for reconstructing 2-D or 3-D homicide and other crime scenes. Database and computer-aided design (CAD) are an integral part of this system in which digital files replace paper documents.

Investigators can use this software to record and reconstruct evidence. More than 500 CSIRR symbols are used to construct crime scene drawings. A built-in calendar and chronological capability enable the user to organize the names of case investigators and witnesses, and information such as the names of places regarding an investigation. Digital photographs and audio and video images are searchable, as is information about suspects and victims ("Technology" 1996).

EVIDENCE PACKAGING

Evidence is packaged in a variety of ways. Handguns and rifles are placed in tie-down boxes, which prevent these weapons from shifting during transit. Shifting could cause the loss of fingerprints. Knife tubes, which are three inches by eighteen inches, are large enough for most knives. Only one end of a tube is open and there is a core of rigid foam inside, into which a person can secure the knife. Evidence strips and a biohazard label are affixed to the tube before it is transported. Syringe tubes are one inch by seven inches in size. These tubes, like knife tubes, are open only at one end, contain a core of rigid foam, and include evidence strips and a biohazard label. Barrier drug pouches, which vary in size from four inches by six inches to twelve inches by sixteen inches, are made of polyester. They can be sealed with an impulse heat-sealer to prevent narcotic gases from leaking; these sealers look somewhat like large staplers. Evidence cans, ranging in size from 0.5 ounces to four ounces, can be used for transporting small items such as shell casings. Evidence jars have white lids for convenient marking; these jars are as small as two ounces and as large as sixteen ounces. Glassine envelopes, which are two inches by three-and-a-half inches, are used for trace evidence. Evidence slide boxes, similar to matchboxes, are used for small items ("Evidence" 2001).

MOBILE EVIDENCE DRYING STATION (MEDS)

The Mobile Evidence Drying Station (MEDS) looks like a garment rack on wheels. The MEDS, however, is used for an extremely important forensic purpose: to preserve the chain of evidence. The MEDS is lightweight and mobile, and is equipped with locking wheels, and a locking mechanism for evidence security. It provides a secure and protected drying area for temporarily storing bloodstained evidence associated with homicide or sexual assault cases. Victim and suspect clothing can be protected from cross-contamination and tampering while waiting to be packaged for submission to a laboratory. The MEDS can accommodate large items such as bedspreads and comforters. No assembly is required, and it is less expensive than a drying room. The MEDS includes accessory bags for jewelry, money, and other small items that are to be entered into evidence ("Mobile" 2001).

REMOVING THE BODY

After detectives, forensic experts, and the medical examiner or representative complete their investigation at the crime scene, the victim is placed onto a clean white sheet or plastic body wrap. The sheet or body wrap is wrapped around the victim to prevent anything on the body, which might later be of value in the investigation, from being lost as the body is moved. After the wrapped body is placed into a body bag, also known as a disaster bag, it is placed onto a mortuary cot and then wheeled to a medical examiner's van, referred to in street language as the "meat wagon," for transport to the morgue. If the decedent is not placed in a clean body bag, trace evidence, possibly from the body previously transported in the medical examiner's van, could be mistaken as being from the present victim. This could contribute to a flawed investigation (B and B's 1999; DiMaio 1984; Lange, Vannatter, and Moldea 1997; Randall 1997).

ROLL HIM/ROLL HER

No one at a homicide crime scene should move or "roll" a body from its back onto its stomach, or vice versa, until the medical examiner (ME) has officially pronounced the victim dead and has completed a preliminary examination at the crime scene.

The ME cannot always arrive quickly because of other commitments or because of heavy traffic. This can make investigators impatient because they are eager to proceed with the investigation and there may be important evidence under the body.

Detectives can work on other aspects of the investigation until the medical examiner arrives. They can question witnesses or canvass the neighborhood. One of the duties of detectives is to remove and examine the victim's personal effects. Wallets, rings, necklaces, watches, and eyeglasses are among the items set aside and kept separate from the body (Simon 1991).

12

Forensic Investigation

Forensics is a method of evaluation used by investigators, wherein an item is subjected to intense scrutiny and evaluation such that the item can be introduced into court as evidence. The evaluation may include aspects of law, medicine, physics, chemistry, anthropology, and psychiatry. In this chapter, there are twelve topics that help explain forensic investigation.

ADIPOCERE

Adipocere is a waxy substance that originates in the fatty tissues of a human corpse. Subcutaneous fat, fat under the skin, is the fat most likely to become adipocere. Sometimes water in tissues and fermentation produced by bacteria is sufficient to produce adipocere, which results when fluid body fats solidify and stiffen. Usually, however, adipocere occurs more readily in bodies immersed in water or buried in moist soil. Adipocere remains affixed to bone even after skin rots and drops off. For this reason, adipocere enables a body to retain its original shape.

Adipocere is usually grayish-white in color. However, a body can take on, through absorption, the color of its clothes or the color of the soils the body is located in if the clothes or soils are moist. Adipocere floats on water, is soluble in fat solvents, and fluoresces under ultraviolet light.

The cooler the environment, the longer it takes for adipocere to form, ranging from four to six months in a cool environment to less than a month in a hot climate.

On June 8, 1913, two farm workers were walking by the Hopetoun Quarry near Edinburgh, Scotland. They noticed something bulky in the water. A closer look revealed two small bodies tied together. Professor Harvey Littlejohn, head of forensic medicine at Edinburgh University and Sydney Smith, his assistant, examined the bodies at a mortuary. Virtually all body fat had become adipocere. Smith believed the remains had been in the water from eighteen months to two years. The autopsy revealed the remains were two young boys. One appeared to be between six and seven years old, the other between three and four. Stomach contents indicated that Scotch broth, a thick soup made from beef or mutton with vegetables and pearl barley, had been their last meal. Considering how long the victims had been in the water, and the likelihood that they would have had the broth when the vegetables were fresh, the victims most likely had died in the latter half of 1911. A stamp on a shirt indicated the shirt had belonged to a poorhouse. Patrick Higgins, their alcoholic father, had admitted William and John to the poorhouse after their mother died. He then removed them and left them with a woman, Elizabeth Hynes, after he stopped supporting them financially. Later, he removed them from the care of Hynes. The boys disappeared in November 1911. Higgins contradicted himself when he tried to explain the disappearance to friends. He was tried in Edinburgh in September 1913. A plea of temporary insanity, due to epilepsy, did not prevent him from a death sentence. Patrick Higgins was hanged on October 2, 1913.

Dealing with adipocere can be very unpleasant. When forensic anthropologist Douglas Owsley was a graduate student, he had to work on the corpse of an obese woman. The corpse was in an advanced stage of decomposition and was foaming with adipocere. The odor was intense. Owsley vomited twice, then never again vomited. Perhaps no other odor could be as sickening to him as the odor of adipocere (Evans 1996; Jaffe 1991; Mason 1983; Royte 1996; Simpson and Knight 1985).

AUTOPSY

The homicide detective's job is to find out who killed the victim and why; the forensic pathologist's job is to find out what killed the victim and how.

A vehicle, usually a van, transporting a homicide victim arrives at the morgue, which is often in the basement or one of the subbasements of a building complex. The driver and other employee of the medical examiner's office get out of the van, open its rear doors, and remove the metal stretcher on which the victim lies in a zippered body bag. They maneuver the wheeled stretcher onto a scale built into the floor of the morgue. This scale takes into account the weight of the victim and of the stretcher. If a body is not weighed when it arrives at the morgue, the body is weighed and measured after it is removed from its refrigeration unit.

The morgue, even when it is not in a hospital, smells like one. There is everywhere the strong smell of chemicals, including formaldehyde.

Stainless steel refrigeration units for temporarily housing the dead are set into the walls. The dead, in addition to homicide victims, also include suicide victims and other individuals who appear to have died under suspicious circumstances. The door to each unit is approximately two feet by two feet. To prevent bodies from decomposing, the temperature in the units is around 40 degrees Fahrenheit.

The attendants place the body into an empty refrigeration unit. When it is time for the autopsy, the victim is wheeled on a stretcher to an overhead camera. Photographs are taken and the body is moved to a stainless steel autopsy table. There are pipes along both sides of the table, from which water flows to the drainage end of the table, carrying blood and body materials the pathologist does not need to keep. A nearby X-ray is used to determine if there are bullets or bullet fragments in the body.

At the drainage end of the table, there is a stand that contains a scale for weighing body organs, a board for cutting these organs, and jars for storing organ specimens. If there is no microphone suspended from the ceiling and used to record the pathologist's remarks as the autopsy is performed, the pathologist wears a portable microphone for this purpose.

After a clothed homicide victim is placed on the autopsy table in the autopsy suite, the pathologist carefully examines the victim's clothes. This is done because most homicide victims are shot or stabbed to death and there are holes or tears in the clothes of most of these victims, unless the victim was shot only in the head.

The pathologist examines the clothes to match holes and tears with wounds. The pathologist knows the victim died as the homicide detectives and the pathologist thought when the locations of holes and tears match up with the locations of wounds. There are cases where a perpetrator or perpetrators dressed a victim or changed the victim's clothes. A pathologist keeps this in mind during an autopsy. Clothes are also examined to determine if they should be tested for gunpowder residue. The pathologist carefully removes the clothes, one by one, keeping in mind trace evidence. Bullets and bullet fragments can sometimes be found in the victim's clothes whether or not the victim is X-rayed.

When sexual activity is suspected, vaginal swabs, oral swabs, and anal swabs are taken to determine if ejaculate is present. It may be possible later to link semen to a particular suspect. Chemical tests can determine if a homicide victim fired a gun, even if investigators do not find a gun at the crime scene.

After removing the clothes, the pathologist examines the nude body, noting the color of the hair and eyes, and noting any birthmarks, tattoos, scars, bruises, contusions, lacerations, or scratches. An autopsy assistant is present to indicate, on a rough paper sketch of a body, any trauma the pathologist finds.

The pathologist uses a scalpel to make an incision extending from the top of one shoulder to the end of the breastbone—the sternum. The same type of incision is made from the top of the other shoulder to the sternum. The next step is to make an incision down the middle of the abdomen to the pubis, an area of bone in the pelvis. The pathologist then peels back the skin and uses an electric saw to cut through the ribs in order to remove the breastplate.

When there are bullet or knife wounds, the pathologist follows wound tracks. The trajectories of bullets and directions of knife blades are of interest. Entrance and exit wounds are matched. Bullets and bullet fragments are removed. This is done either by hand or by using one or more instruments that cannot damage the bullets or bullet fragments and render useless any ballistic test results. The pathologist can distinguish fatal from nonfatal wounds and knows if death was relatively instantaneous or took longer.

The removal of the breastplate provides the opportunity to examine internal organs. The organ tree is lifted as a single entity out of the body's central cavity and set aside. This procedure, called a "modified Rokitansky," has its origins in the Europe of the late 1800s and the work of two pathologists, Carl von Rokitansky and Rudolf Virchow.

The heart, liver, pancreas, spleen, and other organs are weighed, examined, and dissected. If the person undergoing an autopsy is a woman, her uterus is examined. If she is pregnant, the pathologist and homicide detectives know pregnancy can be a motive for homicide or suicide.

An electric saw is used to cut the top of the skull. This procedure is somewhat like cutting one end of a cantaloupe to expose the inside. The skin of the scalp is pulled forward over the face. This allows any head wounds to be tracked. The brain, pinkish-gray in color, is removed, weighed, and examined.

Samples of blood, bile, and urine are collected for testing for poisons, alcohol, and street drugs such as cocaine and heroin. A stainless steel ladle is used for scooping up blood, a syringe for retrieving a sample of urine from the bladder.

Internal parts of the body not required for further examination are placed in a plastic bag and tied. The bag is placed into the chest cavity after the autopsy is completed. The pathologist or an assistant sews up the body and replaces the brain and cut-off part of the skull. Then the body is wheeled to its refrigeration unit to await release to a funeral home.

Like clothing, other evidence, ranging from bullets to fingernail clippings, is placed in various evidence containers and given to detectives to transport to the evidence control unit (Corwin 1997; Cuomo 1995; Gibson 1998; Henderson 1998; Poss and Schlesinger 1994; Sasser 1990; Seligmann et al. 1995; Simon 1991).

CADAVER DOGS

Cadaver dogs, also called "sniffing dogs," detect human remains and can distinguish between the scent of decaying human tissues and decaying animal tissues. These dogs focus on the scent that emanates from a decomposing human body. They detect this scent regardless of the stage of a body's decomposition. The presence of hundreds of individuals in a search area does not impede the efforts of cadaver dogs. Searchers use steel prodding poles to make holes in the earth. This allows the aroma of bacteria to rise to the surface. It is then easier for the dog to detect the scent.

A body under water also decomposes, and the scent of decomposition surfaces. The scent is present as a thin film on the surface of the water. The dog indicates to its handler where the highest concentration of scent is located. A cadaver dog in a boat detects this scent. A search on water is more difficult than a ground search because currents and wind have to be considered. Nevertheless, a cadaver dog on a boat narrows down a search area for divers.

Buried human tissues, covered with traces of dried blood and soil from underneath buried homicide victims, are used to train cadaver dogs. Their powerful sense of smell completely overshadows that of human beings.

The Sigma Chemical Company in St. Louis, Missouri, manufactures pseudo scent used in training cadaver dogs. Pseudo Corpse mimics the scent of a dead body less than thirty days old. Pseudo Corpse II mimics the dry rot scent of a cadaver older than thirty days. The Federal Bureau of Investigation (FBI) uses German Shepherds and other dogs as cadaver dogs.

In 1992, Detective Mark Green and other police officers had information supplied by several individuals regarding the 1984 murders of children near Phoenix, Arizona. The remains of the children were purportedly buried in a plateau southwest of Phoenix.

Detective Green broke open an ampoule of a scent that mimicked the smell of a human corpse and gave a whiff to Judge, a Labrador retriever. Thirty minutes later, at the plateau, Judge began digging furiously and found old diapers and shreds of rotted clothing.

Glen Turpin, a member of the Durham Regional Police Service in Ontario, Canada, and his cadaver dog Jesse, a Belgian Malinois, found a buried murder victim in February 1998. The victim, thirty-six, had disappeared two years earlier and was found buried approximately six feet underground. A twenty-five-year-old Brampton, Ontario, man was subsequently arrested and charged with first-degree murder.

Cadaver dogs are not always successful in their search for human remains. This was the case in July 1998 when Irene Silverman, a New York millionaire, disappeared. The elderly former ballerina lived in her townhouse at 20 East 65th Street in Manhattan before her disappearance. Cadaver dogs took part in an extensive police search for Irene, but she was not found. However, investigators linked her disappearance to Sante Kimes and her son Kenneth. The couple had a long history of criminal activity and faced an eighty-four-count indictment in New York. Both received long prison terms (McQuillan, A. 2000; McQuillan, B. 1998; Muha 1998; Sachs 1996).

CADAVERIC SPASM

Sometimes at the moment of death, a dying person's muscles experience a violent spasm known as a cadaveric spasm. This occurs most frequently in a person's hand grasp. A perpetrator shot by police may grip a gun, knife, or other weapon so tightly that the weapon has to be pried from the perpetrator's hand. A dying individual experiencing this may also tightly grasp other things such as an item of clothing. There are also times when the entire body, at the moment of death, will become rigid.

Among the Los Angeles Police Department (LAPD) photographs of Nicole Brown Simpson is a close-up photograph of her left hand clearly showing cadaveric spasm (DeSola, 1988; Lange, Vannatter, and Moldea 1997; Nice 1965; Simpson and Knight 1985).

CANOE MAKER

Police jargon for the medical examiner is "canoe maker." This is because during an autopsy, the medical examiner (ME) removes internal organs from the cadaver in order to examine and weigh them. To open the rib cage, the ME commonly uses large pruning shears. After the ME has removed the organs, the cadaver resembles an empty shell or canoe (Henderson 1998; *Police* 2000).

CORONER AND MEDICAL EXAMINER

A coroner is a public official, usually elected and still part of the medico-legal system in certain areas of the United States, who investigates suspicious or unnatural deaths. A coroner may not have medical or legal training; in many rural jurisdictions, the sheriff acts as the coroner. The coroner conducts an inquest, an inquiry during which a jury hears evidence and decides if a death resulted from a crime. The jury's verdict is not conclusive, but it may form the basis of a murder indictment.

Since the 1960s, medical examiners have been replacing coroners because most coroners are not as professionally qualified as medical examiners. A medical examiner is a public official, appointed by a state or local government and trained as a physician, who investigates suspicious or unnatural deaths, determining the cause of death and whether or not the death was the result of a crime (*Encyclopedia* 1997; *World* 1997).

DECOMPOSING BODIES INDOORS

One of the most disturbing things about being a homicide detective is being near a "stink stiff," a decomposing body, at an indoor crime scene. The smell of a corpse that has been decomposing in a hot environment for a week is especially overwhelming. The overpowering odor of decaying flesh, combined with the sour-sweet, iron-like smell of blood, saturates everything. Maggots and flies have colonized the body.

Often the deceased is in an apartment or house for several days before someone finds the body. A pet dog or cat that has not eaten for several days may also be present. When this is the situation, the unfed pet eats the decedent's flesh and feces.

A stink stiff on a bed or sofa liquefies, especially in a room in which all the doors and windows are closed and the temperature is high. The body fluids seep into the mattress or sofa. A severely bloated corpse, if not handled very carefully, will explode, splattering everything and everyone around it. This compounds the mess if the victim was shot in the head with a large-caliber gun, and brain matter is already all over the floor, walls, and ceiling. Brain matter and other parts of the body may cover trace evidence. Investigators must be especially cautious as they move throughout the room, taking care not to destroy evidence by stepping on it or by inadvertently leaning against it.

The smell of death clings to clothes, which have to be dry-cleaned. The smell clings to skin. Detectives shower after they leave the death scene. Some detectives have aftershave lotion in their cars, pour it on the sleeves of their shirts, and inhale, temporarily blocking out the nauseating odor of death. Investigators have used different methods over the years to prevent vomiting at homicide crime scenes: lighted cigars, burning coffee grounds, buckets containing ammonia-soaked rags, spraying the surroundings with disinfectants, dabs of Vicks VapoRub or similar ointment under each nostril, and putrefaction masks, face masks for filtering organic vapors coming from a decaying body.

There are surprises at the scene of homicides. Tulsa, Oklahoma, homicide detective Charles W. Sasser was examining a corpse whose mouth was open. Suddenly, a mouse scurried out of the mouth (Buchanan 1987; Dillmann 1989; Gates and Shah 1992; Hirschfeld 1982; Lawrence et al. 1989; McKenna and Harrington 1996; Rachlin 1991; Sasser 1990).

DIATOMS

Diatoms are one-celled plants found in saltwater, in freshwater, and on moist soil. They are golden or golden-brown algae either circular or oblong in shape and have a glasslike appearance because of their silica content. In oceans, diatoms are a part of plankton, a mass of drifting organisms. Diatoms can help investigators determine the cause of death of a person found in a river, lake, or ocean. Diatoms, which vary from two to five microns in size, may penetrate the deepest body organs of a person who drowns. Drowning is likely the cause of death when a person has diatoms in his or her lungs and there are no indications of postmortem wounds caused by boats, propellers, rocks, or fish. Diatoms are not found in a dead person's tissues when they are not present in the water from which a dead person is recovered. After an autopsy is performed, samples of the lungs, brain, kidneys, liver, and bones can be soaked in strong acid to dissolve soft tissues and diatom skeletons. The diatoms can then be identified under a microscope. Diatom counts expressed per 100 g of human tissue may suggest a decedent drowned. Twenty diatoms per 100 microliters of pellet from a 10-g lung sample indicate that a person drowned. Diatoms in the liver are also highly indicative that drowning was the cause of death. Sometimes, however, up to 10 diatoms per 100 g of human tissue are present in a normal liver of a deceased person whose cause of death was not drowning. There would be small amounts of plankton in a person's tissue after rapid drowning or drowning in freezing water. When a dead person is placed in water, or a person dies in water but drowning is not the cause of death, this person may have diatoms in his or her lungs. Diatoms will not likely be found in other organs because the absence of a heartbeat prevented the diatoms from circulating past the lungs.

Specific crime scene factors may provide additional evidence in establishing the cause of death. Neatly folded clothes and a suicide note, both left near water in which an apparent drowning victim is found, indicate a probable suicide. A high blood alcohol level, determined at the autopsy of a person recovered from water, indicates a probable accident. Gunshot, knife, or other wounds on a body discovered in water may be the cause of death, when there is no indication at autopsy of diatoms having penetrated further than the lungs (*Academic* 1998; Ludes 1996; McLay 1990; Miller 1998; Perper and Wecht 1980; *World* 1996).

FLOATERS

A clothed corpse dumped into a lake may float for a short time, if the air in the clothes produces sufficient buoyancy. After the body sinks, gas from decomposition enables what remains of the body, the "floater," to resurface. As the flesh decomposes and gas escapes, the corpse will again sink.

Cold water slows down putrefaction and months may pass before a corpse resurfaces as a floater. Warm water speeds up putrefaction; in such conditions, a few days may pass before a dead body resurfaces. A corpse trapped in plants or in a submerged vehicle may never come to the surface.

Normally, a body that resurfaces is in a facedown position. The back will become adipocere, also known as "grave wax"; the opposite side will become a skeleton.

Jim Blundell, Bob Hoffman, and Ken Walls, three fishermen in their twenties, were fishing on the shore of Dumfoundling Bay in Miami, Florida, on the morning of August 7, 1976. Blundell paused to gaze about and noticed a fifty-five-gallon steel drum in a canal leading to the Intracoastal Waterway. The drum was wrapped with heavy chains. He left his fishing partners to investigate. As soon as Blundell peered into one of the holes in the drum, he smelled, then saw, the remains of a corpse.

It was determined at the Dade County Medical Examiner's offices that the corpse was that of a man. The victim had been gagged with a washcloth kept in place with adhesive tape wrapped around the head. There was a rope knotted around the neck. Asphyxiation was the cause of death. The coroner speculated the killer or killers had also shot the victim in the stomach, then a knife had been used to remove the bullet. A slit in the torso extended from chest to navel, and the legs had been cut off at the thighs, then the legs and body had been stuffed into the drum.

The drum would have remained submerged in nearly thirty feet of water if gases had not formed in the body, due to decomposition, and caused the drum to surface. If Blundell had not seen and examined the drum, it would have sunk in the near future because the body gases would have dissipated, leaving the drum without any buoyancy. The body may never have been found.

A fingerprint on file at the FBI indicated the body was that of Johnny Roselli, seventy-one, a gangster residing with his sister, Edith Daigle, in Plantation, Florida. Roselli, a former gunman for Al Capone in Chicago, Illinois, during Prohibition, had been involved in an alleged CIA–Mafia conspiracy to assassinate Fidel Castro during the early 1960s. Roselli was concerned he might go to prison or be deported if he did not cooperate with government investigations. He had already testified in Washington, D.C., before the intelligence committee chaired by Senator Frank Church. Certain people did not approve of Roselli's behavior. This disapproval was enough to have him killed. His killers were never found.

The U.S. Coast Guard and St. Petersburg Police in Florida were contacted on June 1, 1989, by a fisherman after he saw from his boat three bodies floating in Tampa Bay. The bodies, badly decomposed, were those of three females who had been hog-tied with rope. There was a cinder block tied around the neck and duct tape over the mouth of each body. Each victim was wearing a T-shirt and bathing suit top. The suit bottom of each female was missing.

Examination of a car near the shore indicated the three dead females were vacationers from Ohio. Joan Rogers, thirty-eight, was the oldest victim. The two younger victims were her daughters, Michelle, seventeen, and Christie, fifteen. They were staying at the Days Inn in St. Petersburg. Husband and father Hal Rogers had remained in Ohio to work on their farm.

Stomach contents of the victims and information provided to investigators by Days Inn staff indicated the mother and daughters had died approximately forty-eight hours before their bodies were discovered. A note in the car stated how to get from the Days Inn to where the car was located.

Jana Monroe, an FBI profiler, appeared on the television program *Unsolved Mysteries* to discuss the case, but none of the thousands of leads generated by the program produced any results. She then had the handwriting from the note placed on billboards in the Tampa–St. Petersburg area. It was only a couple of days before three individuals separately contacted police and stated the handwriting was that of Oba Chandler. Each individual had sued Chandler because he had installed for them faulty aluminum siding. He had responded in his own handwriting to their charges.

Two other women, who had almost met the same fate as Joan Rogers and her daughters, said a man similar to Chandler wanted them to come on his boat. One woman went with the man; the other one refused to go. She had a strong hunch there was something wrong about going aboard. The woman who went with the man later reported he tried to rape her and threatened to drown her in Tampa Bay. Oba Chandler, a man in his mid-forties with a previous criminal record, was eventually sentenced to death for the Rogers murders. As of November 2002, the Florida Supreme Court had upheld Chandler's three convictions and death sentences.

Unlike the bodies of Johnny Roselli and the Rogers women, some floaters are bloated and discolored to the extent that they look only vaguely human. Fish eat the eyes. Hands, feet, or other body parts break away from the rest of the body when police divers or other rescuers are not careful in retrieving the bodies.

Separate polyethylene bags are used to bag body parts found separately, or bodies that fragment, when they are being recovered (Adcock 1984; Davis 1996; Douglas and Olshaker 1995; Iserson 1994; Kessler and Weston 1953; Rachlin 1991; Rappleye and Becker 1991; Williams, Jaffe, and Marro 1976).

OUTDOOR SEARCH METHODS

There are five different search methods police use to locate physical evidence outdoors. The strip method involves roping off an area into a rectangle, then searchers, at the same pace, walk along paths parallel to each other. The grid method search defines an area as a rectangle; searchers walk along parallel paths horizontally and vertically. In the spiral method, searchers follow each other along a path, the path spiraling in toward the center of the search area. The area to be searched, when using the zone method, is divided into four rectangles; these rectangles are divided into smaller quadrants, and a searcher searches each major subdivision.

The wheel method search entails viewing the search area as a circle divided into pie-shaped sections. Searchers start at the center then go outward along the radius. Searchers are frequently police academy recruits under the supervision of experienced police officers (O'Maley 1994).

STOMACH AND SMALL INTESTINE CONTENTS

The stomach and small intestine contents of a homicide victim can be studied at autopsy, and conclusions can be made from them regarding the victim's approximate time of death. Usually, the stomach empties its contents four to six hours after a person eats a meal, and the small intestines empty twelve hours after a meal. Therefore, a homicide victim whose stomach is full of food with evidence of little digestion died shortly after eating the meal. The victim whose stomach is empty died four to twelve hours after his or her last meal. The victim whose stomach and small intestines are both empty died twelve or more hours after the last meal. Stomach and intestine contents, as an indicator of approximate time of death, should be used cautiously because severe injury or emotional trauma can completely arrest the digestion process. This occurs when a person lapses into a coma due to a sudden head injury.

Detectives keep in mind the approximate time of death when they ask suspects to account for their whereabouts. A homicide detective at a crime scene who suspects murder by poison or suicide by the ingestion of drugs will request an examination of stomach and small intestine contents. Samples of food extracted from the stomach and small intestine of the victim should undergo toxicological analysis. Results of the analysis should be compared with drug-specific toxicological data (Borman 2000; Eckert 1997; Geberth 1996; O'Hara and O'Hara 1994).

TIME OF DEATH

Determining the time of death depends on the cause of death and how and where the body was left. There is no single, consistently accurate method for determining the time of death. The more specific the time of death, in the opinion of a medical examiner, the easier it is for an attorney, during cross-examination, to effectively dispute the time.

Normal body temperature is 98.6 degrees Fahrenheit, but in a dead person, this temperature drops approximately one and a half degrees Fahrenheit per hour. Cooling is slower in a person wearing heavy clothing, and an overweight person cools at a slower rate than a lean person does.

The preferred way to establish the time of death is to rely on the comments of one or more reliable witnesses. This method is relatively easy to use in a hospital or at the scene of a motor vehicle accident. The most reliable estimate is between the times when the decedent was last seen alive and the time the decedent's body was discovered.

The time of death can also be estimated by noting some of the changes a body undergoes after death. These changes, however, cannot indicate a specific time. After a death occurs, a body begins to cool and becomes more rigid (rigor mortis). This rigidity takes place anytime from fifteen minutes to fifteen hours after death.

The blood moves to those parts of the body nearest to the ground, the skin in those areas becoming a purplish color (livor mortis). This takes place approximately within two hours after death, blood tending to clot in the tissues after this time.

A person has probably been dead a few hours if this person's body is warm and limp, dead a few additional hours if it is cool and stiff, and dead a day or longer if it is cold and limp. These estimations, however, do not apply to decomposed or skeletonized bodies because these processes take much longer.

There are other things for investigators to consider, depending on the location of the dead person. How much mail is in the decedent's mailbox? What is the most recent date on newspapers at the decedent's address? Is the decedent dressed for work or for leisure activity? Does food on the table indicate breakfast, lunch, or dinner? Is there on the premises a calendar with recent notations? Also, family, neighbors, coworkers, friends, and others should be interviewed regarding the decedent's activities.

A core temperature can be taken by inserting a thermometer into the decedent's rectum, liver, or ear canal. If rectal temperature is to be taken, clothing should be carefully moved to one side or completely removed, not cut. Anal swabs should be taken before the thermometer is inserted. Otherwise, the thermometer could cause contamination and destroy evidence.

Checking the joints of the fingers and the larger joints determines the amount of rigor mortis. A high degree of rigor is present in the fingers when it is difficult for the medical examiner to easily flex the fingers. A leg, arm, or other body part in rigor mortis, which does not appear to be in a proper position relative to the rest of the body, may indicate that the body was moved.

After a person dies, the heart no longer pumps blood, and blood pools (settles) in the lowest parts of the person's body. Blood is "unfixed" immediately after death. This means that the blood moves when the body is moved. Blood becomes "fixed" and does not move after a few hours. If an investigator pushes his or her finger on an area where blood has settled and the area blanches (turns white) easily, the blood is unfixed. When a body is discovered on its back, but livor mortis is evident in the abdomen, the body was moved (Nickell and Fischer 1999; Randall 1997; Vanezis and Busuttil 1996).

13

Sketches, Photographs, and Videotaping

"Seeing Is Believing." It is a normal component of a homicide investigation to make three types of visual records of a crime scene: sketches, photographs, and videotapes. Each method has specific advantages and disadvantages, although together they often portray a scene from many perspectives. An experienced investigator creates accurate and specific representations of the crime scene for admission in court as evidence. In this chapter, we discuss sixteen methods of preparing and presenting visual evidence.

35 MM CAMERA

A 35 mm single-lens reflex (SLR) camera and certain accessory equipment are sufficient for taking basic crime scene photographs. The accessory equipment consists of a 50 mm lens for close-up photography, an electronic flash, a flash extension cord, close-up filters, a teleconverter, and a tripod. The 35 mm camera and accessory equipment are adequate for photographing blood splatter; invisible bloodstains, latent bite marks, and shoe print evidence.

A moderate wide-angle lens, used with a 35 mm camera, enables the photographer to adequately cover a ten-foot by twelve-foot room with four photographs, one taken from each corner of the room.

A macro lens is commonly used when photographing close-up physical evidence at indoor crime scenes. The camera with a macro lens is mounted on a tripod to reduce distortion. A photograph is taken with a measuring device. A second photograph is taken without the device. The measuring device and evidence to be photographed should be the same distance from the film plane. The item of evidence or the scale could otherwise be out of focus.

A Polaroid camera does not produce photographs of a quality required for professionally documenting a crime scene. Nevertheless, a Polaroid can be used to instantly obtain a photograph of a homicide victim. This photograph can be shown to various individuals in order to confirm the victim's identity (Douglas 1992; Mallion 1993; Staggs 1997).

CAMERA FILTERS

It is sometimes necessary to photograph fingerprints on objects that have multicolored backgrounds. Beer and soft drink cans are examples of such objects. Camera filters can help reveal the definition in latent fingerprints. The forensic photographer observes the object through various color filters, then chooses the filter that provides the best contrast between the latent fingerprint and the background. For example, a number twenty-five red filter, placed over the camera lens, eliminates a red-colored background (Redsicker et al. 1994; Staggs 1997).

CLOSE-UP PHOTOGRAPHS

Close-up photographs depict clearly the details of evidence at a crime scene. A close-up photograph shows more closely, than does a mid-range photograph, a gun, or other object.

After a close-up photograph is taken of a weapon, chalk contrasting in color with the gun is run back and forth over the serial number and identification markings of the gun. The excess chalk is wiped away. The rest of the chalk affixed to the gun makes the serial number and markings more readable. The gun should again be photographed to ensure the availability of before-and-after photographs. If this is not done, a defense attorney can raise the matter of evidence tampering (Mallion 1993; Nickell and Fischer 1999; Staggs 1997).

FACES

InterQuest, Inc., a Montreal, Quebec, company, manufactures FACES, a software program used to produce composite photographic images. This software was launched in the fall of 1998. FACES can create simulated photographs, including simulated photographs of homicide suspects. As an alternative to sketches produced by police artists, FACES might replace these artists.

The person who uses FACES, whether alone or in the presence of a crime victim or other person, has access to approximately 4,000 computerized facial features, skin types, and hair types stored in a database. The features and types are combined to represent a suspect's face. The creation of the image begins with the selection of a type of head. Each facial feature, skin type, or hair type has a category and a number. For example, a "pointed" head is number 106; "even" lips are number 312. FACES automatically combine selected facial features.

A woman who was brutally raped reported the rape to the Canton, Michigan, Police Department. There she used FACES to create a composite picture of the rapist, a procedure that took her forty-five minutes. *Michigan's Most Wanted* aired a segment about the rapist. Within days, Mitchell Dean Sproessig was arrested, charged, and subsequently received a life sentence for the rape.

FACES played a major role in the identification and arrest of Nicholas Stoumbelis, thirty, suspected to be the South Florida Rapist, an individual allegedly responsible for the torture and rape of twelve young girls. According to Detective Bob Edgerton of the North Lauderdale Police Department, FACES will likely be in laptops used by North Lauderdale police. Victims and witnesses will use FACES at crime scenes ("Software" 2000; Tuck 1999).

IDENTI-KIT

The Identi-Kit, a composite production device, has been widely used by police in North America to create composite facial descriptions of possible suspects. In 1940, Hugh C. McDonald of the Los Angeles Police Department (LAPD) devised the first usable Identi-Kit. McDonald later cooperated with the Townsend Company of Santa Ana, California, to improve the usability of Identi-Kit. By 1960, Identi-Kit was used by many police forces worldwide.

Identi-Kit, now available from Smith & Wesson, consists of a manual, booklet, and transparencies. The transparencies are numbered and are depictions of facial features. Numbered photographs in the booklet correspond to transparencies. There are thirty-four noses, twenty-six chins, and 177 hairstyles. There are also other transparencies, including hats and age lines. Features, whether in the booklet or in the box containing transparencies, are grouped together. For example, all the eyes are grouped together, all the noses together. Identi-Kit is relatively equivalent to Photo-Fit, which is widely used in the United Kingdom and other European countries (Kind and Overman 1972; Lane 1992; Wells 1988).

IDENTI-KIT 2000

A witness to a homicide or another person with information potentially valuable to detectives can be interviewed, and the information obtained from them can be used to electronically create a facial composite. Identi-Kit 2000, which accomplishes this task, is used with an IBM-compatible PC or laptop. It takes only minutes for a witness to see a face generated that corresponds to the description given by the witness. The core of the Identi-Kit 2000 is a facial feature database periodically updated and representing all major races and both genders. The operator uses multiple edit commands to move, shade, add, remove, or otherwise alter a feature. All facial composites can be printed; also, Identi-Kit 2000 can create custom wanted bulletins, send a composite to a fax machine, or send the file to another Identi-Kit 2000 user (Smith & Wesson 2000).

MID-RANGE PHOTOGRAPHS

Mid-range photographs depict the location and relationship of evidence and other items at a crime scene. A mid-range photograph shows the victim and evidence, such as a gun, in relation to the victim (Staggs 1997).

OVERVIEW PHOTOGRAPHS

Overview photographs depict a crime scene as the photographer first saw it. Several complete sets of photographs are taken before the crime scene is disturbed. The photographer is cautious not to destroy evidence. Neither investigators nor their equipment should be in these photographs.

Photographs of buildings in which the crime took place should include shots of all points of entry and exit. Vehicles, street signs, and address plaques are photographed in relation to the crime scene building. Aerial photographs are occasionally useful.

Interior overview photographs show a view of the entrance, a room as it appears when a person enters it, and each corner of each room. These photographs should overlap regarding content, and are usually taken with a wide-angle lens. Moreover, these photographs depict potential items of evidence.

Photographs are also taken of hallways and stairwells when a crime scene is in an apartment or office (Staggs 1997).

PHOTO-FIT

Photo-Fit, also known as the "Penry Facial Identification Technique," was invented in Britain in 1971, by Jacques Penry. Photo-Fit is a composite production device that has been used widely by police in the United Kingdom and other European countries to create composite facial descriptions of possible suspects. Photo-Fit is relatively equivalent to Identi-Kit, which has been used in North America. Photo-Fit, however, uses photographs of features, instead of transparencies, and has a greater number of features. Entries in Photo-Fit are organized within features according to their similarity. Neither Identi-Kit nor Photo-Fit can produce a multidimensional likeness. This negative characteristic is the reason why both devices produce relatively poor-quality likenesses (*Crimes* 1994; Owen 2000; Wells 1988).

PHOTOEVIDENCE SCALES

Photoevidence scales are used in photographs to indicate size or distance. Crime scene photographers use evidence scales when blood at crime scenes is photographed. Photoevidence scales typically have black numbers on a yellow background. These colors are easy to see in black-and-white as well as in color photographs. A standard thirty-six-inch scale has vertical numbers on one side, horizontal numbers on the other side (Staggs 1997).

PHOTOGRAPHIC EVIDENCE

Crime scene photographs must fairly and accurately represent people, places, and things. These photographs document facts, record evidence, permit reconstruction of crimes, and may reveal evidence not initially noted by investigators at crime scenes. Crime scene photographs must be taken carefully with the knowledge that they will be used as evidence in court. These photographs should not include paper arrows or rulers for scale. A competent defense attorney can argue the addition of these items altered a crime scene, and the photographs should not be admitted as evidence. Therefore, two sets of photographs should be taken with and without items that help explain the photographs (Mallion 1993; Nickell and Fischer 1999).

PHOTOGRAPHS AND COINS

When a ruler is not available, a coin can be used in a crime scene photograph to indicate size and distance relationships between different objects. For example, a coin can give the viewer of a crime scene photograph an idea of the size of a scratch on a person in relation to the rest of the person's body. A coin can also be used to indicate size and distance relationships regarding tool marks and pry marks (Mallion 1993).

PHOTOGRAPHS OF CROWDS

Crowds at a crime scene are photographed because the perpetrator may be among the curious onlookers. Subsequent examination of the photographs may also reveal potential eyewitnesses. Photographs are also taken of nearby vehicles and their license plates. The perpetrator's vehicle may be at the scene, and the perpetrator may return after the crime scene has been processed and police have left (Douglas 1992).

POLAROID PHOTOGRAPHS

The body of David Madson, a thirty-three-year-old architect, was found on May 3, 1997. Anglers came across Madson near an abandoned farmhouse next to East Rush Lake, Minnesota, approximately forty-five miles north of Minneapolis. Madson had been shot three times by killer Andrew Cunanan.

Investigators took Polaroid photographs of Madson's body in order to show the pictures to citizens in Rush City, hoping someone might identify Madson. Polaroid cameras are commonly used to quickly obtain a photograph of a homicide victim at the crime scene or at the morgue. Investigators then have something to show people who might have known the victim.

Polaroid cameras, however, are not used to take crime scene photographs for use as evidence in court. Polaroid quality does not compare favorably to the quality of photographs taken with a 35 mm camera. For example, experience has shown that Polaroid cameras have been of limited value in photographing bloodstain patterns (Clarkson 1997; Corwin 1997; Orth 1999; Redsicker et al. 1994).

SKETCH

There are three main types of crime scene sketches. The projection sketch, in which everything is drawn on one plane and viewed from above, is the most frequently used crime scene sketch.

A rough sketch is done at the crime scene after photographs are taken but before anything is moved. Although this sketch does not have to be made to scale, it must have accurate measurements, indicating distances of objects from one another. The measurements are taken by at least two individuals using a tape measure. The individual who will testify in court is the person who should record and keep track of measurements.

A finished sketch is done later in a police department office by a police sketch artist or someone with an aptitude for drawing. The finished sketch is based on the rough sketch and is done to scale. It has a legend, which explains the symbols used to identify objects. A scale of 0.25 inches per foot to 0.50 inches per foot can be used, depending on the size of buildings to be represented. A scale of 0.50 inches per ten feet can be used to depict outside areas.

The sketch should also include the name and title of the sketcher, the date and time the sketch was produced, the type of crime committed, an identification of the victim or victims, the investigating agency's case number or numbers, the names of persons who took the measurements, the precise address of the place sketched, and a compass indicating directions (DePresca 1997; Geberth 1997).

VIDEOTAPING

Although videotaping can provide investigators with a visual record of a crime scene, videotapes should be used as an adjunct to still photographs, not as a replacement for them. Videotapes, like still photographs, may be admitted as evidence in court. They can also be used to train rookie investigators about crime scene investigation techniques.

An advantage of videotapes over still photographs is that videotapes provide continuous coverage of an investigation. An advantage of still photographs over videotapes is that still photographs are generally of better visual quality than videotapes.

Videotaping should continue uninterrupted to ensure there are no gaps that a defense attorney can bring to the attention of the court and weaken the prosecution's case. The operator should indicate in a log the amount of time elapsed when tapes or batteries were changed.

The first item on videotape should show information that describes the particulars of the tape. The particulars include the location, the date of taping, and the name of the video camera operator. There should also be an introduction by an investigator. The audio should then be turned off because an inadvertent negative remark by an investigator at the crime scene could be used by the defense in court against the prosecution.

Panning slowly and widely provides a long-range view of the crime scene. Taping with the lens partially zoomed in gives a mid-range view. Zooming tightly produces a close-up shot. These are the same three types of shots used when taking still photographs at a crime scene (Berg and Horgan 1998; Staggs 1997).

14

Forensic Experts

Forensic experts are scientists and professionals with specialized training in forensic investigation techniques. Forensic experts assess items of evidence against established and historical scientific data to establish the continuity, integrity, and validity of the evidence. Forensic entomologists, experts in insect behavior, and forensic palynologists, experts in pollen and spores, are frequently called upon to help solve homicides. Forensic entomologists use data about insect life cycles to determine the time of death of a victim. Forensic palynologists use information about pollen and spores to determine if pollen at a crime scene is present on a suspect's clothing. In this chapter, we look at six ways forensic experts use their specialized knowledge to link victims and perpetrators.

EXCAVATION AND PHOTOGRAPHY OF BURIED BODIES

The preferred route, whenever possible, to the site of a buried body is the route used by the person who found the body and contacted police. This person is typically a farmer, hunter, construction worker, hiker, or utility employee. The route should be marked in order to preserve as much as possible the surrounding area. The same route should be used when entering and leaving the crime scene. An evidence technician should accompany the forensic photographer. Clothing, tire tracks, or anything else that could be used as evidence in court should be photographed and preserved. Aerial photographs of the burial site should also be taken.

At the scene, investigators superimpose on the site a grid made of stakes and string, usually oriented northward. This is followed by a scale drawing, which has corresponding squares. The drawing has two views: top and side. The top view is an aerial view. The side view indicates depth and elevation.

A hand trowel or flat-bladed spade is used to remove soil in even layers of approximately four to six inches. The dirt that is removed is sifted twice: first through a quarter-inch mesh screen, then through a finer window screen. Every item discovered should be photographed twice before it is removed: once with and once without a ruler and north indicator. An item should not be removed from a screen, placed in the excavation, and photographed there. This procedure is incorrect and constitutes false documentation (Boyd 1979; Nickell and Fischer 1999).

FORENSIC ENTOMOLOGY

A forensic pathologist determines the time of a victim's death by studying livor mortis, the pooling of blood in the victim, and rigor mortis, the stiffening of the decedent's body. This expert also examines the stomach contents, which reveal the time of consumption and digestion of food, and body temperature, which begins to drop when a person dies.

There are, however, other important ways of finding out when a homicide victim died. A forensic entomologist, an expert whose knowledge of insect behavior can be used as evidence in court, uses data about insect life cycles to determine the time of death.

European researcher J. P. Megnin published in 1894 a work about entomology, corpses, and legal medicine. He stated that a body exposed to air undergoes certain changes. The appearance of specific insects at the body correlates with specific changes in the body. This pattern of insect behavior and body decomposition recurs consistently. Identifying specific insects enables entomologists to estimate the time of death.

A human body begins to internally decompose minutes after death. Blowflies are attracted to a fresh cadaver's gases, blood, and fecal matter. These flies search for openings in which to lay their eggs. Eggs are laid in the mouth, nose, eyes, bullet wounds, stab wounds, anus, and genitalia. The eggs hatch into maggots that eat for several days, then become pupae. Adult flies emerge from the pupae. This entire process may take a week in warm weather.

The forensic entomologist collects fly larvae to rear under controlled conditions. Then literature and insect reference collections are used to help identify the adults. After the entomologist determines the details of the larvae, especially the developmental period, the entomologist knows when the mother fly of a specific species was at the location of the corpse.

Although fungi and bacteria contribute to decomposition, insects play a larger role. Insects that colonize a corpse normally appear in the following order: flies, beetles, wasps, ants, and spiders. As insects eat the corpse, enzymes secreted by these insects contribute to the liquefaction of the corpse. Beetles and moths do not appear at the corpse until it has for the most part dried out.

Various factors influence the rate at which insects colonize a corpse. Access to a clothed body is partial, and it is nonexistent to a body covered with soil. Although flies cannot reach a body buried under a very thin layer of soil, these flies may lay some eggs on the soil. The larvae that hatch can burrow down to the body.

It is difficult for flies to get to a body in the trunk of a car during summer and even more difficult to reach a body in a burned-out car during fall.

A body that is exposed to insects can be reduced to 20 percent of its live weight in less than a week (Beil 1995; McKeown 1991; Slack 1992).

FORENSIC EXPERTS AND BURIED BODIES

Teams of forensic experts work at body excavation sites to solve homicides. An archeologist is an expert in the systematic excavation of buried bodies. This person knows how to perform an excavation without damaging or destroying potential physical evidence. A pathologist is knowledgeable about various types of death and how they are caused. The botanist examines root systems and estimates how long vegetation has been damaged; this procedure can help in developing a timeline regarding the most likely time of death. The entomologist provides information about the life cycles of dead insects found at the site. Information about this can also help establish a timeline. An anthropologist comments on different aspects of skeletal remains, such as the skull and pelvis. The information generated by these five experts, combined with information provided by detectives, is vital in solving a case (Boyd 1979).

FORENSIC PALYNOLOGY

A woman was killed in May 1959 in central Sweden. A palynologist, an expert in the study of pollen and spores, wanted to know if the victim was killed where her body was discovered or if she was killed somewhere else and dumped. The palynologist studied dirt attached to the victim's clothing. The dirt did not contain pollen from plants in the area where her body was discovered. This indicated that she was killed somewhere else, then dumped. A second opinion was given regarding the pollen samples. According to the second palynologist, the woman could have been murdered in May. This was before plants in the region where she had been killed had pollinated. Both opinions were admitted as evidence. Although it is not known if the murder was solved, this homicide illustrated one of the earliest cases in which pollen data was accepted as forensic evidence in court.

A homicide, committed in Austria in 1959, also illustrated the value in homicide investigation of forensic palynology. Police working a missing person case found a suspect who had a motive to kill the missing person, a man who disappeared near Vienna while he was on vacation. A pair of boots with mud on the soles was found in the suspect's room. Dr. Wilhelm Klaus, a geologist, analyzed the boots and learned that the mud on them contained certain types of pollen. This enabled Klaus to determine where the victim likely walked in order to get mud on his boots. A small area north of Vienna had soils containing the type of pollen found on the suspect's boots. The suspect confessed when he was confronted with this evidence. He showed investigators where he killed and buried the victim. This was where Klaus indicated the body would be found.

A suspect in another homicide case claimed his gun could not have been the murder weapon because, according to him, the gun had not been removed from storage in months. Swiss criminalist Max Frei examined the weapon. Grease on it contained two types of pollen. Both were from plants that were pollinating when the murder was committed. This contradicted the suspect's claim regarding the last time he cleaned the gun and put it into storage. Frei successfully linked the suspect to the murder (Bryant and Mildenhall 2000).

HUMAN DECAY RESEARCH

Insects colonize a corpse almost as soon as a person dies, especially the corpse of a person who dies outdoors. A forensic entomologist can study the life cycles of insects and determine how long a body has been at a particular location. Detectives can use this information to determine more accurately where the decedent was during the last few days, or even hours, of his or her life.

Research into human decay, and how information about this decay can help solve homicides, is conducted at a number of universities. Dr. William Bass, who began his career in 1971 as a forensic anthropologist, established at the University of Tennessee the Body Farm, four acres of fenced woodland. There are donated corpses throughout the Body Farm, along footpaths, under trees, in culverts, and in automobiles. Some corpses are buried and used in training cadaver dogs. After the bodies have decayed to the point at which there is no more flesh, and insect life cycles can no longer be studied, Bass keeps the bones for further study. Interestingly enough, the bones are kept in boxes in an office beneath Neyland Stadium at the University of Tennessee.

Bass helped solve a homicide that detective Mike Lett of the Knox County Sheriff's office was working. Lett was dispatched to see a man who had come across a human skeleton near the Fourth Creek Treatment Plant near Knoxville. After a preliminary investigation at the scene, Lett asked the dispatcher to send Bass to the location. As Bass and Lett looked at the skeleton, Bass pointed out a number of things to the homicide detective: the skeleton's wide pelvis, its pointed chin, the narrowness of the nasal area, and damage to the skull. Bass told Lett it appeared the skeleton was that of a woman who had been beaten to death.

Bass took the bones with him for further study. His subsequent examination led him to conclude the skeleton was that of a white female who was between thirty-eight and forty-three years of age. She was approximately five feet and one-and-a-half inches tall, had an upper denture plate, and had been dead from three to five months.

Lett compared Bass's description of the dead woman to missing person's reports and identified the woman as Mary Francis Holt. Bass's description was very accurate: Holt was white, forty-eight years old, and five-feet one-inch tall; had dentures; and was last seen alive three months and three weeks before her skeleton was found. Blunt force trauma to her skull was the cause of death.

Penn State entomologist Ke Chung Kim uses dead pigs to study insect life cycles. Pigs have a nearly hairless body and decay much the same way human beings decay. Kim offers a workshop to law enforcement officers who learn how to collect insect clues at a crime scene. The officers then send the insect evidence to an expert (Gannon 1997; Johnson 1990).

INSECT CRIME SITE KIT

Dael Morris of the Royal Ontario Museum (ROM) worked in 1991 toward establishing an insect crime site kit for Toronto, Ontario, police. The kit would enable police to collect flies and maggots at homicide crime scenes. Thermometers, small aerial nets, lightweight forceps, and vials are some of the items used in this investigative work.

The insect crime site kit can help investigators in the study of insect life cycles. These life cycles are crucial in determining a victim's time of death (McKeown 1991).

15

Body Fluids

Blood, semen, and saliva are examples of body fluids found at a crime scene. Under poor lighting, tar and rust can be mistaken for blood. When a substance is found, forensic experts use specialized procedures to establish whether the substance is a body fluid and whether the body fluid is from the victim, the perpetrator, or both. In this chapter, we discuss nine topics that indicate that body fluids at crime scenes can be as important as bullets and fingerprints.

BLOODBORNE PATHOGENS

Investigators at homicides where there is considerable blood are especially at risk for exposure to HIV (human immunodeficiency virus) and hepatitis B. Exposure to HIV usually leads to AIDS (acquired immunodeficiency syndrome). The major ways of being exposed to AIDS are through blood, semen, and vaginal secretions. The immune system of a person with AIDS cannot adequately resist invasion by microorganisms, which cause various illnesses from which the AIDS-infected person eventually dies. The HIV virus can survive outside the human body from three to fifteen days, depending on whether the virus is in a liquid or dry state. Hepatitis B, transmitted in the same way as HIV, causes liver damage, resulting in jaundice, cirrhosis, and occasionally liver cancer.

The likelihood of airborne particles at a crime scene is especially high when dried blood evidence is collected. Investigators with cuts or sores should be extremely cautious. These individuals should use double-layer protective clothing to avoid infection. Disposable booties, gloves, eye goggles, and facemasks reduce the risk of infection. Needles, sticks, and sharp-edged objects should be handled with great caution.

There should be no eating, drinking, smoking, or use of cosmetics. Contaminated items should be removed to one collection point, placed into biohazard bags, and then destroyed at an appropriate place such as a hospital. All nondisposable clothing and all equipment should be cleaned. Bleach or an alcohol solution can be used for this purpose (Bevel and Gardner 1997; "Police" 1987).

BLOODSTAIN PATTERNS

There may be a large amount of blood near the body of a homicide victim who has a head injury or a cut throat. This blood may be from a severed jugular vein. If there is a pool of blood beside or underneath the body, this indicates the decedent did not move very far after being injured. A trail of blood indicates the victim was attacked in one location and died in another location. The victim may have run after being attacked with a knife or blunt object, or may have been dragged to where the body was found.

Blood on a wall or furniture may be from spurts that originated in a medium-sized artery. Bleeding from the vein of a victim at rest is slow, steady, and produces a pool. Bleeding from the vein of a victim who is walking produces separate drops with wide spaces between them. Flat surfaces, such as walls, sometimes have linear streaks of blood that are wider at their lower end, with separate drops that look like exclamation mark dots. Blood emanating in spurts from a wound produces these types of bloodstains.

A single drop of blood, falling vertically from a vein onto a flat surface, produces a circular stain. The stain looks like a perfect circle when the drop falls a relatively short distance. The periphery of the stain becomes increasingly irregular as the distance increases, and short projections eventually radiate from the periphery.

A drop of blood not falling vertically produces a stain that looks like an exclamation mark. If a victim with an injured hand is in a room, and moves the hand upward in a sweeping motion in the direction of a wall, a bloodstain that looks like an exclamation mark will appear on the wall. The "dot" in the "exclamation mark" will point upward. If the victim moves the hand downward, the dot will point downward. If the long axis of a stain is in a horizontal position, it is possible to determine the direction of the drop—forward or backward.

Smears of blood trail off in the direction of the smear and may preserve the impression of a finger or palm, possibly of value in identifying a suspect (Cuomo 1995; Polson, Gee, and Knight 1985; Vanezis and Busuttil 1996).

CASTOFF BLOOD

The weapon in a homicide that results from blunt trauma is a hammer, pipe, or other blunt object. A fist or knife is sometimes the weapon repeatedly swung at the victim. The weapon strikes the victim and exposes blood at the site of impact, the blood adhering to the weapon. The blood projected from the weapon while the weapon is in motion is called castoff or inline staining. Centrifugal force sends the blood out and away from the weapon. The blood impacts on nearby surfaces, including walls or ceiling. A linear pattern on a wall indicates motion up the wall. Elliptical droplets indicate motion down the wall. More blood is cast off when the murder weapon is swung upward than when it is swung downward. Castoff bloodstains appear as uniformly distributed trails, in other words, along linear patterns.

The number of times the victim is struck is at least one more time than the number of bloodstains noted by investigators. The first swing of the weapon by the perpetrator is not included in the count because this swing breaks open the skin, at which time no significant amount of blood adheres to the weapon or casts from the weapon (Bevel and Gardner 1997; Eckert 1997; Fisher 1995).

DRY BLOODSTAINS

A clean razor blade or sterile scalpel is used to scrape dry blood from a nonporous surface into a sterile container. When dry bloodstains are on a porous surface, such as a fabric, the entire article should be sent, unaltered in any way, to the crime lab. When it is inappropriate because of size to transport an entire article (such as a couch), a portion of the article representing an adequate amount of bloodstain is removed and forwarded to the lab. A cotton swab or gauze pad moistened with distilled water is used when handling traces of dry blood that cannot be scraped into a container or sent on a piece of fabric. The stain softens and soaks into the swab or pad. It is placed, after drying, into a sterile test tube or other container for transportation to the lab (Geberth 1997).

FECAL MATTER

Advancements in forensic science is the reason why fecal matter has more evidential value than it had in the past. Amylase, starch, and bacteria are a few substances that can be detected in feces. Large amounts of feces at a crime scene should be removed with a small clean shovel, air-dried, then placed in a sterile container. A small amount of feces should be removed with a cotton swab or a gauze pad moistened with distilled water, then air-dried or scraped into a container.

D. O. Morris and J. H. Block, with the Department of Environmental, Populations, and Organismic Biology at the University of Colorado, Boulder, linked a suspect to a rape–homicide victim by comparing fecal matter from the suspect's clothing to fecal matter from the victim's clothing. They hydrated the scrapings of fecal matter and microscopically examined them. The cells observed were then compared to known food specimens. Specific foods were identified and a connection was established between the suspect and the victim (Chayko and Gulliver 1999; Eckert 1997; Geberth 1996; Norris and Block 2000).

SEMEN STAINS

Female homicide victims who are raped or sexually assaulted in other ways may have semen left on their bodies by a perpetrator. For example, a nude or partially nude victim may have semen on both breasts.

A wet semen stain should be swabbed at the crime scene or drawn into an eyedropper or hypodermic syringe, then placed into a sterile test tube. A swab or cotton gauze pad is used for smaller quantities that are still moist. After immediate air-drying, they are placed into a sterile container. When a dry semen stain is on clothing, the entire article of clothing is sent to the lab. Caution is exercised not to contaminate the stain. A dry semen stain on a body is removed with a cotton gauze pad moistened with distilled water. After the pad is air-dried, it is placed into a sterile test tube or other container.

Although an ultraviolet (UV) light can be used to detect semen stains at a homicide crime scene, UV light does not always produce results. Dried semen can be particularly difficult to detect. In such a case, methylumbelliferyl phosphate (MUP) can be applied on an area thought to contain hidden semen stains. MUP reacts with the enzymes in semen and forms a substance that appears very bright when exposed to UV light. A section of a mattress containing semen stains would then be removed to the crime lab, where a sample of the semen would be frozen and preserved (Geberth 1996; Houde 1999).

SPITTLE OR SALIVA

A homicide victim may have bite marks on his or her body. Spittle or saliva is removed with an eyedropper or cotton gauze pad and then, after drying, is placed into a sterile test tube or other clean container (Geberth 1997).

VISUAL IDENTIFICATION OF BLOOD

It is not always easy to visually identify blood, especially when lighting is inadequate. Paint and jam can be mistaken for blood; rust and tar stains can look like blood. It is particularly difficult to visually identify blood on dark fabrics. Chemicals affect the color of blood. For example, soap can turn blood a greenish-brown color. A borax solution may speed up the removal of the stain. Regardless of the method criminals use to remove bloodstains from clothing, criminals very rarely succeed (Polson, Gee, and Knight 1985).

WET BLOOD

At a crime scene at which there is wet, pooled blood, an eyedropper or hypodermic syringe is used to collect and transfer blood to a sterile container, for example a sterile test tube. The container should immediately be transferred to a refrigeration unit or laboratory. This blood should not be frozen. In some jurisdictions, sodium azide or EDTA can be added to prevent blood from spoiling.

If there is only a small amount of wet blood at a crime scene, a cotton swab or gauze pad is used to collect a specimen. The swab or gauze pad should not be placed in a sterile test tube, or other clean container until the swab or gauze is dry because microorganisms in moisture can destroy or alter blood evidence (Geberth 1997).

16

Test Methods

A test method is a scientific procedure that can be used at a crime scene or within a laboratory to identify, establish, or verify body fluids, if a suspect fired a weapon, or if the suspect is telling the truth. Test methods help homicide detectives answer specific questions regarding blood, semen, urine, fingerprints, and other items associated with a homicide investigation. Current DNA profiling techniques have proven effective in convicting guilty persons while exonerating wrongfully convicted persons. In this chapter, we look at thirteen test methods for establishing the guilt or innocence of homicide suspects.

8-HYDROXYQUINOLINE

8-hydroxyquinoline, a trace metal detector and a carcinogenic chemical, is used to determine if a victim fired a gun. The victim's hands are sprayed with special attention to the palm, trigger finger, and thumb. A photograph is taken with black-and-white film and ultraviolet light as the light source. If the victim cocked the hammer, a photograph may reveal on the victim's thumb an impression of the hammer (Douglas 1992).

ALFRED L. CARTER

For thirty years, physicist Alfred L. Carter specialized in experimental particle physics at Carleton University in Canada. In 1982, the

Royal Canadian Mounted Police (RCMP) approached Carleton regarding the application of physics and mathematics in the study of blood spatter at crime scenes. This was the year Carter became interested in this subject.

He created the "Back Track" computer program seven years later. This software analyzes bloodstain patterns. "Tracks," a computer program that was created in the same year as Back Track, applies the laws of physics in the study and simulation of bloodstain patterns. Investigators can determine a number of things from bloodstain patterns, including the type of weapon used in a homicide, the number of times the weapon was used, and the velocity of impact when the victim was struck, whether with a bullet from a firearm or with blows from a blunt object such as a baseball bat.

A blood-spatter analyst can use Back Track to analyze up to fifty bloodstains on twelve different surfaces. The analysis involves the computerized use of strings to represent the flight paths of blood droplets. These droplets do not travel in straight lines. However, if the droplets are viewed from above, as in a bird's-eye view, their flight paths appear as straight lines. Strings are attached to suitable stains and extended into space. The strings, as a group, converge in the direction of the source of projected blood. Strings can accurately represent rapidly moving droplets, which have flat, stringlike trajectories.

The flight paths of blood droplets that fall on to a flat surface, such as a floor or ceiling, are straight lines. The patterns created by these droplets can be analyzed with the tangent method. This method is used when bloodstains are on horizontal surfaces. The flight paths of blood droplets, when projected onto these surfaces, are straight lines. This method does not require the time-consuming work involved in mounting strings at the crime scene. The tangent method, however, is not useful for vertical surfaces such as walls because the flight paths of droplets, when projected onto vertical surfaces, are curved lines.

In 1991, Carter and his son Brian established Forensic Computing of Ottawa, Inc., to market their software. With financial aid from the RCMP, Carter developed, in 1992, a procedure that uses digital imaging technology in the analysis of blood spatters. In 1999, he became a distinguished member of the International Association of Bloodstain Pattern Analysts (IABPA) (Bevel and Gardner 1997; *Bloodspatter* 2000).

BENZIDINE TEST

One way of determining if a stain is blood is by using the benzidine test. This test is very sensitive even when blood is barely visible. The first step is to rub a small piece of filter paper on the area suspected of being a bloodstain. The second step is to treat the filter paper with a solution containing benzidine, a carcinogenic organic chemical. If the filter paper turns a vivid blue color, the stain is blood (Kind and Overman 1972; Ragle 1995).

DNA AND WRONGFUL CONVICTIONS

Witnesses sometimes lie under oath. Lies, incompetent defense attorneys, and questionable scientific evidence contribute to wrongful convictions. However, DNA evidence can exonerate a wrongfully convicted individual. DNA evidence became acceptable in court in the late 1980s.

After DNA test procedures were improved, prosecutors used this method to eliminate suspects before these suspects were wrongfully charged. During the 1990s, DNA testing established that sixty-nine individuals in North America went to prison for crimes they did not commit. In January 2000, Illinois Governor George Ryan imposed a moratorium on executions because DNA evidence had exonerated thirteen prison inmates. In January 2003, he commuted the sentences of 167 condemned inmates.

The Innocence Project at the Benjamin N. Cardozo School of Law in New York uses DNA evidence to exonerate wrongfully convicted inmates. Barry Scheck and Peter Neufeld, civil rights attorneys, established and direct the project. Since 1995, students at law schools throughout the United States have investigated and established wrongful convictions. There were twenty DNA-based exonerations in 2001.

Gary Dotson of Chicago, Illinois, was the first man in the United States to be exonerated of rape on the basis of DNA evidence. He was exonerated on August 14, 1989, after spending more than a decade in jail. Cathleen Crowell, his presumed victim, had lied to police that Dotson raped her. Crowell feared she might have become pregnant the previous day when she had consensual intercourse with her boyfriend. A rapist, not her boyfriend, would be a plausible explanation if she became pregnant and had to tell her parents (Dwyer, Neufeld, and Scheck 2000; Scheck, Neufeld, and Dwyer 2001; Willing 2002).

DNA PROFILING

In England during the early 1950s, English researchers M. H. F. Wilkins and Francis Crick, and American researcher John Watson, were studying the acids that comprise the cell nucleus. Their work subsequently paved the way to the discovery of DNA (deoxyribonucleic acid). DNA, a "genetic fingerprint," is unique in every person except identical twins, and it uniquely defines every person. DNA is found in every cell that has a nucleus. This excludes red blood cells, but not other cells present in blood. Seminal fluid, hair, urine, perspiration, vaginal fluid, and tooth pulp are sources of DNA.

The DNA molecule looks like a twisted ladder or double helix, a spiral form. The "ladder" has four chemical subunits or bases: guanine (G), adenine (A), thymine (T), and cytosine (C). These subunits comprise the "ladder's steps." A always pairs with T, G always pairs with C, and base-pair combinations of A-T and G-C form the steps of the double-stranded DNA helix. There are more than 3 billion base pairs in human DNA. A small portion of base pairs determines a person's unique traits.

British geneticist Alec Jeffries developed DNA profiling in 1985. DNA profiling, also called "DNA fingerprinting," is a procedure that involves extracting DNA from biological evidence, such as saliva, at a crime scene, then comparing this evidence to a DNA sample obtained from a suspect. Analysis at a lab such as Cellmark Diagnostics in Germantown, Maryland, determines if the crime scene DNA and the suspect's DNA match. It was first used successfully to help solve the murders of two teenage girls in England. One girl was raped and murdered in 1983; the other girl was raped and murdered in 1986. Semen and blood on both victims indicated the same perpetrator. Police learned from information, which originated at a pub, that a man gave them a false blood sample. This man was arrested and a true blood sample was later obtained. His unique gene pattern matched perfectly the DNA obtained from semen found at the crime scenes of both homicide victims.

RFLP (restriction fragment length polymorphism) is an important DNA testing procedure used in criminal investigation. DNA genetic material is extracted in the lab from crime scenes, victims, and suspects' tissues or body fluids. The extracted material is mixed with enzymes in order to cut the DNA into fragments. These fragments are placed in a special gel and then exposed to an electrical charge, which sorts the fragments according to size. Genetic tracers search for, then lock onto, specific fragments of the DNA. The tracers reveal a pattern, and each evidence sample has a pattern that can be compared with a sample from the victim and a sample from the suspect.

PCR (polymerase chain reaction) is also a major DNA testing procedure. In the lab, DNA is extracted from the crime scene victim's, and the suspect's, samples. Part of the DNA molecule is amplified in a test tube to produce billions of copies. This can be done in a few hours. Then the amplified DNA is analyzed. The analysis of the evidence sample is compared with the analysis of the sample from the victim and the sample from the suspect. When the patterns in the samples are compared, the profile identifies distinctive features of the samples.

The first person to be convicted based on DNA evidence in the United States was Timothy W. Spencer, who had murdered four women in Richmond, Virginia. He died in the electric chair at the Greensville Correctional Center in Greensville, Virginia, on April 27, 1994 (Bennett and Hess 2001; Berg and Horgan 1998; Blanket 2003; Fisher 2000; Kane, Anzovin, and Podell 1997; Linedecker 1995; Scott 1998; Weston, Lushbaugh, and Wells 2000).

DUSTY HESSKEW

By 1994, Dusty Hesskew, then forty-five, of the Austin, Texas, Police Department, had been a police officer for twenty-two years. Hesskew, experienced in both homicide and child abuse investigation, also used his expertise in bloodstain analysis in his work. He had studied, in 1985, at the Corning Forensic Institute, where Herb MacDonell, pioneer bloodstain analyst, taught bloodstain analysis.

Hesskew used a pig carcass, stuffed with animal remains and unused human blood, to represent a human chest cavity. He produced bloodstains for comparison with actual stains by shooting, bludgeoning, or in other ways attacking the human substitute. This was done because different weapons have different effects on the distribution of blood at homicide crime scenes. A Styrofoam human head containing pig or calf brains took the place of a human head.

Hesskew later focused his work on family violence and stalking investigations (Dingus 1994).

EDTA

EDTA is an abbreviation for ethylenediaminetetraacetic acid. EDTA is a preservative that protects substances, including blood, from rapid deterioration. EDTA is not intended to protect blood for a long time, only until the blood is placed in a refrigerated facility. Laundry detergents and paints contain EDTA. EDTA can be detected in a person who has eaten preserved foods. It can also be found on washed clothes. Blood from a homicide crime scene should be placed in a vial, have EDTA added to it, then get transported, the sooner the better, to a laboratory for analysis (Clark and Carpenter 1997; Lange, Vannatter, and Moldea 1997; *Stedman's* 1995).

FRANK BENDER

Frank Bender, a former commercial photographer, preferred to paint and sculpt than to continue to work in commercial photography. He took night classes at the Pennsylvania Academy of Fine Arts and learned about anatomy at the Philadelphia Medical Examiner's Office.

Pathologist Dr. Halbert Fillinger was extremely impressed with the unique talent he almost immediately saw in Bender. Bender could reconstruct with remarkable accuracy the facial features of a dead person he had never seen by using the person's skull and non-hardening clay. He could also study a photograph of a person who disappeared years ago, then recreate the facial features of the person as the person would look at the time of the reconstruction.

In 1989, at the request of *America's Most Wanted*, Bender worked with Richard Walter, a Michigan prison psychologist and profiler. Bender created a bust of John List, who, in 1971, killed his family in New Jersey and then disappeared. The bust was shown on *AMW*. List was arrested by the FBI eleven days later. In addition to having worked with *America's Most Wanted*, Bender worked on cases for Interpol and the U.S. Marshals Service and shared information with the FBI and Scotland Yard. Bender could not explain his rare and valuable talent (*Frank Bender* 2000; Rubin 1998).

PARAFFIN TEST

Synonyms for the paraffin test include the dermal nitrate test, nitrate test, diphenylamine test, and Gonzales test. The premise of this test is that a chemical solution of diphenylbenzidine and diphenylamine, applied to warm paraffin that has been brushed on a person's hand, will reveal if the person recently fired a gun.

This is because nitrates are expelled when a gun is fired, and they appear on the hand of the person who fired the gun. If the test is positive for nitrates, the person tested fired a gun. Although this may be true, nitrates are present in many other substances, including urine, cigarette ash, and fertilizer. Therefore, this test is essentially of no value in court. However, a homicide investigator could convince a perpetrator who does not know anything about this test of its validity. This could give the investigator a psychological advantage in dealing with the perpetrator (Jaffe 1991; Kessler and Weston 1953).

PHENOLPHTHALEIN TEST

The phenolphthalein test is a presumptive test used if something is suspected of having blood on it. The first step in the test procedure is to apply distilled water on a cotton swab. The swab is then applied on an area thought to contain blood. The second step is to put a drop of phenolphthalein on the swab. A "false positive" results if the swab turns pink, and no further tests are necessary. If the swab does not turn pink, a drop of hydrogen peroxide is put on the swab. The test is positive for blood if the swab immediately turns pink. However, this test does not distinguish human from animal blood (Bugliosi 1996; O'Hara and O'Hara 1994).

POLY LIGHT

A poly light is an alternate light source used to study stains. It produces wavelengths that cause certain chemicals to glow. Seminal stains, saliva, and urine are some of the stains a poly light will reveal as a glow or fluorescence. Although a poly light does not identify a stain as specifically urine or saliva, it indicates which stains require further study. An acid phosphatase test, for example, can confirm that a particular stain is semen (Cox 1998).

POLYGRAPH

When a polygraph (lie detector) test and a homicide suspect meet certain conditions, the test is valid well over 90 percent of the time. Not everyone, however, meets the conditions that qualify a person to take a polygraph test. Exceptions include persons who are extremely angry, women who are over three months pregnant, individuals who are seriously mentally ill, people who are seriously mentally deficient, individuals afflicted with severe pain, prisoners on death row, and persons with a heart condition unless they have written permission from a doctor. This is because a polygraph examiner cannot obtain realistically accurate results from a polygraph test administered to a person who has a psychological or physiological pathology (or a condition that causes intense physiological changes, such as pregnancy). The suspect should be asked in a positive way to take the test. The examiner should introduce him or herself, explain the test procedure, and then establish a certain rapport with the suspect. The polygraph examiner assumes that the person he or she examines experiences certain physiological changes in response to questions and that the polygraph, a scientific diagnostic instrument, reveals to the examiner when the examinee lies.

Breathing, blood pressure, pulse rate, and galvanic skin response reflect changes when a person replies "no" to questions when the correct response is "yes." It is fear of detection, not guilt, which causes the physiological changes measured by a polygraph. The examiner can, in order to eliminate false confessions, ask the suspect questions only the real killer and police can truthfully answer.

The more familiar the examiner is with the crime scene and other aspects of the homicide, the more qualified he or she is to formulate a variety of questions to ask the examinee. Only the examiner and the person being examined should be in the examination room during the examination.

A person may be emotionally drained after committing a homicide. This person should not take a polygraph test the day the homicide was committed because the polygraph may not accurately reflect any emotional response. There should be at least one day between the time the suspect was questioned by detectives and the time the suspect is given the polygraph test. If the suspect is examined immediately after being questioned by investigators, the polygraph may indicate misleading responses. Overly erratic emotional responses may be too difficult for the examiner to interpret.

The suspect should be told to do certain things the day before the examination: get a good night's sleep; continue to take, if applicable, prescribed medication; not wear any bulky clothes; eat a light meal; and not rush to the examination. Anyone who has contact with the suspect on the day of the examination should not say or do anything to upset the suspect.

A polygraph examination must be repeated approximately 10 percent of the time. The examiner can give an opinion 95 percent of the time regarding the truthfulness of the examinee's replies. For example, O. J. Simpson denied on tape killing his wife, Nicole, and her friend, Ron Goldman. To test the truthfulness of this claim, the television program *Hard Copy* hired Ernie Rizzo to test the stress in Simpson's voice. Rizzo used a lie detector called the psychological stress evaluator. Police and the military also use this instrument. Rizzo stated the lie detector indicated Simpson was lying. On the other hand, the tabloid the *Globe* had the same tape analyzed by Jack Harwood, who used Verimetrics, a different type of lie detector. Police also use Verimetrics. According to Harwood, Simpson did not commit the murders (Bunn 1996; James 1991; Murphy 1980).

SODIUM AZIDE

Sodium azide is a crystalline solid that is either white or colorless. It is soluble in water, highly toxic, and decomposes when heated. Like EDTA, it is added to blood to preserve it for analysis (*Concise* 1996; *Hawley's* 1993).

17

Persons of Interest (POI), Perpetrators, and Pyromaniacs

A person of interest (POI) is not immediately considered a suspect; however, he or she may exhibit suspicious behavior regarding a homicide. A POI initially may not have the means, motive, and opportunity to commit a homicide, whereas a perpetrator has all three. A pyromaniac may set a fire, send in the alarm, and then return to the scene as an onlooker. The pyromaniac may ask questions or offer conjecture specific to the cause of the fire. In this chapter, we explore eighteen aspects of suspect behavior.

DIXIE CUPS

Higher-ranking members of street gangs assign lower-ranking members to do certain things, such as commit murders. The lower-ranking members, known as "Dixie cups," are literally disposable as far as higher-ranking members are concerned.

The Homicide Investigation Unit (HIU) in New York successfully prosecuted street gangs by working with Dixie cups. This unit, composed of detectives and prosecutors and headed by assistant district attorney Walter Arsenault, plea-bargained with Dixie cups for information. Numerous informants were paid in cash. As a result, one drug gang called the Jheri Curls was convicted of multiple counts of murder (Toobin and Croce 1994).

LINEUP

The lineup is one procedure that police use to identify the suspect in a crime. A witness discreetly views, through a one-way window, a group of individuals who look similar. The lineup allows the witness to identify the suspect without being influenced by police to focus on a particular person in the lineup. A lineup should not be used if the witness knows the suspect and recognized the suspect when the crime was committed.

At least six individuals, one of whom is the suspect, are brought into the lineup room. Neither the investigator nor the lineup participants say or do anything to reveal which of the participants is the suspect. All the lineup members look similar in terms of race, sex, height, and other characteristics.

Before the investigator and witness enter the room, the suspect should be allowed to choose where to stand in the lineup. Furthermore, before the investigator and witness enter, the witness is told the suspect may not be in the lineup. Moreover, the witness is instructed not to, in any way, indicate a decision. Although the witness can indicate a selection on a form, the witness must not discuss the selection with anyone until the witness and investigator have left the room. The investigator decides when, how, and where to inform the suspect about the witness's selection.

The lineup participants do not talk in the lineup room, unless requested to, by the investigator. Before the witness enters the room, the members are told if they have to demonstrate certain characteristics or behavior, for example, wear hats or walk in a certain way. If the witness wants the lineup members to perform a certain action, the witness quietly asks the investigator.

When there is more than one witness, each witness, with the assistance of the investigator, attempts to identify the suspect. Only after this, two or more witnesses are permitted to confer with each other. When a suspect's attorney is present at the lineup, the attorney is there only as an observer. The attorney is not permitted to in any way take part in, modify, or influence the lineup (O'Hara and O'Hara 1994).

LINEUP STAND-INS

Lineup stand-ins are individuals who look like suspects. New York Police Department (NYPD) homicide detective Carolann Natale needed individuals for lineups. She and her partner drove, during the late 1970s, through the Times Square area. They looked at the crowds for appropriate people. These people resembled a suspected killer and a material witness. Natale and her partner called out to men who drank from pint bottles concealed in paper bags or men who milled in front of peep shows. The two detectives got what they wanted by driving cooperative men to the Midtown North Precinct on West Fifty-fourth Street, then, after the lineup was over, driving the men back to Times Square. The men who cooperated were motivated by a cash payment of $5.00. There was a five-dollars-for-five-minutes agreement for them to act as lineup stand-ins (Hirschfeld 1982).

ERNESTO MIRANDA

Ernesto Miranda was arrested, in March 1963, for raping and kidnapping an eighteen-year-old woman. The victim identified Miranda in a police lineup. Police questioned him for two hours. During questioning, however, Miranda was not told he had the option of remaining silent or having a lawyer present. He confessed and was convicted, but then appealed. The U.S. Supreme Court in *Miranda v. Arizona* (1966) reversed the conviction. Because of the ruling, suspects must be clearly informed of their rights before being questioned by police. Otherwise, their statements are not admissible in court. In 1972, in Phoenix, Arizona, Miranda was killed in a skid row card game.

Immediately after the *Miranda* ruling, homicide clearance rates in New York began to decline sharply. The average rate of clearing homicides in New York for the years 1960 through 1965 before *Miranda*, was 87.6 percent. The highest clearance rate was 90.2 percent in 1962; the lowest clearance rate was 83.3 percent in 1965. This occurred although the number of homicides had increased from 390 in 1960 to 634 in 1965.

Miranda had been in effect for six months at the end of 1966. During that time, the homicide clearance rate in New York dropped to 78.1 percent and continued to decline each year through 1972. The rate was 68 percent in 1969 and 56.7 percent in 1972. In other words, the rate dropped 26.6 percent between 1965 and 1972 (Berg and Horgan 1998; Gelb 1975).

MODUS OPERANDI (MO)

The expression "modus operandi" (MO) means "method of operation." A criminal typically commits a crime according to an identifiable MO. An MO is learned behavior that is established while a criminal committed a crime. A criminal uses a particular MO because it enables him or her to reach certain objectives.

Police, through MO files, know when the same method of operation was used to commit two or more crimes. An MO file might contain information about a rapist-murderer who, every time he raped and then murdered a victim, left the body lying on its side and facing a particular direction. The first person to develop an MO file was August Vollmer, a police training and management reformer and former chief of police in Berkeley, California (Douglas 1992; Keppel and Birnes 1997; McArdle and McArdle 1988; Salottolo 1970).

OFFENDER BEHAVIOR AT CRIME SCENES

There are three general categories of offender behavior demonstrated at crime scenes: disorganized, organized, and a combination of disorganized and organized.

The disorganized offender is a loner who may be mentally retarded or psychotic. This person may not wash or change his clothes for days. He acts out because of anger, drugs, or alcohol, and he spends little or no time planning his crime. His victim may be a relative, a friend, or an acquaintance. The disorganized offender uses any available weapon. He leaves the victim's body at the crime scene and makes little or no effort to conceal the body. This killer often leaves the weapon at the crime scene, which is likely within walking distance of where he lives or works. If this individual is not apprehended, he may evolve into an organized offender.

James Odom and James Lawson, Jr., convicted rapists, illustrate the behavior of disorganized offenders. They met as inmates at a mental institution in California. After their release, they got together in South Carolina, where they abducted a female convenience store clerk at gunpoint. In an isolated location, Odom raped the clerk and Lawson cut her throat, then he mutilated her dead body. The body was easily discovered, and within days the two killers were arrested.

The organized offender appears to other people to be good-natured and well intentioned. He is extroverted, articulate, and often very concerned with his appearance, but he is also self-centered, deceitful, manipulative, and deliberate. This offender has his own weapon and means of restraining the victim, such as a rope, and usually kills someone who cannot be directly linked to him. He attempts to conceal the victim's body and avoids leaving fingerprints and body fluids at the crime scene. He removes evidence, including shell casings, when he leaves the scene. Although he kills in one location, he transports the dead victim to another location for disposal. This offender is not necessarily concerned if the victim's body is discovered, but he can be very excited about publicity regarding the victim and the impact of the murder on the community.

Edmund Emil Kemper, III, an organized offender, murdered his grandparents in 1963 when he was fourteen, spent seven years in a maximum security hospital in California, then, in 1969, was released into his mother's custody. Within nine years of his release, he killed eight more people: six female hitchhikers, his mother, and a friend of his mother. Kemper, who purportedly had an IQ of 131, spent months planning the murder of the six female hitchhikers, students at the University of California, Santa Cruz. He used an affable persona when he approached the first coed. On April 2, 1973, as his mother slept, he bludgeoned her with a hammer, sawed off her head, had sex with her body, and cut out her larynx. He used her severed head for dart practice. Patient and attentive to detail, Kemper never left a crime scene in disarray. He was in Pueblo, Colorado, when he called Santa Cruz police several times and waited to be arrested. At first, Santa Cruz police did not believe that he was a killer. It was Colorado police, who, at the request of Santa Cruz police, responded to Kemper's call and arrested him. Kemper's motive for turning himself in appeared to be that he did not enjoy being free. He received seven life sentences in Vacaville State Prison in California.

John Douglas and Robert Ressler of the FBI's Behavioral Science Unit (BSU) saw the need for a third category regarding types of offender behavior at crime scenes. The third category applies to crime scenes and offenders that have a combination of organized and disorganized characteristics. Ted Bundy was usually cunning, cautious, and methodical when he killed. However, on Super Bowl Sunday, 1978, he spontaneously committed murder. He killed two sleeping coeds and injured two others at the Chi Omega sorority house at Florida State University in Tallahassee. Then on February 9, 1978, he abducted twelve-year-old Kimberly Diane Leach from her junior high school, cut her throat, and left her body under a shed. Bundy was arrested several days later while drunk and driving a stolen car (Levin and Fox 1991; Michaud and Hazelwood 1998; *Murder* 1991; Vorpagel and Harrington 1998).

PERSON OF INTEREST (POI)

A person of interest (POI) differs from a suspect because no information links a POI to a specific crime. A POI is investigated for various less important reasons, including that a POI looks like a suspect, drives a car similar to a suspect's car, has a violent criminal history, frequents a specific crime scene area, or is reported to police by someone who is suspicious of the POI, such as a friend or relative (Henderson 1998).

PERSONATION

Unusual behavior not necessary to commit a crime is called personation. The perpetrator committing his or her first homicide kills a victim, then leaves the crime scene. The perpetrator of a second homicide, however, kills a victim but does not leave the crime scene until certain other things are done. The perpetrator of the second homicide engages in unusual behavior that comprises personation. This perpetrator, if the victim was a woman, might insert the woman's umbrella into her vagina. Alternatively, this perpetrator might defecate near the body. He or she attributes unique meaning to the crime scene that only he or she understands (Douglas 1992).

PYROMANIAC

A pyromaniac, also known as a "firebug," is a person who is compelled to impulsively start fires; experiences sensual pleasure from this activity; and, unlike an arsonist, does not have a motive, least of all insurance money. A pyromaniac generally sets small fires, possibly along a daily route, for example, a route to a local store. This person uses matches rather than a time device. Any place the public has access to, such as an alley or hallway, is of potential interest to the pyromaniac. Cellars and storage areas in isolated parts of buildings are also of interest.

A pyromaniac likes to set fires after dark and, unless apprehended, sets an increasing number of fires of increasing danger. This individual may exhibit pyromania by first setting a fire in a field, then setting another fire in a vacant building, then setting another fire in a building in which there are people. Although an arsonist may choose to set a fire in a building when there are people in it, a pyromaniac does not care either way. The fire itself is the only important thing.

Typically, a pyromaniac sets a fire, leaves the scene, then returns when fire engines and a crowd are present. The pyromaniac may also play the role of a hero by dialing 911 to report the fire. There may be an excited or dazed look on this person's face. The eyes may appear glassy.

Photographs of the fire and crowd may reveal a known pyromaniac. These photographs, when compared to photographs of other fires, may reveal unknown persons who are present at numerous fires. Often a pyromaniac has an orgasm while setting or watching a fire. Theft of women's clothing in a particular neighborhood may be associated with a fire set by a pyromaniac in that neighborhood.

A pyromaniac may carefully observe an investigator who questions people at a fire scene. This pyromaniac may avoid coming into contact with the investigator or may ask the investigator questions about the fire, hoping to find out how much the investigator knows (Fitch and Porter 1968; Redsicker and O'Connor 1997; Schultz 1978; Weston, Lushbaugh, and Wells 2000).

SHOW-UP

When the suspect in a crime is stopped by police at the scene of the crime or near the crime scene, and a witness confronts the suspect in the presence of police, this confrontation is known as a "show-up."

It is usually preferable to have a suspect identified in a lineup because a lineup is fairer to the suspect than is a show-up. A lineup, however, is not always practical, especially when there are several or more suspects. Detaining several or more suspects involves detaining innocent individuals. A show-up is also preferable to a lineup when a seriously injured victim may die and there is not enough time to arrange a lineup.

At the scene of the show-up, the suspect if possible should not be in handcuffs because this can prejudice the witness. The role of the investigator is to have the witness state that the suspect is or is not the perpetrator. The investigator should not discuss with the witness the circumstances of the suspect's arrest, nor should the investigator comment on the identification while the suspect or witness is present (O'Hara and O'Hara 1994).

STAGING

Serial and other criminals try to avoid capture by altering crime scenes. This attempt to deceive police about what actually occurred is called staging.

Criminals do not always do staging. A family member without a criminal record will sometimes stage a crime scene to protect a family member who is a victim. This staging is done to avoid embarrassing the victim and the surviving family members. A rape-murder at home is a location where a crime scene might be staged. This is done to decrease the amount of pain experienced by the survivors.

As another example, the victim of an autoerotic fatality is frequently nude or dressed in female clothes when discovered by a family member. This victim may be undressed, then dressed in male clothes, to spare the rest of the family from embarrassment and pain, before police are called.

Investigators at this type of death scene should look for eye bolts in the ceiling or worn spots caused by rope on beams. These observations help investigators determine precisely what occurred (Douglas 1992; Douglas and Olshaker 1995; Keppel and Birnes 1997; Ressler and Shachtman 1992).

STAGING ERRORS

The perpetrator who stages a crime scene is more likely than not to make mistakes that investigators will notice. This perpetrator, unintentionally, will do things that do not make sense to investigators.

The surroundings will not accurately reflect what investigators know from experience defines a particular crime scene.

If an "intruder" enters a house and kills the wife and children, then escapes without seriously harming the husband, investigators become suspicious. In the absence of life-threatening injuries, it appears the husband may be the "intruder" (see the Jeffrey MacDonald case, chapter 18). If a person slips in a bathtub, hits his or her head, and subsequently drowns, investigators become suspicious if the autopsy reveals multiple injuries to the decedent's head. In such a case, a homicide was made to look like an accident. If a woman is found dead and her dress is pulled up, implying sexual assault, but an autopsy indicates no evidence of sexual assault, investigators become suspicious. Someone who knew the woman, rather than a stranger, would carry out this type of action to make the homicide appear to be a random crime (Douglas 1992).

STALKERS

Most stalkers are men, and many have a history of inadequate heterosexual relationships. These individuals, obsessed with their victims, dwell on fantasies of romantic involvement.

Stalkers usually want to possess their victims. During the early stages of stalking, they attempt to contact the person they "love" by means of telephone calls, regular mail, or e-mail. Some stalkers follow their victims on foot or by car. These stalkers may secretly watch their victims. They sometimes confront victims and attempt to give them a present or attempt to physically prevent them from leaving a place.

Stalkers who are reserved may state they merely want to talk. Stalkers who are aggressive may use obscene language or threaten to harm victims or their families. It is virtually impossible for victims to reason with stalkers because stalkers are delusional and have their own logic. Some of these individuals are psychotic.

In 1990, California was the first state to pass antistalking legislation. This was primarily because of lobbying by celebrities. Actress Theresa Saldana was stalked, then stabbed multiple times, in 1982, by Arthur Richard Jackson, who became obsessed with her after seeing her in the movie *Raging Bull*. In 1989, actress Rebecca Schaeffer was shot dead by Robert John Bardo. She had starred in the television series *My Sister Sam*. Bardo videotaped every episode, had photographs of her, and sent more than forty letters to her (Laird 1992; Shillington 1993).

SUSPECT'S GUILT OR INNOCENCE

There is a widespread belief, commonly held by homicide detectives, that it is usually easy to distinguish between an innocent person charged with homicide and a guilty person charged with the same crime. When these two individuals are questioned, their behavior will be quite different. The innocent person will protest his or her innocence, will worry, and may cry. The guilty individual will be very relaxed, will be nonchalant, and will easily fall asleep. People who fake innocent behavior often anticipate questions that detectives will ask and provide answers that have too many details. Detectives sense that these individuals have rehearsed their answers (Appleby 1998).

UNDOING

A perpetrator engages in undoing, a form of personation, when the victim is closely associated with the perpetrator or the victim represents to the perpetrator a significant person. A family member, an extramarital lover, or a friend is typically a significant person. A son who kills his mother, then attempts to make her appear as if she is still alive, illustrates undoing. The son might wash his mother's body, dress her in clean clothes, then position her on a couch in such a way as to make her appear as if she is sleeping. Undoing occurs because a part of the killer cannot or does not want to accept that the victim is dead. The killer may give the impression to others, or state directly to others, that the victim is still alive. If the killer leaves the body in an extremely dry and hot location, the body will mummify in about a year and will remain mummified for years if it is not disturbed (Bennett and Hess 2001; Douglas 1992).

WANT

On August 9, 1969, five people were found murdered at 10050 Cielo Drive in the Bel-Air section of Los Angeles, California. The victims were Voytek Frykowski, Abigail Folger, Jay Sebring, Steven Parent, and actress Sharon Tate Polanski.

Although there were four vehicles in the driveway, there should have been one more, Sharon Tate's Ferrari. Since it was possible the perpetrators could have escaped in the Ferrari, police broadcasted a "want." The car was to be located and examined regarding the homicides. The police later learned that the perpetrators were members of the Charles Manson crime family (Bugliosi and Gentry 1974).

WORKING OFF A BEEF

The informant who makes a deal with police by giving them information to have charges dropped or a sentence reduced is said to "work off a beef." The vast majority of informants do this. Informants can be relied on repeatedly if they are treated properly, paid when money is a part of the deal, and have their identity protected.

Although informants can provide police with extremely valuable information, informants, if not effectively controlled, can bring about deadly situations. In 1994, in Massachusetts, career criminal Henry Marshall was released from prison as an informant for the FBI. Three months after Marshall was released, he violated his parole, and during the robbery of a tavern in Washington, he killed tavern owner Dennis Griswold.

Still, the importance of informants cannot be emphasized enough. Manny Mata, a Los Angeles Police Department (LAPD) officer, and his partner, Tony Perez of the U.S. Marshals Service, worked together on a special assignment. In 1984, they arrested thirteen homicide suspects in less than six weeks. This was accomplished primarily because of information provided by informants. The informants and suspects were Cuban criminals who came to the United States in 1980 during the Mariel boatlift (Katel 1995; Sabbag 1992).

YELLOW SHEET

Yellow paper has been used to record criminal charges. Although official arrest records are still referred to by some police officers as yellow sheets, yellow sheets today are more likely to be white computer printouts (Ryan 1995; Wallance 1981).

18

Case Profiles

A case profile summarizes the events and circumstances leading up to, and the evidence collected during, the investigation of a crime. Throughout past decades, it has been demonstrated that perpetrators follow repeatable and often predictable patterns. Police databases contain thousands of case profiles, listing modus operandi (MO), aliases, and signatures of known and unknown perpetrators, which are used to profile current suspects. In this chapter, we review twenty-two case profiles collected over six decades.

BELT PARKWAY CASE

New York Police Department (NYPD) Lieutenant Vito DeSerio was driving on the Belt Parkway in Brooklyn, New York, on Friday morning, July 8, 1967. His destination: the 122nd Squad on Staten Island. It was 08:40 and in front of him was a Camaro, its driver a teenage girl.

At Plum Beach, the Camaro, without signaling, moved toward the center lane. It crossed the center and service lanes and stopped in bushes bordering the parkway.

When DeSerio approached the Camaro, the girl was moaning, her head slumped forward. Her eyes were rolled back. He saw the name "Nancy McEwen" on her license. She was from Garden City, Long Island. There was nothing in her wallet to indicate a medical condition and no marks on her body.

Fifteen minutes later, an ambulance took her to Coney Island Hospital, where doctors were unsuccessful in reviving her. However, they noticed a small hole, with no blood, on the left side of McEwen's head. Her hair had obscured the hole.

Albert Seedman, deputy chief inspector of Brooklyn South Detectives, arrived at the crime scene in thirty minutes. The death of Nancy McEwen had an odd twist. Seedman had a talent for solving odd-twist cases.

All the windows of the Camaro, except the left rear window, were up. There were no glass fragments. The bullet had to come from the Sheepshead Bay side of the Camaro. The shooter could have shot McEwen from reeds that slope down to Plum Beach or from a boat on the bay. A hunter may have been in the reeds and dunes, hunting rabbits, pheasants, or ducks, and a stray bullet from the hunter's gun may have hit her.

Seedman ordered members from emergency services and ballistics to find the shell casing by searching the beach and dunes. Patrolman Brockstein from the Sixty-first Precinct told Seedman that just after dawn, while routinely checking the Plum Beach parking lot, he saw on a dune a beautiful, well-dressed woman, holding a shotgun. Another woman and a man were nearby. They had cameras. Brockstein learned that all three individuals were photographing a fashion layout. The shotgun, a double-barreled .410, was being used as a prop by the model who was holding it. Brockstein confirmed the firing chamber was empty, noted the license plate number of the photographer's car and the license plate number of another car being polished by two Puerto Ricans, then Brockstein left to continue patrol.

George Heffernan, a tow truck driver who regularly worked out of the parking lot, told detectives he saw the model and photographers at approximately 08:45. Detectives used the license plate number of the photographer's car to identify the photographer as James Brooks of Manhattan. Brooks stated he and his wife, who worked together, borrowed two shotguns from Abercrombie and Fitch. Detectives did not smell any freshly burned powder when they examined the shotguns at the Brooks residence.

Although Seedman knew McEwen did not die of a shotgun blast, he was still suspicious of Brooks and his wife. McEwen died 200 feet from the model. Brooks or his wife could have accidentally killed McEwen with a third gun, then disposed of it. The model, Yaffa Turner, of the Eileen Ford Agency, voluntarily came to the Sixty-first Squad Office. She mentioned her agent had a rifle. Detectives investigated, but there was no sign that the rifle had recently been fired.

The Kings County Medical Examiner reported, on Saturday morning, the bullet removed from McEwen's head was a .318-caliber bullet. It was copper-coated and steel-jacketed with a left twist, two lands, and grooves. Seedman sent a ballistics technician with the bullet to the FBI lab in Washington, D.C., for the FBI's opinion.

The search teams on Plum Beach, looking for the bullet's shell casing, did not find it all weekend. On Monday, an ordnance team from Fort Monmouth, New Jersey, used special metal detectors to search for the shell casing, but did not find it.

The next morning, Tuesday, Seedman was in a helicopter over Fort Tilden where he saw a shooting range. The Army stated, and detectives later confirmed, that no one had used the range on the previous Friday.

At McEwen's funeral, the same day, detectives questioned a nervous young man who they determined was a friend of McEwen's anxious to return to work. In addition, on Tuesday, the FBI concurred with the NYPD ballistics finding, adding the bullet that killed Nancy McEwen was fired from an Enfield .303 rifle. Attempts to track down recent sales of Enfield .303s and suitable ammunition were unsuccessful. A hot line was just as unsuccessful. Arrest records, spanning the last five years, in which an Enfield may have been mentioned, were not of any use.

Seedman ordered detectives to canvass every door in Brooklyn to find the owner of the Enfield. There were 3 million people in Brooklyn. Seedman's detectives were astounded. Seedman chose, as the starting point, Knapp Street, north of the Belt Parkway, a mile ahead of where McEwen's Camaro went off the road. Next morning, fifty detectives began the canvass.

In the 2700 block of Knapp, detectives came across Theodore DeLisi, forty-six, the owner of an Enfield. He explained he had been in his boat, off Rockaway Beach, fishing for bluefish. He planned to shoot at sharks that interfered with his fishing. To practice shooting, DeLisi fired twice at a beer can, hitting it the first time, missing it the second time. The second bullet went north across Rockaway Inlet. This bullet passed through the open window of the Camaro and struck McEwen in the head. If the window had been up like all the others, the bullet, by this time, may not have had enough momentum to break the glass and lodge itself in McEwen's head.

Theodore DeLisi was charged, on July 18, 1967, with homicide and discharging a rifle within city limits. Although the homicide charge was subsequently dismissed, DeLisi was fined one hundred dollars on the rifle charge.

The death of Nancy McEwen was ironic. At one time, DeLisi and McEwen lived close together in Whitestone, northern Queens. When she was younger, he often waved to her on his way to work. Although Brooklyn is 240 square miles in size, Albert Seedman knew, somehow, by placing his finger on a map, where to find the solution to this case. He had narrowed down the canvass to one particular block. Detectives who knew Seedman had again seen him demonstrate his unique talents (Seedman and Hellman 1974).

ROBERT A. BERDELLA

Chris Bryson, twenty-two, was married, a high school dropout, a father, and a hustler. At approximately 01:00, Tuesday morning, March 29, 1988, Bryson got into a Toyota Tercel hatchback in downtown Kansas City, Missouri. Robert A. Berdella, thirty-nine, was the driver of the Tercel. Berdella grew up in Cuyahoga Falls, Ohio, and had moved to Kansas City in 1967 to study art.

Bryson was ready to party. He thought there would be sex and drugs. He felt he might earn extra money for his sexual services. Bryson was pleased that Bob (as Berdella had introduced himself) and he were going to Bob's house rather than to a sleazy hotel or lot. On their way to 4315 Charlotte Street, Berdella offered Bryson a beer. There was a cooler in the backseat and Bryson readily accepted the offer. At Berdella's house, Bryson had another beer and smoked a cigarette. Bryson agreed to go upstairs with Berdella, where there was a couch and television.

At the top of the stairs, Bryson fell to the floor as Berdella, who was behind him, struck him in the head with an iron pipe. From this moment on, Bryson was a prisoner and sex toy for Berdella. Bryson was kept tied up, spending most of his time in bed. He was beaten, injected with animal tranquilizer and drain cleaner, shocked with electricity, and sodomized. Berdella took pictures with a Polaroid 600 camera of the torture and kept notes in a stenographer's notebook. The notebook contained details about his sexual acts, torture methods, and names of drugs injected into his human sex toys. Berdella told Bryson to cooperate because in the past he had killed uncooperative people.

At approximately 10:30 on April 2, 1988, while Berdella was out of the house, Bryson managed to untie his wrists and feet. Naked, he escaped from a second-floor window. A water department meter man across the street asked a neighbor to call police.

During the subsequent investigation of Berdella, luminol was used to detect hidden bloodstains. Luminol, introduced in 1937 by Dr. Walter Specht of Germany, can reveal blood that has been wiped or washed away. The reaction of luminol to peroxidase in blood hemoglobin produces a blue-white luminescent glow. The darker the setting in which luminol is used, the brighter the luminescence. A plastic spray bottle is used to apply luminol, as a fine mist, to a surface suspected of having hidden traces of blood. The initial glow lasts only a few seconds. More luminol has to be sprayed when photographs are taken for crime lab retention or court proceedings. Luminol does not stain or corrode sprayed articles.

Not everything that becomes luminescent when sprayed with luminol is blood. Luminol also gives false positives. It reacts to various substances, including bleach, certain dyes, and copper compounds. However, it does not react to other bodily fluids, including saliva and urine.

After investigators cleared Berdella's basement of clutter, they sprayed the basement with luminol. The luminol revealed, in one corner, a circular puddle-like shape. There was no indication that anyone had tried to clean up this area. Investigators then retrieved from Berdella's gardening shed two plastic barrels and a plastic bucket. They took the barrels to the relatively dark basement. None of the three containers had any obvious bloodstains. However, sprayed luminol was clearly visible in all the containers.

By the time the investigation was over, investigators found human skulls, pictures of the torture and rape of young men, and an envelope of teeth in Berdella's house. Investigators found a human head buried in his yard.

Berdella had killed, over four years, six young men. He dismembered the bodies, then put the parts in garbage bags, which were later taken away by garbage collectors.

Robert A. Berdella, Jr., sadistic serial killer and former crime watch program participant, claimed he did not know the motive for his crime. Nevertheless, he received life in prison without parole. He died at forty-three (Fuhrman 1997; Hetzel 1990; Jackman and Cole

1992; "Luminol" 1998; Lytle and Hedgecock 1978; O'Hara and O'Hara 1994; Sigma 1998).

ALAN BERG

June 18, 1984, was the last day of Alan Berg's life. Berg, age fifty, was a former lawyer who became a radio talk show host in Denver, Colorado, in 1971. Over the years, the chain-smoking Berg was rude, impatient, abrasive, and irreverent with his callers. Many callers did not like his controversial remarks about religion, sex, and politics. He criticized the Christian religion. He criticized Father's Day. He just as easily enraged the Left as the Right. He insulted and cut off callers. There were death threats against Berg, some resulting from on-air arguments with callers.

Ironically, Berg received, in the late 1970s, awards for being the most disliked and most liked radio personality in Denver. And KOA, Berg's employer, was a powerful radio station. In the greater Denver area alone, KOA had a potential listening audience of 1.6 million. At night, KOA could be heard in thirty-eight states.

Judith Lee Berg was Berg's ex-wife; they were divorced in 1978. She was in Denver on June 18, having arrived from Chicago, Illinois, for her parents' wedding anniversary. She and Berg dined at a restaurant in Lakewood, a Denver suburb. Then Berg dropped her off at the Cherry Creek shopping center in Denver, where her car was parked.

He pulled into his driveway on Adams Street, parked his car, and stepped onto the pavement. A volley of .45-caliber bullets struck him from a distance of approximately six feet, knocking him onto his back and creating thirty-four entry and exit wounds. Police and an ambulance arrived. Berg was pronounced dead at 21:45.

Four months later, the FBI found the murder weapon, a .45-caliber MAC-10 machine pistol. This weapon was at the home of Gary Lee Yarbrough in Sand Point, Idaho. Yarbrough, a member of white supremacist organizations, was arrested. David Lane, Bruce Pierce, Richard Scutari, and Jean Craig, four alleged perpetrators, were charged with violating Berg's civil rights. Investigators chose these lesser charges because they did not have enough evidence to charge the alleged perpetrators with murder and have the charges upheld. After thirteen days of proceedings, Lane and Pierce were found guilty. Scutari and Craig were acquitted. Yarbrough was found guilty of assaulting three FBI agents.

Berg's murder was an example of a hate crime, a crime perpe- trated because of, among other reasons, a victim's race, ethnicity, or religion. Ironically, the topic Berg was to have discussed next day on his show was something that he strongly supported: gun control ("Denver's" 1984; Larson 1994; Levin and McDevitt 1993; Singular 1987; White 1985).

TED BUNDY AND ANN RULE

Ted Bundy was twenty-four and a university student in 1971. He would be forty-two and on death row in Florida in 1989. There he would be executed for multiple murders. Ann Rule was almost forty and a mother of four in 1971. She would be fifty-eight in 1989 and al- ready a best-selling writer of true crime.

Ted and Ann met in 1971 at the Seattle Crisis Clinic. He was a work-study student; she took telephone calls from people in dis- tress. Ted also answered telephone calls and was planning to attend law school. She was working on advancing her career as a freelance writer.

Ann liked Ted almost from the moment she met him. Brilliant, hardworking, sensitive, trustworthy, and patient are some of the words she used to describe Ted. It appeared most people liked Bundy. Ted and Ann were a good team. Both were interested in law. Ann had been a police officer in the 1950s. Both were also interested in psychopathology. Ted was studying psychology at university.

Ann did her volunteer work for four hours once a week from 22:00 to 02:00. Ted was there several nights a week. He walked with Ann to her car when she left at 02:00 because he worked until 09:00 and he did not want any harm to come to her. He stood by until Ann was in her car, the doors were locked, the engine was running, and she was driving away.

Ann stopped doing her volunteer work in the spring of 1972. Her writing career and family took precedence. She saw Ted less fre- quently after this.

To learn later that Ted may have murdered at least thirty-eight young women in Washington, Utah, Colorado, and Florida was in- comprehensible to Ann. Someone like Ted Bundy is not likely to be the prime suspect in a homicide investigation during its initial stages. Everything about Bundy, or an individual with a similar persona, prompts investigators to consider someone else as the most likely suspect. As another example, forensic psychiatrist Park Dietz once spent three days with serial killer Jeffrey Dahmer. Dahmer's outward manner was normal and Dietz did not note anything odd about him.

This can also be said of Ted Bundy (Frank 2000; Rule 1980).

CAREER-GIRL MURDERS

In 1963 Janice Wylie, twenty-one, Patricia Tolles, twenty-one, and Emily Hoffert, twenty-three, were three young women sharing apartment 3-C in Manhattan's Upper East Side. Janice was an aspiring actress working for *Newsweek* magazine, and Patricia was an apprentice researcher working for *Time* magazine. Emily recently moved to New York and was to begin work in two weeks as a teacher. Before moving to New York, Emily was a resident of Cambridge, Massachusetts. She lived near Beverly Samans, a twenty-three-year-old graduate student, living at 4 University Road, who had been murdered by the Boston Strangler on May 6, 1963. Emily was in the process of moving to another apartment.

At approximately 09:30 on Wednesday, August 28, 1963, Janice was alone in the apartment. Usually, she was out during the day. She had planned a trip to Washington, D.C., on this day, but cancelled the trip for financial reasons.

When Patricia arrived home at approximately 17:30 that evening, she unlocked the door to the apartment and entered the foyer. She stopped before walking into the living room. The living room was in disarray. Patricia hurried to the nearby apartment—two blocks away—of author Max Wylie, Janice's father. They returned together to the girls' apartment. Patricia had also called the police. The door of Emily's bedroom was half open. Max pushed the door back with his knee, not wanting to smudge any fingerprints that might be on the doorknob. There were two twin beds in the bedroom. The first bed had been disturbed. The second bed was soaked in blood. The girls were lying close together, side by side, at the foot of the second bed, facing in the same direction, bound with torn bed sheets. Emily, who was dressed, had knife wounds in her neck. Janice, who was nude, had been stabbed in the heart, and was struck in the head with a soft drink bottle, which now lay broken and nearby. She had been eviscerated.

The crime scene was bloody even by investigators' standards. After Dr. James A. Brussel, an army psychiatrist accustomed to the sight of blood, was shown crime scene photographs of the murders, he was unable to eat dinner that evening.

Investigators under the supervision of Chief of Detectives Lawrence McKearney uncovered a number of events. For several weeks, Janice had been receiving obscene telephone calls and veiled threats at work. There was no evidence of forced entry through the apartment door. The perpetrator, after leaving blood smears in the bathroom sink and on towels, apparently left the apartment with clean hands. The perpetrator left two bloodstained kitchen knives in the bathroom sink. One bloodstained knife was left in the kitchen.

According to Dr. Milton Helpern, chief medical examiner of New York, both victims died shortly before noon. There was no indication, in either victim, of any recent sexual activity.

It was assumed that Janice or Emily could have willingly let the perpetrator into the apartment, although the perpetrator probably left through a service door, which Max found ajar when he first entered the apartment. The girls normally kept the service door bolted shut from the inside. Initially, it appeared this crime could have begun as a burglary that escalated into a sadistic homicide when Janice, Emily, or both interrupted the burglar. However, a canvass of all apartments in the building did not reveal any evidence of actual or attempted break, enter, and theft (BET). A detective demonstrated, with a collar tab, how easy it was to open the apartment door without a key by sliding the collar tab along the door jamb.

The vital break in the case occurred eight months later in late April 1964. George Whitmore, a nineteen-year-old, marginally literate black male, confessed to murdering Janice Wylie and Emily Hoffert. Earlier, Whitmore confessed to police that he mugged a young girl and stabbed a Brooklyn woman. Police found a snapshot of Janice Wylie in his pocket. However, according to Dr. Brussel, Whitmore, childish and sloppily dressed, was not the killer. Brussel interpreted multiple stabbing, evisceration, and a finger-created smear down each of Janice's thighs as indicators of ritualistic homicide. Brussel believed Whitmore's confession was phony. Phony confessions to police are common. Individuals who make these confessions are frequently people who secretly wish they could commit the crime. However, their inhibitions, sexual or other, prohibit them from committing the crime.

A few weeks after Whitmore's arrest, he claimed the police forced him to confess by beating him, and he recanted his confession. The National Association for the Advancement of Colored People (NAACP) and the American Civil Liberties Union (ACLU) came to Whitmore's defense. Accusations of police brutality and racial discrimination intensified. The case against Whitmore was dismissed in January 1965, because the defense proved that, on the day of the murders, he was in New Jersey.

On January 26, 1965, Richard Robles, a burglar and heroin addict, was arrested and booked for the Wylie–Hoffert murders. During the fall of 1964, Nathan and Marjorie Delaney, a husband and wife in their thirties who were drug addicts and knew Robles, told police about Robles. Nathan wanted a deal. He would tell police who killed Janice and Emily, if the prosecution would be lenient during his upcoming court appearance on a narcotics charge. The Delaneys became convinced Robles was guilty when Robles, under the influence of heroin at the Delaney's apartment, talked about girls, knives, and blood. The police, with the cooperation of the Delaneys, bugged the Delaneys' apartment and recorded conversations between the Delaneys and Robles. Robles's comments about the murders were incriminating. This heightened police interest in him as the likely killer.

Dr. Brussel felt, once again, police had the wrong person. Brussel perceived Robles as someone who was shy with women, had a weak sex drive, and had no previous record of sexual offenses. In addition, Brussel, as a physician, knew that heroin relaxes the user and depresses the user's sex drive.

While talking with authorities, Robles recounted the following events. He chose at random to burglarize apartment 3-C, claiming he had never before seen Janice or Emily. After he unlocked the door and walked in, he saw Janice, who was nude. Initially, she was surprised, then relaxed. She became friendly and welcomed his presence. After talking briefly, she sexually encouraged him. Robles and Janice consensually engaged in various sexual acts for approximately an hour. Suddenly he was compelled to sadistically stab her. He claimed he killed Emily to silence her after she returned to the apartment. Then he left and hailed a cab downstairs, taking it to the

Delaneys' apartment. However, all of Janice's known male friends stated to police that Janice's alleged behavior, as described by Robles, was incompatible with the Janice they knew.

Richard Robles went on trial in October 1965. Jack Hoffinger, Robles's attorney, requested access to transcripts of conversations between the Delaneys and Robles. Hoffinger believed these transcripts might contain new evidence favorable to his client. When Justice Irwin D. Davidson refused to grant Hoffinger access to the transcripts, Hoffinger argued Robles was being used as a substitute for George Whitmore, who police no longer considered as a suspect. Robles was sentenced to life in prison on December 2, 1965. Nathan Delaney received a suspended sentence for cooperating with police in the arrest and conviction of Robles. As of 2003, Robles was still in prison. The relatives of Janice Wylie and Emily Hoffert continue to lobby that he remain there. After Robles was sent to prison in 1965, Dr. Brussel continued to contend Robles was not the real killer (Brussel 1968; *Crimes* 1986; Frank 1966; Gado 2003; Gaute and Odell 1979; "The Girls" 1964; *New York* 1993).

ESTHER AND RENE CASTELLANI

Rene Castellani, a radio personality, and his wife Esther, a sales clerk, were living in Vancouver, British Columbia, in 1964. In August, their daughter Esther and Esther Sr.'s parents went on a vacation to San Francisco, California. Rene remained in Vancouver because of business reasons.

Several weeks after the vacation, Esther complained about occasionally feeling nauseous. By New Year's, her symptoms included abdominal pain and dizziness. A physician attributed her condition to bad eating habits. In March, Rene telephoned the doctor to tell him Esther was vomiting and had abdominal pains. The doctor treated her for nausea. In May, Esther was again violently ill. The doctor, believing she had an ulcer, placed her on a diet.

On May 23, Dr. Bernard Moscovich, a specialist in internal medicine at Vancouver General Hospital, examined Esther. The next evening, Rene and Esther's mother drove Esther to the Vancouver General Hospital emergency department. From then until early July, her health went from bad to better and from better to bad. Numb and painful hands and feet, burning in the neck, occasional vomiting, and severe diarrhea were among her symptoms. Several specialists concurred she had a viral infection. Her breathing became shallow and rapid and she coughed up mucous. Her heart failed and she died on July 11, 1965. Rene was at her side.

Rene agreed to an autopsy, which was performed by pathologist Frank Anderson. The autopsy confirmed Esther died of heart failure, but for no apparent reason. After Dr. Moscovich studied Esther's medical history, however, he concluded arsenic could have caused Esther's death. When chemist Alexander Beaton conducted toxicology tests on tissues preserved at Esther's autopsy, he discovered one thousand times the expected amount of arsenic.

Vancouver City Police were contacted. Homicide detectives who interviewed Rene found him to be very cooperative.

After Esther's body was exhumed, forensic pathologist Thomas Harmon studied samples of peripheral nerve tissue. He concluded Esther had been slowly poisoned. Eldon Rideout, head of the toxicology lab, analyzed Esther's hair roots, using a procedure called Fisher's method. He concluded someone had been administering arsenic to Esther for approximately seven months. The largest doses were administered while she was in the hospital. The arsenic could not have come from embalming fluid or from the soil in which the coffin was buried.

The ongoing police investigation revealed Rene had been having an affair, since summer 1964, with a female coworker.

Eldon Rideout sent to Norm Erickson, a biologist at the Ontario Center of Forensic Sciences, samples of Esther's complete hairs for neutron activation analysis, a method of dating the ingestion of arsenic. This helped correlate Rene's visits to the hospital with a decline in Esther's health.

Less than nine months after Esther died, Rene applied for a marriage license so he could marry the coworker with whom he was having an affair. Six days later, on April 6, 1966, he was arrested and charged with first-degree murder. He was tried and sentenced to be hanged, but in 1967 the British Columbia Court of Appeal granted a new trial. Two years later, he was found guilty for the second time. By this time, the death penalty had been repealed in Canada. He was paroled in May 1979, remarried, and told acquaintances about having killed Esther. However, he stated she had been terminally ill with cancer and he had committed euthanasia. Five years later, in 1984, Rene died of cancer (Barrett 1994).

MIA CLARK

Although Will Rogers died in 1935, it was in 1940 that his estate provided funding for Rogers House, a home for retired silent film performers. In July 1957, the house burned to the ground. Seventeen residents died, in spite of efforts by firefighters to combat the blaze.

Also in 1957, Nick Lubbock was a forensic technician with expertise in chemistry, physics, and ballistics, and he was head of the central Los Angeles Police Department (LAPD) laboratory. Lubbock disagreed with the fire chief and other individuals who thought the fire at Rogers House was an accident. According to Lubbock, arson caused the fire. The point at which the fire originated was too small and too hot for an accidental cause. The source was designed to start the fire.

Lubbock had a reputation for hunches that paid off. He theorized something innocuous-looking was the source of the fire. This source was in open view in an open common room and could be extremely small and easily overlooked.

Lubbock's file of notes and drawings was three inches thick. He had a reference library and archives in his weekend retreat, a house in southwest Los Angeles. He had information in his archives regarding three other retirement home fires in which residents died. These fires were classified as accidents. Lubbock disagreed, because he saw similarities between these fires and the Rogers House fire. In San Diego, California, nine people had died in a fire in a multistory structure. There was a well-ventilated common room on the second floor. The San Diego fire chief's notes indicated a lit cigarette started the fire. Ten people died near Palm Springs, California. The fire started on the sun veranda, destroying most of the building. A relatively small source was the likely cause of the fire. The third fire occurred in another retirement home near Palm Springs, where a gasoline pump and underground tank exploded. Twenty-four people died in the building. Apparently, the fire started in the day lounge where several people were napping. A fire inspector believed the source of the fire was no longer than an inch. He based his opinion on intense charring on a shelf that otherwise had very little fire damage.

After spending a month investigating the Rogers House fire, Lubbock contacted the lieutenant in charge of homicide at the West Hollywood station. Lubbock told the lieutenant that the common factor

in all four fires was a staff member, Mia Clark, a geriatric nurse. She
was an employee at each of the homes when they burned down. Retirement home personnel records and photographs of staff were
kept together. Lubbock saw the same face, but two different aliases.

With help from homicide detectives Tony Rogan and Phil Hanna,
Lubbock located Mia Clark, but not without difficulty. She had her
mail forwarded from one place to a mailbox, then to another mailbox. The detectives waited at the last mailbox until she arrived to
pick up her mail, then they contacted Lubbock so all three men
could follow the middle-aged woman to her home. She reluctantly
allowed the investigators to enter her sterile-looking house. Rogan
told her about the seeming coincidence that she was present each
time there was a fire at one of the homes. Hanna showed her, from a
distance, a sheet of paper he claimed was a search warrant—it was
not. Rogan asked her questions in the living room as Hanna and
Lubbock searched the rest of the house. In the dining room, where
Clark wanted to watch the search but was kept out of the way by Rogan, Lubbock found in a drawer a cardboard box approximately the
same size as a package of cigarettes. Inside the box was a bottle of
purple crystals, a bottle of glycerin, headache capsules, and a pin.
There was another box with the same contents in another drawer.
Lubbock put the second box in his pocket and left with Rogan and
Hanna. It is a matter of conjecture whether or not detectives in 2003
would, due to legal restrictions pertaining to search and seizure, be-
have like Rogan, Hanna, and Lubbock did.

Rogan, who had contacted police in other states, including Colorado, learned from police in Denver that Mia Clark was a mentally
unstable woman with a criminal record for starting a fire at a retirement home in Denver. There was no apparent motive. Rogan, during the continuing investigation, learned that Clark was a former
high school chemistry teacher.

One day, after a lot of thought, Lubbock emptied a couple of the
capsules, then filled one half of one empty capsule with purple crystals. He put five or six drops of glycerin into another half capsule.
After this, he carefully placed the second half capsule over the end
of the first one. He used a tiny strip of adhesive tape to keep the two
half capsules from coming apart.

Lubbock pushed a pin through the end of the capsule containing
the crystals and into the part containing the glycerin. The glycerin
flowed into the crystals. Approximately ten seconds later, white

smoke followed by intense heat appeared at the punctured end of the capsule.

Mia Clark made it clear she had no intention of being defended in court and that she had nothing further to add. When Lubbock successfully demonstrated in court how to generate the intense heat, using the crystals, glycerin, capsules, and pin, Hanna observed an unusual look in Clark's eyes, and he also saw she was suppressing an urge to laugh. A psychiatrist stated that although Clark was mentally disturbed, she knew right from wrong.

At her trial, which lasted less than a week, she was found guilty of murdering sixty people. Before she could be sentenced, she committed suicide in jail. She had removed all the buttons from her prison dress and stuffed them down her throat, suffocating herself (Miller 1998).

CHRISTINE AND PETER DEMETER

On July 18, 1973, at 21:45 in Mississauga, Ontario, wealthy property developer Peter Demeter, forty, drove up to their house in his wife's Mercedes and stopped in front of the double garage. Their house was located at 1437 Dundas Crescent, a dead-end street on one side of a ravine. Dr. Sybille Brewer, a friend from Hartford, Connecticut; her two German nieces; a Canadian girlfriend of the girls; Viveca, the teenage daughter of a relative of Peter's; and Beelzebub, the Demeter's dog, were also in the Mercedes. They had just returned from a postsupper shopping trip to the Yorkdale Shopping Center approximately twenty-two miles away. Now it was time to go into the house to have coffee and dessert.

As the automatic door slowly opened to reveal the inside of the garage, there, lying on the garage floor in a pool of blood beside the door of the Demeter's other vehicle, a Cadillac, was Christine Demeter, thirty-three, a model and the wife of Peter Demeter.

Peter's immediate reaction was that his wife had a terrible accident. She had fallen, as far as he was concerned, while attempting to retrieve a hose from the garage rafters. Another hose, the hose being used to put water into the swimming pool, was leaking. When he rushed into the house to call police, he found their three-and-a-half-year old daughter, Andrea, in the living room watching TV. When police arrived, Peter was not crying over the loss of his wife. He was impatient and irritable, wanting police to remove Christine's body.

Police Superintendent Bill Teggart and other officers noted the blood on the garage floor was still fresh, having seeped away from the body toward the garage door. With this in mind, they speculated that Christine died shortly before Peter and the others arrived from the shopping trip.

There were specks of blood on the Cadillac's door above Christine's head. This appeared consistent with blood having radiated upward, indicating a weapon had impacted her head. Investigators saw bloodstains on the front seat of the car. Apparently, at one point Christine had been inside the car. There was a defense cut between the thumb and index finger of her left hand and bruises on her thighs, shins, and right knee. The seat of the backless hostess gown she was wearing was covered with grime. This indicated she had been dragged or had struggled. There were no suspicious fingerprints in the garage, but the rear door was ajar. After the house and its contents were examined, robbery was ruled out as the motive.

Police saw this death as a homicide, not an accident, but Peter could not have been the perpetrator. He was, by all accounts, over twenty miles from the scene of the murder when the murder took place. Besides, he had witnesses who could back him up.

Police asked Peter how he hurt his hand. He told them he hurt it fixing the swimming pool filter. However, Dr. Brewer and others told Superintendent Teggart that Peter hurt his hand on the garage door spring, while attempting to fix the door.

The day after Christine died, police bugged Peter's telephones. The same day he hired lawyers. Police monitored and recorded conversations between Peter and his lawyers. Although his defense team hired someone to search for electronic bugs, none were discovered.

The more police investigated, the more they found out about Peter, Christine, and their six-and-a-half-year marriage. Police learned each spouse was insured with a million-dollar insurance policy. Gigi, the Demeter's former maid, told police Peter had a girlfriend, Marina Hundt, twenty-nine, a Viennese model. Gigi left the Demeter household because of the Demeters' marital problems. Peter physically and verbally abused Christine even before they were married.

Before Peter met Christine, he knew Marina in Austria where, in 1965, he first asked her to marry him. On one particular occasion, Peter slapped, choked, and threatened Marina with a gun. Rather than marry Peter, Marina married another man. Yet, in June 1973, Peter spent a week with Marina in Montreal, Quebec. Marina believed Peter was going to divorce Christine.

It appeared to investigators that while Peter was at Yorkdale, he made two telephone calls. One call was to the killer; the other call was to Christine. This call was to give her a reason to go to the garage where the killer was hiding. When confronted by the killer, she could not hide in the Cadillac because its windows were rolled down. She could not drive away because the car battery was dead. The struggle resulted in seven skull fractures and cost her her life.

It was a coincidence that on the day Christine died, Rita Jefferies was walking in Toronto's Yorkville district, when Csaba Szilagyija, her former Hungarian boyfriend, drove by and waved to her. Rita recalled Csaba told her earlier in the year that all he had to do to make a lot of money was to kill Christine Demeter. Csaba knew the Demeters because Peter helped him move to Canada and helped him find work in the late 1960s. Csaba had lived with the Demeters for a year and a half. Rita felt Csaba was boasting about his opportunity to kill Christine, and she had not taken him seriously.

For three or four years, Peter had conversations with Csaba about the feasibility of different ways of killing Christine. Csaba used to interpret Peter's comments as an intellectual game rather than an actual plot. Therefore, when Csaba was approached by police, he agreed to wear a wire so police could monitor and record conversations between him and Peter. Because Csaba did not want Christine dead, the least he could do now that she was dead was to cooperate with police and work against Peter. Csaba had the wire at Christine's funeral on July 23.

On July 16, Peter allegedly had wanted Csaba to prevent Christine and Gigi from spending time together because Christine was going to be murdered that afternoon.

When Peter told Teggart, less than a week after the murder, someone had phoned anonymously and said Andrea was going to be killed next, Teggart played along because he knew, due to the electronic surveillance, no such call was made.

In 1972, Peter had apparently asked Ferenc "Fredi" Stark, one of his construction employees, to arrange an accident in which Christine would die. Stark refused, but told Peter about "the Duck," a

Hungarian whose real name was Imre Olejnyik. The plan was for Christine to go alone to a vacant townhouse owned by Peter located in the east end of Toronto at 52 Dawes Road. Christine would be carrying a roll of architectural drawings containing a $10,000 payment for work done by the man she would be meeting. She would enter the townhouse where the killer, the Duck, would kill her by making her death look as if she fell down a flight of stairs. When this was supposedly going to take place, Peter would be at a meeting at Toronto City Hall. However, the Duck met her outside and took the drawings, telling her he had already seen the townhouse and there was no reason to go inside a second time. The Duck was a crook, thief, and con man, but not a killer.

On August 17, 1973, Teggart arrested Peter. The trial was held in London, Ontario. The case was almost dismissed due to a lack of evidence. For example, there was no murder weapon that could be presented in court.

A few weeks after the trial began, Julius Virag, a Toronto underworld figure, contacted police to say he knew who killed Christine. The killer was supposedly the Duck. Three weeks later, police tracked him down and arrested him. Maria Visnyiczky, his common-law wife, was pleased to cooperate with police, telling them that the Duck in the past had beaten her.

Stark also told police he was approached at a construction site in 1971 or 1972 by Christine and Csaba, who invited him to talk business at the Demeter residence. She was prepared to pay him $3,000 for a rifle, but Stark refused. Apparently, the rifle would be used to kill Peter. Joe "The Tractor" Dinardo, a boxer and enforcer, also testified that Christine offered him $10,000 to kill Peter, but Dinardo, like Stark, refused. Charges against Stark were dropped because he agreed to testify against Peter.

On December 5, 1975, the jury found Peter Demeter guilty. He received a life term, but was eligible for parole in ten years.

By 1983, Peter was given day parole, which entitled him to live in a halfway house in Peterborough, Ontario. He was free during weekdays. At this time, he approached Michael Lane, an ex-convict, of Peterborough and Anthony Preston of Hamilton, Ontario. Peter wanted Lane and Preston to arrange the murder of his cousin, Stuart Demeter, twenty. Stuart was the son of Peter's uncle, Dr. Steven Demeter, who, after Peter's first prison sentence, was made guardian of Andrea, Peter's daughter.

Lane went to police, who fitted him with hidden recording devices. Police found a note with Peter's fingerprints on it in Preston's apartment. The note had fifteen demands, which if met by Stuart's parents, would save Stuart's life. Most of the demands were financial. By 1988, Peter was serving three life sentences for these crimes. Then, in July 1988, he received two more life sentences. These two sentences were given because of a plot by Peter to kidnap and murder the sixteen-year-old daughter of attorney Toby Belman. Belman wanted to freeze some of Peter's financial assets because he failed to pay legal bills resulting from the Stuart Demeter case.

On March 19, 1999, Peter was denied temporary passes from prison by a National Parole Board panel (Barrett 1985; Cox 1988; "'Evil'" 1999; Jonas and Amiel 1977; Jones 1995; "The Trial" 1974).

LOUIS-GEORGES DUPONT

Trois Rivières, halfway between Montreal and Quebec City, Quebec, had a serious crime problem in the late 1960s. Prostitution and municipal politics were part of the problem. Organized crime was a dominant force.

There was a new police commission in Quebec in the summer of 1969. This commission traveled to Trois Rivières to investigate police corruption. Detective Sergeant Louis-Georges DuPont, a police officer with a spotless reputation, testified in secret. The commission concluded that Trois Rivières police were ignoring the prostitution problem. The commission added that Georges Gagnon, head of detectives, was incompetent.

Jean Methot, legal counsel for city hall, approached Detective Sergeant DuPont to investigate an underworld connection with gambling. DuPont, who agreed to look into the matter, left the Trois Rivières police station on November 5. He told other officers he was leaving to work on a case.

Three days later, police contacted the local media to tell them DuPont was missing. Two days later, on November 10, police found him in his unmarked car. He was in the front seat, dead of an apparently self-inflicted gunshot wound to the chest.

DuPont's wife and his two sons, Jacques and Robert, maintained DuPont was murdered, but had no idea who committed the murder. Jacques and Robert began an investigation into their father's death.

There was a suicide note at the scene of the "suicide," but no pen. There was no blood on the car seats. Police removed the car seats, but did not see a bullet hole. Later in the same day police, after being told by pathologist Dr. Jean Houle that there was no bullet in DuPont's body, returned to the car and found a bullet in the front seat. Ballistics experts stated the bullet was severely damaged and could not be matched with DuPont's gun. Yet, the bullet had supposedly traveled through DuPont's body without striking any bones and stopped in a soft car seat. Furthermore, the bullet that killed DuPont was of a different type than the type of bullets in his police-issued revolver. In addition, DuPont's fingerprints were not found on his revolver.

Police told Dr. Houle that DuPont had been depressed.

Although police refused to reopen the case, Jacques and Robert DuPont during their continuing investigation gained access to photographs of their father's autopsy. It appeared their father could have been shot in the back. Dr. James Ferris, a forensic pathologist, at Vancouver General Hospital in Vancouver, British Columbia, indicated that DuPont's clothing was torn outward as if pushed from behind. Pathologist Dr. Lewis Roh concluded DuPont's death was a homicide.

In 1993, the DuPont family asked Claude Ryan, Quebec public security minister, to reopen the case. Ryan asked the Quebec Provincial Police (QPP), who asked Dr. Jean Houle, who had performed the original autopsy. Houle maintained that DuPont's death was a suicide. Then, in 1994 the DuPont family contacted the newly elected Parti Québécois government. Serge Menard, the new minister of public security, asked the QPP for another report. He asked the DuPont family to contact a third independent pathologist. Menard stated he would commission a public inquiry if he came to doubt the death was a suicide.

In December 1995, the Quebec Superior Court ruled in favor of a public inquiry. The inquiry, presided over by Quebec Court Judge Celine Lacerte-Lamontagne and held in Trois Rivières, began on June 18, 1996. On August 16, 1996, Judge Lacerte-Lamontagne ruled that the body be exhumed. Her decision was based on the expert testimony of forensic anthropologist Kathleen Reichs. Reichs stated that a well-preserved sternum might be used to reconstruct gunshot wound trauma. Dr. Michael Baden, former chief medical examiner of New York and an expert witness at the O. J. Simpson trial, acting on behalf of the DuPont family, supervised the exhumation of the body of Detective Sergeant DuPont on August 26, 1996. According to Baden, the fatal bullet entered DuPont's body from the front, traveled through his breastbone and heart, then exited through DuPont's lower back. This investigation, however, failed to determine if DuPont died as the result of suicide or murder (Contenta 1996; Johnston 1996; "Murder" 1996; "One Clean Cop" 1996).

YVONNE FLETCHER

There were police and demonstrators in St. James's Square in London, England, on the morning of April 17, 1984. The police were there to maintain order in front of the Libyan People's Bureau. There was to be a demonstration against the Mùammer Gadhafi regime. The demonstrators were to protest the public execution in Libya, two weeks earlier, of two students from Tripoli University whom Libyan authorities saw as traitors. Approximately seventy demonstrators in London were to carry banners and shout slogans for no more than forty-five minutes.

When the shouting began, two groups of Gadhafi supporters, each numbering approximately two dozen individuals, headed toward the anti-Gadhafi group. Police positioned themselves between the two groups.

At 10:18, the sound of what appeared to be shots was heard. Police were not certain because the Libyans in the past had played recorded sounds of automatic weapons fire. Police officers then saw police officer Yvonne Fletcher lying on the pavement. Their initial reaction was that she had fainted. Then they saw the blood. Just after she was shot in the back, gunfire from inside the embassy wounded eleven demonstrators who were Libyan exiles.

A police sergeant resuscitated Yvonne three times, then at 10:40 she was rushed by ambulance to Westminster Hospital. She never regained consciousness. She died from a bullet wound. The bullet had been fired from a Sterling submachine gun.

Police wanted to search the embassy but could not do this without permission from the Libyans inside the embassy. Furthermore, if police stormed the embassy, this would be a violation of the Vienna Convention. This convention states in part that representatives of a host country cannot enter a foreign embassy in the host country. Furthermore, diplomats are immune from prosecution.

The Libyans were told that diplomatic relations would be terminated. All personnel had to be out of the bureau by midnight, April 29.

The evacuation of the embassy began at 08:47, April 27. A diplomatic bag was used to return the murder weapon and ammunition to Libya. This bag and other bags could not be opened if the British government was to adhere to the Vienna Convention.

Thirty Libyans had left the bureau by 11:00 . Police entered the bureau at 04:10 on April 30, aware the bureau might be booby-trapped, but no booby traps were found. Police found a spent cartridge case, Beretta pistols, Browning pistols, ammunition clips, pistol grips for submachine guns, and ammunition. However, nothing could be done to apprehend the perpetrator of the homicide of police officer Yvonne Fletcher (Ashman and Trescott 1987; Fido and Skinner 1999; Stern 1996).

KITTY GENOVESE

Kitty Genovese, twenty-eight, was a barmaid at Ev's 11th Hour Bar in Queens, New York. On March 13, 1964, she left Ev's at 02:55 and walked to her car, which was parked at the curb.

Earlier she had gone out with a young man by the name of Louis Respo because it was her night off. It had been their first date together. Respo and Kitty had dinner at his brother's home. Later they had a drink at a bar called the Nitecap. Although Respo wanted Kitty to have a last drink at his place, she declined.

At 02:00 he dropped her off at Ev's, where she talked briefly with regular patrons before going to her car. As she headed home, she apparently did not see the small car following her.

Kitty pulled into the parking lot of the Kew Gardens station of the Long Island Railroad. The parking lot was near the rear entrance of a second-floor apartment, above an upholstery shop, that she shared with Marie Lozowsky. As she stepped out of her car, she sensed something was wrong. She began hurrying down the street. Then, in front of a card shop a man wearing an overcoat and hat attacked her with a knife.

Kitty's screams and pleas for help woke up Milton Hatch, who lived in a seventh-floor apartment across the street. Hatch looked down at Kitty and her attacker, and yelled at the attacker to let Kitty alone. The attacker ran to a nearby car, got in, and backed up, stopping in a bus zone in front of Isaac Hartz's house. The car looked to Hartz like a 1960 Rambler.

Kitty was now lying under a street lamp that flooded her with light. People inside apartments, on both sides of the street, were watching her. At 03:20, Kitty got up and slowly walked toward the upholstery shop. As she rounded the corner, Emil Power, looking out of his apartment, saw her stagger. She slipped inside a doorway a few doors from her apartment, and fell on her back in the narrow stairwell.

Ten minutes later, neighbors saw the man in the overcoat return, but this time he was wearing a different hat. He was walking normally, checking different doors. As Emil Power was about to telephone police, his wife told him not to, stating thirty people must have already called.

Neighbor Harold Kline was indecisive about what he should do. Then at 03:55, thirty-five minutes after Kitty's first scream, he called the 102nd Precinct from another neighbor's apartment.

Two minutes later, the first patrol car from the 102nd Precinct pulled into the parking lot, stopping near Kitty's Fiat. At 04:05, detectives Mitch Sang and Mike Pokstis from the 102nd Squad arrived. Kitty's legs were spread apart. She was moaning very softly. Police wondered if she had been raped.

She died in an ambulance en route to Queens General Hospital. It was a few minutes before 05:00. When she was examined at the morgue, she had knife wounds in her back, stomach, chest, right breast, throat, and palms of her hands.

By 07:00, forty detectives and technicians were at the crime scene. An uncooperative potential witness, who was an all-night elevator operator, was taken to the 102nd Precinct station house. After twenty-one hours, he gave his name as Robert Bodec. Bodec was released when he refused to cooperate further. Other neighbors, however, were more cooperative. Thirty-eight people knew what happened to Kitty.

The case began to receive increasing publicity, including a front-page story in the *New York Times* on March 27; *Witness*, a play in San Francisco, California; a CBS special by Mike Wallace called "The Apathetic American"; and a book, *Thirty-Eight Witnesses*, by Abe Rosenthal, *New York Times* Metropolitan Editor.

A train conductor, bus driver, bread deliveryman, pizza parlor employee, and bartenders were questioned. None were of help to investigators nor could investigators find a murder weapon. But when police talked to milkman Tom Daley, he told them he saw a seemingly relaxed young man at approximately 04:00 walk out from behind the stores on Austin Street, where Kitty's apartment was located. Police decided to temporarily keep this information confidential.

As the investigation continued, investigators learned that Kitty was a lesbian. This prompted police to consider the possibility that Kitty was killed by a jealous lover. Jealousy is one of the most common motives for murder. Police experience had shown there is more jealousy in homosexual than in straight romances and an increased likelihood of violence in the former. Several witnesses believed the killer might have been female. Detectives subsequently questioned all the women, mainly gay, Kitty had known.

Detectives checked out every patron of Ev's that they could find who had ever talked to Kitty. No detective in Queens could remember an MO like this one.

On March 18, at 11:00, Dan Fulton, who lived in an apartment in the East Elmhurst section of Queens, became suspicious when he saw a relaxed-looking young man remove a TV from a neighbor's apartment. The man told Fulton he was helping a neighbor move. Fulton saw the man place the TV into the back seat of a 1960 Corvair. Whistling, the man returned to the apartment. Jack Green, a friend of Fulton's, ripped off the distributor cap of the Corvair as Fulton phoned the 114th Precinct. Green returned to his apartment. The young man returned to the Corvair, but left when he could not start it.

At 11:25, Fulton and Green were in a patrol car with patrolmen Daniel Dunn and Pete Williamson. They were looking for the young man when they spotted him six blocks away. When the patrolmen stopped him, he cooperated. After all of them returned to the Corvair, the patrolmen found in it another TV, several small appliances, and pornographic pictures.

The man was identified as Winston Mosely, twenty-nine, of Richmond Hill, Queens. Mosely admitted to detectives at the 114th Detective Squad room that he stole the TVs for resale at his father's repair shop. Mosely appeared to be a calm person. Detective John Tartaglia saw him as an intelligent individual and learned Mosely had held the same job for ten years. Mosely's wife also worked and they owned their own home. This burglary suspect did not come across as a burglar.

When Mosely was questioned further, he confessed to having attacked two women, Suzanne Vernon and Laura Foxx. After Mosely confessed to shooting Annie May Johnson, police did not believe him. Johnson had been stabbed with an ice pick. Mosely insisted convincingly he shot Johnson eight times with a single-action .22-caliber rifle and had not touched her with a knife or ice pick. Johnson's body was exhumed in South Carolina. Mosely's claims were confirmed when the body was X-rayed. Medical examiner John Furey had been wrong about the cause of death. He should have X-rayed the body at the time of autopsy. The bullet wounds at that time looked like stab wounds.

Mosely was arraigned before Judge Bernard Dubin in Queens Criminal Court on March 19, 1964. Mosely went on trial at Queens County Courthouse on May 28, 1964. Sidney Sparrow, Mosely's attorney, claimed Mosely had multiple personality disorder. On June 8, the jury, after eight hours of deliberation, found Mosely guilty. He was sentenced by Judge Shapiro to death in the electric chair three weeks later, but three months later, the state Court of Appeals commuted his death sentence to life imprisonment.

In 1968, Mosely escaped from Dannemora Prison by overpowering two guards in the parking lot of the hospital where he was treated for self-inflicted knife wounds. Before surrendering to police from a suburban house he was holed up in, he raped a hostage. He was later sent to Attica State Prison to be a maximum-security prisoner.

One aspect of Mosely's personality is seen in the following account. Ten minutes after leaving Kitty Genovese to die, he was in his car, waiting for a traffic light to change, when he saw a man asleep in his car, the engine idling. Mosely stopped at the curb, went to the man's car, and gently tapped on the window. When the man rolled down the window, Mosely cautioned him he could die of carbon monoxide poisoning or someone could hurt him.

The man thanked Mosely for his concern. Then Mosely continued on his way home (Rosenthal 1964; Sabljak and Greenberg 1992; Seedman and Hellman 1974).

CINDY JAMES

On June 8, 1989, Gordon Starchuk, a construction worker, was operating a jackhammer in the 8100 block area of Blundell Road in

Richmond, a suburb of Vancouver, British Columbia. He had to uri-
nate; he saw an abandoned house nearby, and approached it
through waist-high grass. Starchuk stopped when he saw someone
sleeping on the ground. He walked closer. What he saw was a dead
woman. Her skin was dry, cracked, and partially skeletonized. Feeling nauseous, Starchuk ran to tell the construction crew he had
found a dead body, probably the body of a missing nurse whose
picture he had seen in newspapers. Royal Canadian Mounted Police (RCMP) investigators Jerry Anderson and Jack Henzie, pathologist Sheila Carlyle, and Simon Fraser University entomologist Gail
Anderson went to the crime scene. Jerry Anderson immediately
recognized the body of Cindy James, a forty-four-year-old nurse
who had worked at the Richmond General Hospital and who had
been missing for two weeks. She had serious psychological problems. While alive, she had been treated by a number of psychiatrists, and she was the ex-wife of psychiatrist Roy Makepeace.

Anderson knew her because of an ongoing investigation. Over
many years, she had been victimized. Cindy was first attacked in
1983 when two men stabbed and strangled her in her garage. Police
did not find the attackers. In 1983, she hired Ozzie Kaban, a private
investigator, to protect her. Over seven years, there were nearly one
hundred obscene telephone calls, threatening letters, arson attempts, attempted break-and-enters, and sadistic assaults directed at
Cindy. In 1988, police found her unconscious in her car. Her hands
were tied behind her back. There was duct tape across her mouth; a
black nylon stocking was tied around her neck.

Cindy was reported missing to Richmond RCMP on May 25 by
her friends Tom and Agnes Woodcock, two weeks before her body
was discovered. The Woodcocks and Cindy planned to spend the
night of May 25 at her house, but when the Woodcocks arrived,
Cindy was not home. Richard Johnston, Cindy's downstairs tenant,
told the Woodcocks that Cindy left the house at approximately 16:00
to go shopping. That was the last time he saw her.

The crime scene was adjacent to a busy street near a major inter-
section. This location was not the usual place a perpetrator would
dump a body, yet there were no signs of a struggle. Cindy's right
knee was partially under twigs and blackberry bushes. Her coat was
nearby and lay neatly spread on the ground. The outer side of the
coat was face down. A killer would not usually do this with a victim's coat. A black nylon stocking was used to tie her hands and legs

behind her back. Investigators observed the ligature could be slipped off easily. There was a black nylon stocking around her neck. This stocking was wrapped once under and twice over her hair. Someone used a sharp knife to cut her blouse. A closer examination of cuts indicated they were starting points for a person who, after making the cuts, then tore the blouse. Although there was a blood-stain on the front of the blouse, there were no underlying wounds. On the side of her right arm, there was a puncture wound, probably caused by a hypodermic needle.

Cindy's car was found parked in the middle of the parking lot at Blundell Center, approximately a mile from the crime scene. Cindy had previously been to this mall and was known by Bank of Montreal employees who worked at a branch office there. Cindy was an extremely cautious person who preferred to park directly in front of the bank. Both her bank machine card and a transaction slip were under the car. Investigators surmised these items were purposely placed there. It was unlikely both the card and slip would be in the same location if they accidentally fell out of Cindy's hand; for example, the slip might have fluttered away from the card. There was blood on the car door. Police did not find anyone who saw or heard a violent struggle in the parking lot, suggesting an injured and bleeding person. Her purse, four bags of groceries, and two sets of keys were in the car, which was locked.

Crime scene investigators speculated that Cindy might have walked from the parking lot to the location where her body was discovered.

When pathologist Carlyle examined Cindy's body at the crime scene, Carlyle believed strangulation was the probable cause of death. During the autopsy on June 9, there was no indication of hemorrhaging in blood vessels in Cindy's neck, indicating she was not strangled. Carlyle did not find wounds corresponding to the cuts and tears on the front and back of Cindy's blouse. The ligatures removed from Cindy's body were sent to Robert Chisnall, a knot expert in Ontario. He concluded that Cindy tied herself up. The preliminary toxicology tests were completed by June 29. Cindy had overdosed on flurazepam (Dalmane), a sedative used to treat insomnia.

On July 11, investigator Jerry Anderson told Cindy's family, the Hacks, her death was not a criminal matter. Although she appeared to others to be in a good mood before her death, Anderson knew, from his police experience, that it is common for depressed people to commit suicide, after they emerge from their depression. In Anderson's opinion, another reason she may have killed herself was because close friends and colleagues on whom she depended for support were leaving on vacation, and she felt abandoned.

Cindy was profiled on *Unsolved Mysteries* and the Canadian public affairs program *W5*. Neither the human and technical resources of the Richmond RCMP, Vancouver police, and media nor Ozzie Kaban could identify Cindy's killer.

The British Columbia Coroner's Service held an inquest in 1990 into Cindy's death. Otto Hack, Cindy's father, welcomed the inquest, held in Burnaby, a suburb of Vancouver. He believed his daughter was murdered and the police investigation had been inadequate. Kaban also believed Cindy was murdered. A jury listened to the testimony of witnesses and tried to decide if her death was a homicide, suicide, or accident.

Certain facts were revealed during forty days of testimony over three months. Gail Anderson, relying on her entomological expertise, stated Cindy's body had been at the crime scene as of June 2 or earlier. Toxicologist Heather Dinn reported that twenty 30 mg tablets of flurazepam or up to eighty tablets of a lower dosage were in Cindy's body. This amount was ten times the lethal dosage. A person, other than Cindy, was not likely to administer this amount. There was also ten times the lethal dosage of morphine in Cindy's body.

Using the same lengths of nylon that were used when Cindy was tied up at the crime scene, Robert Chisnall demonstrated in three minutes how she could have tied herself up. Different psychiatrists gave different explanations for Cindy's behavior. Dr. Paul Termansen said she had hysterical personality disorder. Dr. Wesley Friesen stated she was afflicted with borderline personality disorder with features of post-traumatic stress disorder (PTSD). Dr. Roy Makepeace believed his ex-wife had multiple personality disorder (MPD).

May 25, 1990, the last day of the inquest, was the first anniversary of Cindy's disappearance. The jury could not decide if homicide, suicide, or accident was the manner of her death. The investigation would not be reopened. The death of Cindy James remains much more of a mystery than a "whodunit," or a difficult to solve homicide (Hall 1991; Henderson 1998; Mulgrew 1991).

DIANE NEWTON KING

Diane Newton King was the morning anchor at WUHQ-TV in Battle Creek, Michigan. One day at work, she began receiving telephone calls from an anonymous male. He kept asking her to have lunch with him. She refused. A threatening letter appeared in her mailbox at home. The letter stated she should have accepted the lunch invitation. On another occasion, she was visiting her parents in Sterling Heights, Michigan, near Detroit, when her husband, Brad, called to tell her someone had tried to break into their farm home.

On February 9, 1991, Deputy Guy Picketts was dispatched to 16240 Division Drive in Marshall, Michigan, a small town southeast of Battle Creek. There was unknown trouble and injuries.

This was the King residence.

When Picketts arrived at the scene at approximately 19:00, Diane was sprawled on her back in the driveway near the Jeep Wagoneer she had driven home. There was blood on her nose, her eyes were closed, and her body was warm. There were two small-caliber bullet holes in her body. One wound was in her chest, the other one in her groin. Diane's two young children were in the back seat of the Jeep. They were not injured and were too young to identify a perpetrator. The distraught man in the house was Brad King, Diane's husband and the person who made the call for help.

It appeared an obsessed fan stalking Diane had killed her; something stalkers rarely do. Diane was dead on arrival at Oaklawn Hospital.

During the initial investigation, investigators found a spent .22-caliber rifle casing in the loft of the barn. Brad told police he had been walking in a nearby field at the time Diane was killed. Investigators later found in a nearby creek spent shell casings and a .22-caliber Remington Scoremaster rifle.

From the very beginning of this case, investigators, including lead detective Jack Schoder, as well as friends, acquaintances, and colleagues of the Kings, felt the killer was not a stalker. Many people knew Brad had been married before and during their marriage had been unfaithful to Diane. Diane, a very ambitious and domineering person at home and at work, was also the spouse who earned most of the money for the King household. Brad had difficulty keeping a job. Both had undergone marriage counseling.

Police, friends, and others were puzzled by Brad's seemingly feigned emotions or, at times, lack of expected emotion considering his wife had been murdered. A priest, Father Jim Barrett, also noticed this.

It took nearly a year to build a sufficiently strong case against Brad. He was arrested in Denver, Colorado, on January 30, 1992, and charged with Diane's murder. The former police and probation officer was tried, convicted, and sentenced to life in prison (Hoffman 1994).

CHANDRA LEVY

Chandra Levy, a twenty-four-year-old intern at the Federal Bureau of Prisons, had lived alone since September 2000 in a condominium at 1260–21 Street N.W., Washington, D.C. At approximately 09:30, May 1, 2001, Chandra logged onto the Internet, accessed travel sites, and sent e-mail until approximately 13:00, including an e-mail to her parents, Dr. Robert Levy and his wife Susan in Modesto, California. Her parents expected Chandra home on May 9 to receive a master's degree in public administration at the University of Southern California two days later. After Chandra's parents were unsuccessful in contacting her by telephone between May 1 and 6, they contacted police.

Police officers entered her condominium and found her driver's license, credit cards, checkbook, jewelry, and cell phone. There was no sign of a struggle and her luggage was packed; however, Chandra was not there.

During the early stages of the investigation, police believed there were no typical reasons for Chandra's disappearance, such as an unwanted pregnancy, gambling debt, or the end of a relationship.

While in Washington, one of Chandra's classmates, an intern of U.S. Representative Gary Condit, introduced Chandra to Condit, fifty-three, of Ceres, California, a town near Modesto.

Around May 7, rumors began circulating among Chandra's friends and family that she had an affair with a powerful man in Washington. Condit denied to Chandra's parents and to the media that he was this man. Robert and Susan Levy, and Gary Condit, posted a $25,000 reward for Chandra's return. Condit had also given money in 1993 to help find the man who attacked Karen Mathews, a Stanislaus County clerk recorder, in the garage at her home in Modesto, California.

On June 13, 2001, police went to Condit's apartment to talk with him; they were told it was not a good time. On June 23, 2001, on their second attempt, investigators interviewed Condit. Condit told investigators he last saw Chandra on April 24, a day after her internship at the Federal Bureau of Prisons had abruptly ended. He stated that the last time he talked to her on the telephone was on April 29. He added that he and Chandra met at his apartment to discuss her future. He described Chandra as indecisive and he offered to help her find work. He said that she hoped to again work in California and expressed interest in becoming an FBI agent or going to law school.

In July 2001, a series of events occurred. Anne Marie Smith, a United Airlines flight attendant, told Fox News she had an affair with Condit. Linda Zamsky, Chandra's aunt, told the *Washington Post* that Chandra confided in her about the affair. Condit denied Smith's allegation, but admitted during his third interview with police he did have an affair with Chandra. Abbe Lowell, Condit's attorney, announced Condit passed a private lie detector test that indicated he had nothing to do with Chandra's disappearance. Police used cadaver dogs to search for Chandra's remains in abandoned buildings near her condominium, near Condit's apartment, and along the Potomac and Anacostia Rivers, and in Rock Creek Park in northwest Washington, D.C., but the search was unsuccessful. Condit voluntarily gave a DNA sample to police. Police also looked for a possible link between Chandra's disappearance and the disappearance of Joyce Chiang, twenty-eight, an attorney for the Immigration and Naturalization Service (INS). Her body was located in the Potomac River in April 1999, four months after she went missing. Investigators had concluded that her death was a probable suicide.

Voter sentiment about Condit was changing; in August 2001, the largest newspapers in his district, the *Modesto Bee* and the *Fresno Bee*, called on him to resign.

On May 22, 2002, at approximately 09:30, a man walking his dog in the dense woods inside Rock Creek Park discovered skeletal remains, jogging clothes, running shoes, and a Walkman close to a jogging trail near the western edge of the park. The District of Columbia Medical Examiner's Office used dental records to confirm that the remains were those of Chandra Levy. Levy's remains had been impacted by environmental factors for up to thirteen months. Dr. Jonathan Arden, Washington medical examiner, could not find enough medical evidence to determine the cause of Chandra's death, nor could he determine if Chandra died where her remains were found or if she had been brought to that location from some other crime scene. The medical examiner determined that homicide was the manner of death.

On June 6, 2002, private investigators hired by the Levy family conducted a search in the area of Rock Creek Park where Chandra's remains were found and discovered a human leg bone. Four days later, members of the Washington Metropolitan Police Department (MPD) Mobile Crime Unit and recruits from the Maurice T. Turner, Jr., Institute of Police Science used a grid search and a line search in the area where Chandra's remains were located. Certain bones were not located because wildlife may have moved them.

During the ongoing investigation, Assistant Chief Terrence Gainer and other police officials reviewed other attacks on women in Washington, D.C. Two suspects—Albert Cook, twenty-five, of Rockville, Maryland, convicted of raping and murdering a woman jogger in January 2001; and Ingmar Guandique, a twenty-year-old Salvadoran immigrant convicted in February 2002 of attacking two women joggers near the location of Chandra's remains—could not be linked to Chandra's death.

In late September 2002, detectives came to believe that Guandique could be Chandra's killer even though he passed a lie detector test. This was because a Spanish-speaking interpreter, not a bilingual lie detector technician, had administered the test to Guandique. The interpreter could have skewed test results by improperly translating Guandique's answers and possibly altering the questions during translation. Sheila Cruz, the manager of a building where Guandique lived, told the *Washington Post* that around the time Chandra disappeared, Guandique had injuries to his face, including scratches and a swollen lip. A grand jury has since subpoenaed friends of Guandique.

Condit received much negative publicity and was defeated in March 2002, when he attempted to win the Democratic congressional primary in his district, even though police did not officially consider him a suspect in Chandra Levy's death ("Chandra" 2002; Isikoff

2001; Levy 2002; "Polygraph" 2002; Sbranti 2001; Sbranti and Doyle 2001; "Skeletal" 2002; Smalley, Hosenball, and Breslau 2002).

JEFFREY MACDONALD

The consequences of crime scene investigation are far-reaching. Evidence pertaining to a crime scene may be improperly handled, stored, and documented, leading investigators to focus on false leads. Prosecutors and defense attorneys can be misled and innocent persons may be wrongfully convicted while the real perpetrators get away with murder.

The crime scene at 544 Castle Drive, Fort Bragg, North Carolina, was complicated by the actions of the investigators, over several days, beginning on February 17, 1970. Green Beret Surgeon Jeffrey MacDonald, his wife, Colette, and their two young daughters, Kimberly and Kristen, lived at 544 Castle Drive. At 03:45, Jeffrey Mac-Donald dialed the telephone operator. He uttered the word stabbing and wanted military police and an ambulance dispatched to his home. When military police arrived and checked the front door of the MacDonald home, they found the front door locked and entered through the unlocked back door.

Military Policeman (MP) Kenneth Mica found Colette, twenty-six, in the master bedroom. She was lying on the floor, motionless, on her back with her legs spread. She was partially covered with a blue pajama top. She had been struck with a club and had been stabbed with a knife and an ice pick. The word "Pig" had been written in blood on the headboard of the bed. He found Kimberly, five years old, in another bedroom. She had been struck with a club and had been stabbed with a knife. Kristen, age two, was in a third bedroom. She had been attacked with a club and had been stabbed with a knife and an ice pick. All three were dead.

Jeffrey MacDonald, twenty-six, had been struck with a club and had been stabbed. He was laying unconscious on his stomach his head on Colette's left shoulder when Military Police arrived at the scene. MP Kenneth Mica resuscitated Jeffrey MacDonald, who gave his account of what happened.

Jeffrey MacDonald stated that at approximately 02:00, after watching TV and washing dishes, he walked into the master bedroom.

Kristen, who was sleeping beside Colette, had wet the bed. Not wanting to awaken Colette and change the bed sheets, he carried Kristen to her own bedroom. He then returned to the living room, where he fell asleep on the couch. Later Colette's shouting and Kimberly's screams woke him up. He described the four intruders as "acid heads," three males and a female who were standing beside the couch. One of the males, a black man, carried a baseball bat and wore an army fatigue jacket with sergeant stripes. One of the two white males carried a bladed weapon. A blonde-haired woman wore a floppy hat and carried a candle. She chanted, "Acid is groovy. Kill the pigs." Jeffrey struggled with the intruders and lost consciousness in the living room. When he regained consciousness, he went into the master bedroom and removed a paring knife from Colette's chest, then he gave her mouth-to-mouth resuscitation. The resuscitation was not successful. He used his blue pajama top to partially cover her body. He attempted to resuscitate Kimberly and Kristen, without success. Then he dialed the Fayetteville operator, requested help, then passed out.

MPs did not immediately rope off the crime scene. Neighbors and the media were allowed access to the yard. MP Richard Tevere, one of the first MPs to arrive at the apartment, noted the front windows of the apartment were open. Later the same morning, the windows were closed when crime scene photographs were taken. One MP stated the lights in the girls' rooms were on when he arrived. Another MP stated the lights were off. MP Robert Duffy noticed a bureau drawer was open in the master bedroom. Later that day when photographs were taken, the drawer was closed. Garbage collectors were allowed to empty the trashcans before they could be examined for possible evidence. During the investigation, investigators found blue fibers: eighty-one fibers in the master bedroom, nineteen fibers in Kimberly's bedroom, and two fibers in Kristen's bedroom. Later many of the fibers went missing. A piece of skin found underneath one of Colette's fingernails was lost. The paring knife MacDonald said he had removed from his wife's chest was not the apparent murder weapon. There were no fingerprints on the paring knife and there were no fingerprints on the telephones in the apartment. Howard Page, the Criminal Investigation Division (CID) photographer, did not have a fingerprint camera and lighting equipment at the crime scene. Howard Page and Hilyard Medlin, chief CID lab technician, destroyed fingerprints and palm prints. Ralph Turbyfill, another lab technician, used an apartment table lamp for lighting when Page photographed fingerprints. This accounted for numerous out-of-focus and generally poor-quality photographs. MP Mica saw MacDonald's billfold on the living room floor. Later someone moved the billfold to the top of a desk. Later still another person noticed the billfold was no longer on the desk. Investigators did not find fibers in the living room where Jeffrey claimed he struggled with the intruders.

Ten months passed before James Paulsen, one of the ambulance drivers, admitted, at an army investigatory hearing, to stealing the billfold. He stated that he stole the billfold at the time he drove MacDonald to Womack Hospital. A bottle of diet pills and two of Colette's rings also disappeared from the crime scene.

Before CID investigator William Ivory arrived at 544 Castle Drive, approximately eighteen MPs with dirt and grass on their shoes had been inside the apartment. Ivory, twenty-six, who had only assisted in one murder investigation, studied the crime scene. A plastic flowerpot in the living room was upright while the dirt and the plant from the pot were on the floor. The flowerpot was originally on top of a coffee table, which apparently was knocked over when MacDonald struggled with the intruders. Although the table was top-heavy, it was not lying on its heavy face—it was on its side. Magazines, which were reported to be on top of the table before it was knocked over, were neatly positioned on the floor, inconsistent with a struggle. A throw rug located between the living room and dining room was not rumpled—it lay undisturbed. Investigators found the baseball bat, ice pick, and knife used in the murders outside the back door.

Ivory was convinced MacDonald became furious after Kristen wet the bed. He concluded that Jeffrey fought with Colette about the bedwetting, and in a fit of rage, he killed Colette and Kimberly. Ivory found the March 1970 issue of *Esquire*, which had an article about the Tate–LaBianca murders committed by the Charles Manson crime family in August 1969, in the living room. He believed that after Jeffrey killed Colette and Kimberly and realized what he had done, he then killed Kristen to make the crime scene appear as if the entire family had been victimized by mass murderers. He then wounded himself and later lied about the intruders. As early as 05:30, October 17, CID investigators, including CID Chief Franz Joseph Grebner, agreed with Ivory that MacDonald was the perpetrator.

The army formally charged MacDonald with murder, but after an investigatory hearing on October 13, 1970, all charges against him were dismissed. Colette's family, initially supportive of Jeffrey, became increasingly suspicious about his actions and his behavior after he was exonerated.

The 1970 investigatory hearing was a military proceeding. He was tried in civilian court in 1979. MacDonald was convicted in 1979 of murdering his family. His appeals have been unsuccessful and he remains in prison (Nickell and Fischer 1999; Noguchi and DiMona 1985; Potter and Bost 1995; C. Wecht, Curriden, and B. Wecht 1993).

MARILYN SHEPPARD

On July 4, 1954, Marilyn Sheppard, wife of osteopath Dr. Sam Sheppard, was murdered in their home, which looked out on Lake Erie, in Bay Village, Ohio, a suburb near Cleveland. Marilyn, four months pregnant, had been struck thirty-five times with an object, primarily on the face and head. The night before, Sam, Marilyn, and close friends had been watching television when Sam received a call about a seriously ill patient. Sam left for several hours, returned home, and fell asleep on the downstairs couch. He claimed he awoke later because of Marilyn's screams, which came from the upstairs bedroom. Sam apparently entered the bedroom and saw someone standing near the bed. Then a second person struck him from behind and knocked him unconscious. When he regained consciousness, he saw Marilyn was dead. He heard a noise, realized the intruder was downstairs, and chased the intruder to the beach. During a struggle on the beach, the intruder again knocked Sam out. The house had been ransacked.

Dr. Samuel R. Gerber, coroner of Cuyahoga County, and the *Cleveland Press* both believed Sam killed Marilyn. No murder weapon was ever found, but Dr. Gerber stated a surgical instrument was the weapon. Although Sam had injuries, there was doubt that the injuries were genuine. There was belief the injuries, which included broken teeth, a swollen face, and a bruised spinal cord, were self-inflicted. Susan Hayes, a twenty-four-year-old medical technician who admitted she had been Sam's mistress for three years, was the prosecution's final witness. Sam was found guilty of murder and was sentenced on December 21, 1954, to life in prison. Three weeks later, his mother shot and killed herself. Days later, his father died from a bleeding ulcer.

After the trial, the Sheppard family, in 1955, hired Dr. Paul Kirk, a biochemist and criminologist, to study the blood distribution at the crime scene. Kirk used a model of the bedroom in his investigation. Sam's blood was Type A. Marilyn's was Type O. A large spot of human blood in the bedroom was neither Type A nor Type O. This indicated a third person had been in the bedroom. Kirk believed this person, the intruder and killer, struggled with and was injured by Marilyn. There was one place in the bedroom where there was no blood on the wall. This was where the killer had been standing, the killer's body blocking the splatter, preventing it from reaching the wall.

By studying the blood on the wall in relation to Marilyn's position in the bed and where the killer had been standing, Kirk determined two things: which blood on the wall spurted from Marilyn's head as she was struck and which blood was castoff blood, blood projected from the killer's weapon as the killer repeatedly swung the weapon. Kirk also learned the killer was left-handed. Sheppard was right-handed.

There was no blood on Sam's clothing, except a small smudge on the left leg of his pants. He apparently got the smudge when he leaned over Marilyn's body to check her pulse.

When Marilyn was found, her legs were spread apart, her breasts were exposed, her pajama top was pulled up, and her pajama bottoms were pulled down. Her pajama bottoms, which had been pulled down before she was attacked, had relatively little blood on them. Most of the blood was at the bottom of her legs. It appeared to Kirk that Marilyn's death involved a sexual attack. There was nothing to indicate Sam would rape Marilyn.

There were over forty drops of blood in the blood trail that led out of the house. According to Kirk, the blood trail was from the killer's wound, not from the murder weapon allegedly carried by Sam as he left the bedroom, went downstairs, and went outside. Kirk believed the murder weapon could not retain enough blood to create the blood trail. Kirk also believed a cylindrical object, not a surgical instrument, was the murder weapon.

F. Lee Bailey was Sam's attorney at Sam's second trial, eleven years after the first one. At the second trial, Paul Kirk testified that Sam was not guilty. The U.S. Supreme Court overturned Sam's conviction in

1966. Sam died on April 6, 1970, at the age of forty-six, after experiencing personal and health problems that included alcohol and drug abuse. An overdose of pills was the cause of death.

Years after the Sheppard house was demolished, carpenters in Cleveland used photographs of the house to construct parts of the interior in a warehouse. The reason for this was to have a setting virtually identical to the crime scene, in which forensic experts could reenact the murder.

Dr. Michael Sobel of the University of Pittsburgh used a 1950s flashlight to strike a model of Marilyn Sheppard's head multiple times in an attempt to reproduce her fatal wounds. Dr. Cyril Wecht, the medical examiner of Pittsburgh, viewed photographs of the calvarium, the top of the skull. In Wecht's opinion, a blunt force instrument, such as a 1950s flashlight, would produce the type of fracture evident in Marilyn's skull. Wecht agreed with Kirk's observations that Marilyn had been sexually attacked.

Bart Epstein, a student of Kirk's during the 1960s, used his own blood and a special helmet to reenact Marilyn's murder. The blood splatter Epstein produced was remarkably similar in size, spacing, and height to the splatter produced by Kirk.

In 1954, Richard Eberling had a window-washing business in Bay Village. The Sheppards were among his customers. One of Marilyn's rings was in his possession when he was arrested for larceny five years after her murder. He told police during questioning he had cut himself and had bled while working inside the Sheppard's home a few days before Marilyn was killed. Eberling received a life sentence for an unrelated murder and purportedly bragged to other inmates that he had murdered Marilyn.

Dr. Mohammad Tahir, a DNA forensic expert in Indianapolis, Indiana, studied DNA from the crime scene, including Marilyn's hair, Eberling's blood, and later Sam's exhumed body. DNA evidence indicated a third person had to be in the house when the murder was committed because the blood trail in the house could not be attributed to Marilyn or to Sam. Eberling, who could not be excluded as the third person, died from heart failure in 1998, in prison.

Sam Reese Sheppard, the son of Sam and Marilyn, was seven years old when Marilyn was murdered. He spent his adult life attempting to prove that his father did not kill Marilyn. Sheppard, Jr., using the wrongful imprisonment statute, sued the state of Ohio for $2 million, claiming his father was wrongfully imprisoned, but lost the case in 2000 (Bailey and Aronson 1971; Cooper 1973; "The Killer's" 2001).

CHARLES STUART

A sociopath knows the difference between right and wrong, but easily does the wrong thing without remorse because he or she tries to profit from the wrong thing. It is very difficult for most people with a conscience to commit a murder and avoid being caught. A sociopath does not have a conscience. This person murders someone, seeing the murder as a necessary step in a game plan.

A sociopath maintains an extremely convincing façade of normalcy and conformity, always doing the expected thing. Other people easily praise, admire, and respect this type of individual. Yet, a sociopath does not exhibit genuine kindness or compassion. Everything and everyone, including the sociopath's family, is expendable. The sociopath is self-centered, manipulative, and deceitful.

On October 23, 1989, Charles Stuart and his pregnant wife Carol were shot in their car in Boston, Massachusetts, after attending a birthing class at a hospital. Carol, a lawyer, was shot in the head and died. Charles, a fur store manager, was critically wounded, then treated at Boston City Hospital. Charles had used his car phone to call the state police to say a black man was the shooter.

Charles's eulogy to Carol was read at her funeral on October 28 because he was too ill to attend. Columnists, talk show hosts, and politicians praised Charles for weeks as a decent, law-abiding husband and innocent victim. On January 1, 1990, however, Matthew, one of Charles's brothers, told family members who were not already aware of what he was going to say that Charles was directly involved in Carol's death. Matthew knew this because in early October Charles asked Michael, another brother, and friend David MacLean to kill Carol. Matthew told the family that he was going to tell authorities on January 3 about Charles's involvement.

On January 4, 1990, Charles jumped to his death off the Tobin Bridge. A note in which he allegedly stated that he could not stand the allegations made against him was found on the seat of his car, which he had parked on the bridge. He did not confess to the murders. Later it became apparent there was no black perpetrator. Charles was the perpetrator. The mood in Boston changed to anger and bewilderment.

It became clear that from the time Charles was out of high school, his life was a series of lies. Outwardly, he exuded success, but he was not successful. He lied about his education when he was hired by the fur store. He did not attend Brown University, but did spend two months at Salem State College.

Charles loved Carol for what she did for him. She helped him move up to middle-class society and up the social ladder. She became expendable because she was pregnant and intended to stop working. Parenthood would interfere with Charles's dream of becoming a wealthy restaurateur.

He committed suicide after he stopped receiving attention and sympathy from family, friends, and the public, something a sociopath craves. Charles could not stand a long prison term and public humiliation (Englade 1990; Fox and Levin 1990).

GEORGE TREPAL

Forty-one-year-old Peggy Carr, a waitress in Alturas, Florida, became ill in October 1988. Chest pains, nausea, and hair loss were among the symptoms she experienced. Then two other members of her family became ill: her son, Duane Dubberly, seventeen, and her stepson, Travis Carr, sixteen. Their symptoms were similar to Peggy's symptoms.

Tests revealed that Peggy and her sons had been poisoned with thallium, a rare heavy metal. Thallium used to be used in rat poison. However, the Environmental Protection Agency (EPA) restricted the use of thallium in the early 1970s.

Peggy's husband, Pye, and other members of her family were also tested. Tiny amounts of thallium were found in these family members. Peggy, who went into a coma, died on March 3, 1989, after being taken off life support. Duane and Travis survived. The thallium was traced to bottles of Coca-Cola Classic in the Carr home.

Homicide investigator Ernie Mincey, who worked the case, could not find within the Carr family a motive to murder Peggy. Pye mentioned to Mincey a note typed on a Post-It and received by the Carrs five months before the illnesses began. The note gave the Carrs two weeks to forever leave Florida or they would all die. The note was not signed.

Mincey noticed the envelope was addressed to Pye in Bartow, Florida. This was the way to address a letter if it was to be delivered to someone who actually lived in Alturas and who had a home mailbox. Mincey believed someone who lived in Alturas wrote the note. A person who lived elsewhere would very likely not know this was the way to contact the Carrs at home.

Mincey interviewed George Trepal, forty-two, who with his wife Diana, forty-one, lived next door to the Carrs. George and Diana had moved next door to the Carrs in 1982. Mincey learned a number of things, including the fact that Peggy and Diana, two days before Peggy became ill, shouted at each other because Diana did not like the loud music played by the Carr kids. Mincey also learned that Trepal knew the Carrs had been threatened. Something about the way Trepal said this made Mincey suspicious. Besides, the threatening note was not public knowledge. Investigator Mincey ran a criminal record check on Trepal and learned that Trepal was an ex-convict who had been arrested in 1975. He served two-and-a-half years in Connecticut for being the chemist in a methamphetamine operation, for which thallium can be used in the manufacturing process.

Even in his previous prison term, Trepal had complained that the sound from radios was very loud. Trepal, who claimed to be a computer programmer and technical writer, and Diana, an orthopedic surgeon, both belonged to Mensa, an international organization whose members score in the top 2 percent of the general population on IQ tests. George and Diana spent most of their free time with members of the Polk County Mensa chapter. George and Diana participated annually in the Mensa Murder Weekend, in which participants met at a hotel to plot the perfect murder as a game.

Mincey enlisted the help of Susan Goreck, an expert in undercover work for the Polk County Sheriff's Department. Susan met George and Diana, in April 1989, at a murder weekend. Susan posed as "Sherry Guin" from Houston, Texas, who claimed she had run away from her abusive husband. Sherry spent considerable time with George because Diana worked long hours. George and Diana rented their house to their new "friend" Sherry in December 1989, because Diana had a new practice in Sebring, Florida.

Goreck and other investigators searched the house and garage. Laboratory tests revealed that a whitish crystalline substance found in the garage was thallium nitrate. Investigators searched the house in Sebring, and books on poison were among the items found.

A grand jury returned a fifteen-count indictment against Trepal. A trial jury, after six hours of deliberation, found Trepal guilty of first-degree murder. In 1991, he was found guilty of one count of murder and six counts of attempted murder, then sentenced to death. However, as of the summer of 2002, Trepal's death sentence had not been carried out. The Florida Supreme Court at that time was deciding whether or not he deserved a new trial because of questionable work allegedly performed by the FBI laboratory during Trepal's initial trial. Nonetheless, in this case Trepal's intellectual "superiority" had brought about his own downfall (Hallifax 2002; Hewitt and Grant 1991; "Kill" 2000).

KARLA FAYE TUCKER

Karla Faye Tucker's trip to death row began many years before 1998, when she died of lethal injection in a state prison in Huntsville, Texas. Her trip gained momentum when Shawn Jackson, a good friend of Karla's, began seeing a man by the name of Jerry Dean. Karla hated Jerry because in Karla's view, Jerry pretended to be something he was not: tough. Karla arrived home one day to find Jerry's Harley-Davidson in her living room and Jerry and Shawn having sex in Karla's bed. Karla threw Jerry out.

Another time, Jerry obtained photo albums belonging to Karla. He knew the albums meant a great deal to her. Jerry defaced some of the pictures, including a picture of Karla's mother, which he stabbed. The next day, without warning, Karla attacked Jerry, inflicting enough damage to send him to the hospital to have his eyes examined for glass fragments. After this incident, Jerry claimed he put out a contract to have Karla's face burned.

On Friday, June 10, 1983, Karla, twenty-three, and some of her friends began celebrating her sister Kari's birthday. There was sex, food, music, drugs, and alcohol. Danny Garrett, Karla's thirty-seven-year-old live-in boyfriend who wanted to get married (even though Karla was not interested in marriage), was working late that weekend as a bartender. When he arrived home, Karla and Jimmy Leibrant, a friend of Karla's who also had been at the birthday party, agreed with a suggestion Danny made. They should go to Jerry's apartment, steal his motorcycle parts, and scare him. There were in Karla's body, at this time, drugs and alcohol, including heroin, marijuana, Percodan, rum, tequila, and Valium.

Karla and Danny, using a key Karla found in Shawn's jeans pocket, entered Jerry's apartment. Karla and Jerry began struggling in the bedroom, where Jerry awoke when the intruders had walked into his apartment. Danny broke Jerry's neck with a hammer, then left to gather motorcycle parts.

Jerry was making a gurgling noise that was annoying Karla. She took a nearby pickaxe Jerry used in his work as a cable television installer and struck him in the back. The gurgling noise did not stop until Danny struck Jerry several more times in the back and chest. When Jerry was quiet, Karla realized someone else was in the bedroom.

Deborah Thornton, thirty-two, married with a son and stepdaughter, was underneath some sheets against a wall. Deborah had met Jerry earlier that day at a party and had returned with him to his apartment. Karla swung the pickaxe, grazing Deborah's shoulder. Jimmy walked in, saw what Karla was doing to Deborah, and fled. Danny returned to the bedroom, saw the two women struggling, and grabbed the pickaxe. He plunged it into Deborah's shoulder, kicked her in the head, pulled the pickaxe out, kicked her again, and plunged the pickaxe into her chest. Before Karla and Danny left the apartment, Jerry had been struck with the pickaxe twenty-eight times. Both Jerry and Deborah were dead. Each time Karla swung the pickaxe, she later told police, she had an orgasm.

Karla, the daughter of a prostitute, began using marijuana when she was eight years old and heroin at ten. Her mother, Carolyn Moore, urged her to become a prostitute, which she did at thirteen. In addition, at thirteen, Karla learned that Lawrence Tucker, a longshore man, was not her real father; a Greek fireman was her real father. At approximately eighteen, Karla married Steven Griffith; at twenty-one, she left him.

Karla and Danny boasted to Danny's brother, Doug, and Doug's wife, Kari, who was Karla's sister, about the murders. Karla and Danny wanted Doug and Kari to help them kill Jimmy because he knew too much about the murders. After several weeks of fear and tension, Doug contacted Detective Sergeant J. C. Mosier, an old friend and a member of the Houston Police Department. Karla and Danny were subsequently arrested.

Four months after Karla's arrest, she became a Christian. She wrote essays, made antidrug videos targeted at young people, and in 1996, married Dana Brown, a prison chaplain. Religious conversion is common in prison, but there was something special about Karla. She was now attractive, friendly, likeable, warm, and relaxed.

When she appealed her death sentence, she received support from all over the world. The detective who arrested her, former prosecutors, Pat Robertson of the Christian Coalition, and Bianca Jagger of Amnesty International supported her. Even Peggy Kurtz, the sister of Jerry Dean; Ronald Carlson, the brother of Deborah Thornton; the European Parliament; and Pope John Paul II advocated clemency for Karla. Karla received media exposure, which included interviews on *60 Minutes*, *Charles Grodin*, *The 700 Club*, and other programs.

However, in Texas, religious conversion has never constituted grounds for granting a pardon. Every person and organization that could have granted Karla a pardon denied that pardon. This included Texas Governor George W. Bush and the Texas Board of Pardons and Paroles.

Danny Garrett was also convicted, and he also received the death penalty. He died in prison of liver disease in 1993.

Minutes before Karla went to her death on February 3, 1998, she apologized to her victims and expressed love for her family. Karla was the first woman executed in Texas since 1863, and the second woman executed in the United States since 1976, when the death penalty was reinstated. Velma Barfield, a woman who poisoned her boyfriend with arsenic, was also executed on November 2, 1984, in North Carolina (Arrillaga 1998; Gwynne 1998; Hoppe 1998; Kuncl 1995; Lowry 1992; Lowry 1998; Pedersen 1998).

DANIELLE VAN DAM

It was around 23:00 on February 1, 2002, when Damon van Dam, thirty-six, put his seven-year-old daughter, Danielle, to bed at the family's home in Sabre Springs, a suburb of San Diego, California.

On February 2, Danielle's mother, Brenda van Dam, thirty-nine, dialed 911 at 09:39. She told the operator that Danielle went to bed around 23:00, and at approximately 09:39 she found that Danielle was missing from her bedroom. She added that she found the side door of the garage open.

The night Danielle went missing, an eyewitness alleged that Brenda, Danielle's mother, had danced suggestively with David Westerfield, a neighbor of the van Dam's, at Dad's Café and Steakhouse and that David left Dad's café and steakhouse before Brenda. She returned to her home at approximately 02:00 with four other men and women she met at the café and steakhouse.

On the morning of February 2, officers with dogs searched approximately 200 neighborhood homes and could not locate Danielle. Westerfield, a fifty-year-old divorced engineer, was not home when police earlier canvassed the neighborhood. Westerfield had left Sabre Springs on the morning of February 2 in his thirty-five-foot Southwind motor home, and had driven to the Imperial County desert for a weekend camping trip.

On the morning of February 4, David Westerfield took a sports jacket and some bedding to a dry cleaner. The clerk at the dry cleaners noticed that David was acting unusual. Later, on February 4, when police arrived at Westerfield's home, he gave the officers oral and written permission to search his house. The only contact Westerfield allegedly had with Danielle was when he bought Girl Guide cookies from her earlier that year.

The following day, February 5, San Diego police detectives, including detectives Johnny Keene and Maura Mekenas-Parga, returned with a search warrant and searched Westerfield's house, motor home, and sport utility vehicle. The detectives noticed that there was no comforter on Westerfield's bed in his bedroom, or on the bed in his motor home. A fingerprint expert found fingerprints on a cabinet next to the bed in the back of the motor home. The fingerprints belonged to Danielle. Genetic markers in a bloodstain on Westerfield's jacket and on a stain on the carpet of his home matched Danielle's genetic markers. Short, grayish-brown hair, consistent with the hair of the van Dam dog, was found in Westerfield's house and motor home. Loose fibers found in the motor home were consistent with the carpet fibers in Danielle's bedroom.

When detectives left Westerfield's residence, they took with them containers filled with potential evidence. They took Westerfield's sport utility vehicle and the motor home to a police impound. On February 26, as the investigation continued, Westerfield pleaded not guilty to murder, kidnapping, and child pornography charges. One day later, Karsten Heimburger, a milkman and volunteer searcher, found the body of a child under trees near Dehesa Road, not far from the town of El Cajon, twenty-five miles from Danielle's home. A necklace consistent with a necklace Danielle was wearing the night she disappeared, and an earring matching one belonging to Danielle, were found on the body. Although the body was unidentifiable at the crime scene, it was confirmed later by autopsy to be that of Danielle. The autopsy found that she had been sexually assaulted and murdered. Forensic entomologists, testifying for the prosecution and defense, discussed insect life cycles to establish a window of opportunity for Westerfield to be at the location where Karsten Heimburger discovered Danielle's body.

Based on prosecution arguments including that given by entomologists, the defense lost its case and a San Diego Superior Court jury recommended that Westerfield receive the death penalty. He was sentenced to death on January 3, 2003 ("DA" 2002; Figueroa and Reno 2002; Hughes 2002; Judge 2003; Ryan 2002; "The Trial" 2002).

WAH MEE CLUB

The Wah Mee Club was a cocktail lounge in the Chinatown International District, not far from the Kingdome, in Seattle, Washington. The Wah Mee later became a private gambling club that had steel doors. At 12:30 on the morning of February 19, 1983, three immigrants from Hong Kong entered the Wah Mee through the alley entrance. The immigrants, young men in their twenties, were Benjamin "Bennie" K. Ng, Kwan Fai "Willie" Mak, and Wai-Chiu "Tony" Ng. Thirteen men and one woman, Jean Mar, were in the club. Patrons were playing a Chinese game called "paykyo." The two Ngs (not related) and Mak used nylon rope to hog-tie every person in the club, then with two small-caliber handguns shot them in the head. Before the shooters fled with $10,000 they found on the premises, they fired thirty-two rounds into the victims. One victim, Wai Chin, an elderly man, was able to free his hands and managed to crawl outside to safety. A passerby notified police, who found twelve individuals lying dead on the linoleum floor. One person later died in hospital. After medical treatment, the lone survivor, Wai Chin, identified two of the perpetrators. Later, other police sources identified the third perpetrator.

Benjamin Ng could not explain to detectives why there was more than $10,000 in cash, two handguns, ammunition, and a rifle in his girlfriend's apartment. Wai Chin testified against the Ngs and Mak.

Benjamin Ng was sent to prison for life with no chance of parole. Wai-Chiu Ng received seven consecutive life terms. Kwan Mak was sentenced to death. However, in April 2002, Mak's sentence was changed to life in prison without parole (Carter 1999; "Life Sentence" 2003; *Murder* 1991; "Unlucky 13" 1983).

JACK ANDERSON WILSON

Jack Anderson Wilson was born in Canton, Ohio, on either August 5, 1920, or August 5, 1924. Wilson grew up to become a six-foot-four-inch alcoholic who walked with a limp. He had a five-page rap sheet and three different social security numbers. Wilson used numerous aliases, including Jack A. Taylor, Eugene Deavilen, Grover Loving, and Arnold Smith. He was arrested in several states on various charges, including sexual offenses including sodomy. Wilson was arrested numerous times in Los Angeles, California. His first arrest there was on March 22, 1943. A few of his other arrests in Los Angeles were battery on July 26, 1948; burglary on June 12, 1950; and grand theft on February 21, 1951.

The significance of Jack Anderson Wilson as a criminal is that he may have been the killer of Elizabeth Short, who was murdered in Los Angeles in 1947. Short was known as the Black Dahlia because of her black hair and her black clothes. Although approximately fifty individuals confessed to murdering Short, Wilson, in the final analysis, may have been the most likely suspect.

Short, who was born in Hyde Park, Massachusetts, on July 29, 1924, was an aspiring starlet. She moved to Los Angeles in June 1940, at the age of fifteen. She was found dead in a dirt lot in the Leimert Park section at approximately 06:00, January 15, 1947, by a young woman pushing a stroller. Short had been cut in two at the waist and drained of blood. Her face and breasts had been slashed. There were rope marks on her wrists, neck, and ankles. It appeared her body had been washed.

Short met many people as she frequented cafés and nightclubs, often relying on people she met for a place to stay, for food, and for money before she moved on to do the same thing somewhere else in Los Angeles. This lifestyle resulted in her and Wilson's paths crossing. Wilson apparently knew Short had an incomplete vaginal canal and could not engage in normal intercourse.

Wilson fit the description of one of the robbers of a club called the Mocambo. This robbery may have been linked to powerful underworld figures. Short may have represented a threat to Wilson because of what he believed she knew about some of his activities. He may also have detested her because of her sexual inadequacies.

Short's murder resembled another recent homicide case. Georgette Bauerdorf, a Sunset Strip socialite, was murdered in her Hollywood bathtub months before Short's death. Bauerdorf and Short knew each other. Both were U.S.O. hostesses. Bauerdorf mentioned Short in her diary. The body of both victims at one point had been in a tub of water. Both victims had something stuffed into their throat or mouth, strangulating them or causing partial strangulation. Bauerdorf's car, stolen by her killer, was abandoned a short distance from East 31st, near Trinity, the location where Short was purportedly murdered. This was not far from 39th and Norton, where Short's body was subsequently dumped. Wilson, when he was younger, lived for a time with his mother near 31st and San Pedro. He apparently knew this part of the city.

Wilson was a suspect in both murders, but at the time there was insufficient evidence to charge him. In late 1981, Wilson, or Arnold Smith as he was known at the time, revealed to an informant details about the Short homicide that only the killer, police, or coroner could have known. Smith did this indirectly by saying the real killer was Al Morrison, a female impersonator. The informant and police, however, believed Jack Anderson Wilson, Arnold Smith, and Al Morrison were all the same person.

A few days before police were going to interview Wilson, he died in a fire in room 202 of the Holland Hotel, located at 7th and Columbus in downtown Los Angeles. Wilson's death was most likely an accident. During the four years he lived at the Holland Hotel, there were minor fires caused by his careless smoking.

The Elizabeth Short/Black Dahlia murder remains an open case ("The Black Dahlia" 2000; Blanche and Schreiber 1998; Gilmore 1998; Scott 1998).

"Four King-Twenty, 1-8-7 at 7-8-2-5 East Cherry Lane, clear."

Bibliography

Aaron, Roger W. "Gunshot Primer Residue: The Invisible Clue." *FBI Law Enforcement Bulletin* 60, no. 6 (June 1991): 19–22.

AbcNEWS.com. "Chandra Levy Timeline: Washington Intern Missing More than a Year, Found Dead." May 28, 2002, http://abcnews.go.com/sections/politics/DailyNews/levy_timeline.html (accessed September 27, 2002).

Academic American Encyclopedia, 1998, s.v. "diatom," "dum-dum," "dynamite," "evidence."

Adcock, Thomas Larry. *Precinct 19*. Garden City, N.Y.: Doubleday, 1984.

Adelson, Lester. "Homicidal Poisoning: A Dying Modality of Lethal Violence." *American Journal of Forensic Medicine and Pathology* 8, no. 3 (September 1987): 245–51.

Alberta Frequency List. 7th ed. New Westminster, B.C., Canada: J. and M. Communications, 1998.

Allen, Nancy H. *Homicide: Perspectives on Prevention*. New York: Human Sciences Press, 1980.

"America's Weapons of Choice." *Newsweek* 134, no. 8 (August 23, 1999): 36–37.

Anastasia, George. *The Goodfella Tapes*. New York: Avon Books, 1998.

Angell, Elizabeth. "Guns and Their Deadly Toll." *Newsweek* 134, no. 8 (August 23, 1999): 19–21.

Appleby, Lon. "Anatomy of a Homicide." *Toronto Life* 32, no. 1 (January 1998): 80–88.

Arrillaga, Pauline. "For Victim's Family, Execution Brought Satisfaction but No Forgiveness." *Corpus Christi Caller-Times Interactive*, Wednesday, February 4, 1998. www.caller2.com/texas/tex2333.html (accessed February 8, 2003).

Ashman, Chuck, and Pamela Trescott. *Diplomatic Crime: Drugs, Killings, Thefts, Rapes, Slavery, and Other Outrageous Crimes!* Washington, D.C.: Acropolis Books, 1987.

"Assault Rifles from Past Wars Flood the Field." (Toronto, Ontario) *National Post*, Monday, August 21, 2000.

Avila, Oscar. "Tylenol Murders Linger in Shadows: After 20 Years, Case Is Dormant but Not Forgotten." *Chicagotribune.com*, Sunday, September 29, 2002. www.chicagotribune.com/news (accessed February 19, 2003).

Axthelm, Pete, and Ann McDaniel. "Crying amid the Carnage." *Newsweek* 103, no. 18 (April 30, 1984): 24.

B and B's Removal Supplies and Body Bags. 1998. www.bnbmfg.com/html/removal equipment.html (accessed May 26, 1999).

Baden, Michael M., and Judith Adler Hennessee. *Unnatural Death: Confessions of a Medical Examiner*. New York: Random House, 1989.

Bai, Matt. "Cold Case Confidential." *Newsweek* 131, no. 2 (January 12, 1998): 70.

Bailey, F. Lee, and Harvey Aronson. *The Defense Never Rests*. New York: Penguin Books, 1971.

Bardsley, Marilyn. "Paul Bernardo and Karla Homolka." *Crimelibrary.com*. www.crimelibrary.com/serials/bernardo (accessed April 20, 2002).

Barkas, J. L. *Victims*. New York: Charles Scribner's Sons, 1978.

Barrett, Cindy. "A Murderous Proposition." *Maclean's* 98, no. 17 (April 29, 1985): 28.

Barrett, Sylvia. *The Arsenic Milkshake and Other Mysteries Solved by Forensic Science*. Toronto: Doubleday Canada, 1994.

Barthel, Joan J. *Love or Honor: The True Story of an Undercover Cop Who Fell in Love with a Mafia Boss's Daughter*. New York: William Morrow, 1989.

Bartley, Diane. "John Walsh: Fighting Back." *Saturday Evening Post* 262, no. 3 (April 1990): 44–47.

Beil, Laura. "Maggots and Murder: Six-Legged Sleuths Yield Crucial Clues at Scene of Crime." (Montreal) *Gazette*, final edition, Sunday, January 15, 1995.

Bellamy, Patrick. "Charles Ng: Cheating Death." *Crime Library*. www.crimelibrary.com/serial_killers/predators/ng/call_1.html (accessed February 23, 2003).

Bennett, Wayne W., and Kären M. Hess. *Criminal Investigation*. 6th ed. Belmont, Calif.: Wadsworth/Thomson Learning, 2001.

Berg, Bruce L., and John J. Horgan. *Criminal Investigation*. 3rd ed. New York: Glencoe/McGraw-Hill, 1998.

Berry-Dee, Christopher, and Robin Odell. *Lady Killer*. London: True Crime, 1992.

Bevel, Tom, and Ross M. Gardner. *Bloodstain Pattern Analysis: With an Introduction to Crime Scene Reconstruction*. Boca Raton, Fla.: CRC Press, 1997.

"The Black Dahlia." *Case Reopened*. TLC Television, August 24, 2000.

Blanche, Tony, and Brad Schreiber. *Death in Paradise: An Illustrated History of the Los Angeles County Department of Coroner*. Los Angeles: General Publishing Group, 1998.

"Blanket Commutation for All Illinois Death Sentences." *Star Online* (Toronto, Ontario), Sunday, January 12, 2003. http://thestar.com.my/services/printerfriendly.asp?file=2003/1/12/latest9613Blanketco.asp&sec=l atest (accessed February 7, 2003).

Blank-Reid, Cynthia. "Strangulation." *RN* 62, no. 2 (February 1999): 32–35.

Bloodspatter Analysis with Computers. July 20, 2000. www. physics.carleton. ca/carter (accessed November 27, 2000).

"Bodies of Evidence." *New Detectives.* Canadian Learning Television, October 13, 2000.

Boedy, Matthew. "Victims' Families Struggle with Reminder of Murders." *alligator.org*, Friday, August 25, 2000. www.alligator.org /edit/issues/00-fall/000825/b04rolling25.htm (accessed February 20, 2003).

Boei, William, and Daphnee Bramham. "Detective Goes Commercial." *Vancouver* (B.C.) *Sun*, final edition, Tuesday, June 11, 1996.

"The Bolles File." *Newsweek* 89, no. 5 (January 31, 1977): 32.

Borman, Stu. "Crime Specialists Tell Forensic Tales." *Chemical and Engineering News* 78, no. 14 (April 3, 2000): 43 and 46–47.

Bosco, Joseph. *A Problem of Evidence: How the Prosecution Freed O. J. Simpson.* New York: William Morrow, 1996.

Boyd, Robert M. "Buried Body Cases." *FBI Law Enforcement Bulletin* 48, no. 2 (February 1979): 1–7.

Boyle, James J. *Killer Cults.* New York: St. Martin's Paperbacks, 1995.

Brooks, Pierce R. *"...Officer Down, Code Three."* Northbrook, Ill.: MTI Teleprograms, 1975.

Brown, Chip. "The Accidental Martyr." *Esquire* 120, no. 6 (December 1993): 101–16.

Brown, G. I. *The Big Bang: A History of Explosives.* Stroud, UK: Sutton Publishing, 1998.

Bruno, Anthony. *The Ice Man: The True Story of a Cold-Blooded Killer.* New York: Dell Publishing, 1993.

Brunt, Martin. "Meet the Dando Murderer." *British GQ*, no. 131 (May 2000): 146–51.

Brussel, James A. *Casebook of a Crime Psychiatrist.* New York: Bernard Geis Associates, 1968.

Bryant, Vaughn M., Jr., and Dallas C. Mildenhall. "Forensic Palynology: A New Way to Catch Crooks." *Crime and Clues: The Art and Science of Criminal Investigation.* 1998–2000, www.crimeandclues.com/pollen.htm (accessed August 23, 2000).

Buchanan, Edna. *The Corpse Had a Familiar Face.* New York: Berkley Books, 1987.

"The Buddhist Monk Murders." *Medical Detectives.* TLC Television. Thursday, June 20, 2002.

"Buford Furrow Apologizes, Gets Life." *AsianWeek.com.* www.asianweek. com/20010406/news6bufordfurrowlife.html (accessed April 19, 2002).

Bugliosi, Vincent. *Outrage: The Five Reasons Why O. J. Simpson Got Away with Murder*. New York: W. W. Norton and Company, 1996.

Bugliosi, Vincent, and Curt Gentry. *Helter Skelter: The True Story of the Manson Murders*. Toronto: Bantam Books, 1974.

Bunn, Geoff. "Constructing the Suspect: A Brief History of the Lie Detector." *Borderlines* no. 40 (April 1996): 5–9.

Burnside, Scott. "Dial 'M' . . . for Murder: When Big Crimes Hit Kansas, It's the Metro Squad That Gets the Call—A Team of Supercops. Ontario Will Soon Have Its Own Team." *Toronto* (Ontario) *Sun*, final edition, Sunday, October 27, 1996.

Burzinski, John. "AFIS Technology at Your Fingertips." *Blue Line Magazine* 11, no. 3 (March 1999): 9–10.

Cairns, Alan. "Homolka Stays in: Parole Board Cites 'Psychopathy.'" *cnews*, Friday, March 9, 2001. www.argonauts.ca/CNEWSLaw0103/09_karla-sun.html (accessed February 8, 2003).

———. "Karla's Seeing Dollar Signs: Lawyer." *cnews*, Thursday, January 31, 2002. www.argonauts.ca/CNEWSLaw0201/31_karla-sun.html (accessed February 8, 2003).

"The California Killing Field." *American Justice*. A&E Television, Wednesday, September 20, 2000.

Came, Barry. "A Community in Fear: Gays in Montreal Live with Violence." *Maclean's* 106, no. 48 (November 29, 1993): 12.

Campbell, Peter. "Telling a Tragedy." *RCMP Quarterly* 52, no. 2 (Spring 1987): 12–15.

Cantalupo, Joseph, and Thomas C. Renner. *Body Mike: An Unsparing Expose by the Mafia Insider Who Turned on the Mob*. New York: Villard Books, 1990.

Carter, Mike. "Legal Quagmire Lets Wah Mee Killer Dodge Death Penalty." *Seattletimes.com*. February 19, 1999. http://archives.seattletimes.nwsource.com/ (accessed February 6, 2001).

"CaseInfo Product Information." *CI Technologies*. www.citechnologies.com/caseinfoproductinfo.htm (accessed March 11, 2001).

"CertiFINDER Uses News, Public Records to Help Locate Suspects." *Law Enforcement Technology* 26, no. 7 (July 1999): 88–92.

Chayko, G. M., and E. D. Gulliver, eds. *Forensic Evidence in Canada*. 2nd ed. Aurora, Ont., Canada: Canada Law Book, 1999.

Church, George J. "The Other Arms Race." *Time* (Canada) 133, no. 6 (February 6, 1989): 18–22 and 24–25.

Clark, Marcia, and Teresa Carpenter. *Without a Doubt*. New York: Viking, 1997.

Clarkson, Wensley. *Caged Heat*. New York: St. Martin's Paperbacks, 1998.

———. *Death at Every Stop*. New York: St. Martin's Press, 1997.

"Cold-Case Unit Cracks 27-Year-Old Murder." (Toronto, Ontario) *Globe and Mail*, Tuesday, March 30, 1999.

Collier's Encyclopedia, 1996, s.v. "dynamites."

Columbia Encyclopedia. 5th ed., 1993. s. v. "dum-dum."

Concise Science Dictionary. 3rd ed. Oxford: Oxford University Press, 1996.

Conlon, Edward. "The Pols, the Police, and the Gerry Curls." *American Spectator* 27, no. 11 (November 1994): 36–47.

Contenta, Sandro. "Autopsy Fails to Prove Murder; Kin of Police Officer in Trois-Rivières Reject Suicide Theory." *Toronto* (Ontario) *Star*, final edition, Tuesday, September 17, 1996.

Cooper, Paulette. *The Medical Detectives*. New York: David McKay Company, 1973.

Cormack, A. J. R. *The World Encyclopedia of Modern Guns*. London: Octopus Books, 1979.

Cornwell, John. *The Power to Harm: Mind, Medicine, and Murder on Trial*. New York: Viking, 1996.

Corwin, Miles. *The Killing Season: A Summer inside an LAPD Homicide Division*. New York: Fawcett Crest, 1997.

"The Cost of Cool Gear." *U.S. News & World Report* 126, no. 2 (January 18, 1999): 29.

Coulson, Danny O., and Elaine Shannon. *No Heroes: Inside the FBI's Secret Counter-Terror Force*. New York: Pocket Books, 1999.

Count, E. W. *Cop Talk: True Detective Stories from the NYPD*. New York: Pocket Books, 1994.

Cowger, James F. *Friction Ridge Skin: Comparison and Identification of Fingerprints*. New York: Elsevier, 1983.

Cox, Bill G. *Shop of Horrors*. New York: Pinnacle Books, 1998.

Cox, Yvonne. "Sentenced for Murder." *Maclean's* 101, no. 36 (August 29, 1988): 6.

"Crime Scene and Evidence Markers." *City Grafx*. 1998. www. citygrafx. com/police.html (accessed May 26, 1999).

Crimes and Punishment. Reference ed., vol. 6. New York: Marshall Cavendish, 1986.

Crimes and Punishment: The Illustrated Crime Encyclopedia, vol. 2, 1994, s.v. "forensic photography."

Crowley, Kieran. *Burned Alive*. New York: St. Martin's Paperbacks, 1999.

Cuomo, George. *A Couple of Cops: On the Street, in the Crime Lab*. New York: Random House, 1995.

Cyriax, Oliver. *Crime: An Encyclopedia*. London: Andre Deutsch, 1993.

"DA: 'We Believe Danielle van Dam's Body Has Been Found.'" *CNN.com/U.S.* February 28, 2002, www.cnn.com/2002/US/02/27/missing.girl/ (accessed September 27, 2002).

Dannen, Fredric. "The Nine Lives of 'Fat Cat.'" *Vanity Fair* 54, no. 4 (April 1991): 170–75 and 229–31.

Danto, Bruce L., John Bruhns, and Austin H. Kutscher, eds. *The Human Side of Homicide*. New York: Columbia University Press, 1982.

Darden, Christopher A., and Jess Walter. *In Contempt*. New York: Regan Books, 1996.

Darnton, Nina. "Street Crimes of Fashion." *Newsweek* 115, no. 10 (March 5, 1990): 58.

Davis, Don. *Bad Blood: The Shocking True Story behind the Menendez Killings*. New York: St. Martin's Paperbacks, 1994.

———. *Death Cruise*. New York: St. Martin's Paperbacks, 1996.

"Deadly Rampage." *Tampa Bay Online*. www.tampabayonline.net/reports/shooting/home.htm (accessed September 18, 1998).

Delsohn, Steve. *The Fire Inside: Firefighters Talk about Their Lives*. New York: HarperPaperbacks, 1996.

Demaris, Ovid. *The Last Mafioso: The Treacherous World of Jimmy Fratianno*. Toronto: Bantam Books, 1981.

"Denver's Talk-Show Murder." *Newsweek* 104, no. 1 (July 2, 1984): 26.

DePresca, John. "Handling Crime Scene Evidence." *Law and Order* 45, no. 8 (August 1997): 75–79.

DeSola, Ralph. *Crime Dictionary*. Rev. and expanded ed. New York: Facts on File, 1988.

Dietl, Bo, and Ken Gross. *One Tough Cop: The Bo Dietl Story*. New York: Pocket Books, 1988.

Dietz, Mary Lorenz. *Killing for Profit: The Social Organization of Felony Homicide*. Chicago: Nelson-Hall, 1983.

Dillmann, John. *Blood Warning*. New York: G. P. Putnam's Sons, 1989.

DiMaio, Vincent J. M. "Basic Principles in the Investigation of Homicides." *Pathology Annual* 19, no. 2 (1984): 149–64.

———. *Gunshot Wounds: Practical Aspects of Firearms, Ballistics, and Forensic Techniques*. 2nd ed. Boca Raton, Fla.: CRC Press, 1999.

Dingus, Anne. "Wise Blood: From One Stain, Dusty Hesskew Can Solve a Murder." *Texas Monthly* 22, no. 9 (September 1994): 84–88.

Douglas, John, and Mark Olshaker. *Mindhunter: Inside the FBI's Elite Serial Crime Unit*. New York: Scribner, 1995.

———. *Obsession: The FBI's Legendary Profiler Probes the Psyches of Killers, Rapists, and Stalkers, and Their Victims, and Tells How to Fight Back*. New York: Scribner, 1998.

Douglas, John E., et al. *Crime Classification Manual*. New York: Lexington Books, 1992.

Dowling, Donald C., and M. Yasar Iscan. "Scientific Evidence: A Vital Role in Homicide Cases." *Trial* 18, no. 9 (September 1982): 35–37 and 80.

Dunn, William. *Boot: An LAPD Officer's Rookie Year*. New York: William Morrow, 1996.

Dwyer, Jim, Peter Neufeld, and Barry Scheck. "When Justice Lets Us Down." *Newsweek* 135, no. 7 (February 14, 2000): 59.

Dynes, Wayne R., ed. *Encyclopedia of Homosexuality*. 2 vols. New York: Garland, 1990.

Eastham, Michael, and Ian McLeod. *The Seventh Shadow*. Los Angeles: Warwick, 1999.

Eckert, William G., ed. *Introduction to Forensic Sciences*. 2nd ed. Boca Raton, Fla.: CRC Press, 1997.

Eddy, Paul, Hugo Sabogal, and Sara Walden. *The Cocaine Wars*. Toronto: Bantam Books, 1988.

Edwards, Peter. *The Big Sting: The True Story of the Canadian Who Betrayed Colombia's Drug Barons*. Toronto: Key Porter Books, 1991.

———. *Blood Brothers: How Canada's Most Powerful Mafia Family Runs Its Business*. Toronto: Key Porter Books, 1990.

Ellroy, James. *My Dark Places: An L. A. Crime Memoir*. New York: Alfred A. Knopf, 1996.

Encyclopedia Americana, 1997. s.v. "homicide," "medical examiner."

Encyclopedia Americana, 2000. s.v. "bullet," "dynamite."

Englade, Ken. *Murder in Boston*. New York: St. Martin's Paperbacks, 1990.

Eppolito, Lou, and Bob Drury. *Mafia Cop*. New York: Simon and Schuster, 1992.

Evans, Colin. *The Casebook of Forensic Detection: How Science Solved 100 of the World's Most Baffling Cases*. New York: John Wiley and Sons, 1996.

"Evidence Packaging." *Evidence Collection and Protection, Inc.*, 1998. www.crime-scene.com/ecpi/packaging.html (accessed February 8, 2001).

"'Evil' Demeter Is Denied Day Parole." (Hamilton, Ontario) *Spectator*, final edition, Saturday, March 20, 1999.

"Fatal Compulsion." *New Detectives: Case Studies in Forensic Science*. ACCESS Television. Saturday, August 19, 2000.

"The FBI's Drugfire Program." *firearmsID.com*. 1996–2001. www.firearmsid.com/A_drugfire.htm (accessed May 6, 2001).

"Fewer American Officers Killed in the Line of Duty." *Blue Line Magazine* 12, no. 3 (March 2000): 35.

Fido, Martin, and Keith Skinner. *The Official Encyclopedia of Scotland Yard*. London: Virgin Books, 1999.

Figueroa, Ana, and Jamie Reno. "A Tragic Discovery." *Newsweek* 139, no. 10 (March 11, 2002): 42.

Fincher, Jack. "Lifting 'Latents' Is Now Very Much a High-Tech Matter." *Smithsonian* 20, no. 7 (October 1989): 201–2.

Findley, Don. "Ruger's 22 Auto: The First 50 Years." *Gun Digest* 52 (1998): 145–51.

Fisher, Barry A. J. *Techniques of Crime Scene Investigation*. 6th ed. Boca Raton, Fla.: CRC Press, 2000.

Fisher, David. *Hard Evidence: How Detectives Inside the FBI's Sci-Crime Lab Have Helped Solve America's Toughest Cases*. New York: Simon and Schuster, 1995.

Fitch, Richard D., and Edward A. Porter. *Accidental or Incendiary*. Springfield, Ill.: Charles C. Thomas, 1968.

Fletcher, Connie. *Pure Cop: Cop Talk from the Street to the Specialized Units—Bomb Squad, Arson, Hostage Negotiation, Prostitution, Major Accidents, Crime Scene.* New York: Villard Books, 1991.

"Florida High Court Rejects Rolling Appeal in Gainesville Slayings." *naplesnews.com,* Friday, June 28, 2002. www.naplesnews.com/02/06/florida/d788253a.htm (accessed February 23, 2003).

Flynn, Sean. "To Think Like a Killer." *Reader's Digest* (Canada) 150, no. 901 (May 1997): 67–71.

Fort Lauderdale Police Department. "Cold Case Investigations." http://ci.ftlaud.fl.us/police/cold.html (accessed February 8, 2003).

Fox, James Alan, and Jack Levin. "Inside the Mind of Charles Stuart." *Boston Magazine* 82, no. 4 (April 1990): 66–70.

France, David. *Bag of Toys.* New York: Kensington Publishing, 1999.

Frank, Christina. "Stalkers, Serial Killers, and Other Sociopaths: Dr. Park Dietz Explores the Dark Side of the Mind." *Biography* 4, no. 6 (June 2000): 82–85 and 112.

Frank, Gerold. *The Boston Strangler.* New York: New American Library, 1966.

Frank Bender. http://members.aol.com/bender (accessed September 3, 2000).

Fuhrman, Mark. *Murder in Brentwood.* New York: Zebra Books, 1997.

———. *Murder in Greenwich: Who Killed Martha Moxley?* New York: Cliff Street Books, 1998.

Gabriel, Trip. "Deadly Connection." *Vanity Fair* 54, no. 5 (May 1991): 108, 110, 112, 114, and 118.

Gado, Mark. "The Career Girl Murders." *COURTV.com.* www.crimelibrary.com/notorious_murders/not_guilty/career_girls/l.html?sect=14 (accessed February 8, 2003).

Gale Encyclopedia of Science, 1996. s.v. "sulfuric acid."

Gannon, Robert. "The Body Farm." *Popular Science* 251, no. 3 (September 1997): 76–82.

Gates, Daryl F., and Diane K. Shah. *Chief! My Life in the LAPD.* New York: Bantam Books, 1992.

Gaute, J. H. H., and Robin Odell. *The Murderers' Who's Who: Outstanding International Cases from the Literature of Murder in the Last 150 Years.* New York: Methuen, 1979.

Geberth, Vernon J. *Practical Homicide Investigation: Checklist and Field Guide.* Boca Raton, Fla.: CRC Press, 1997.

———. *Practical Homicide Investigation: Tactics, Procedures, and Forensic Techniques.* 3rd ed. Boca Raton, Fla.: CRC Press, 1996.

Gelb, Barbara. *On the Track of Murder: Behind the Scenes with a Homicide Commando Squad.* New York: Ballantine Books, 1975.

Giancana, Sam, and Chuck Giancana. *Double Cross: The Explosive, Inside Story of the Mobster Who Controlled America.* New York: Warner Books, 1992.

Gibson, Candace. "Death of the Autopsy." (Toronto, Ontario) *Globe and Mail*, Tuesday, October 6, 1998.

Gilmore, John. *Severed: The True Story of the Black Dahlia Murder*. Los Angeles: Amok Books, 1998.

"The Girls in 3-C." *Newsweek* 63, no. 18 (May 4, 1964): 24.

Gourevitch, Philip. "A Cold Case." *New Yorker* 75, no. 46 (February 14, 2000): 42–60.

Gralla, Preston. "Hollywood Confidential: PC Crime Fighters." *PC/Computing* 2, no. 1 (January 1989): 180–84, 186, and 188.

Gray, Kevin. "Panic in Detroit." *Details* 19, no. 5 (March 2001): 146–55.

Graysmith, Robert. *The Sleeping Lady: The Trailside Murders above the Golden Gate*. New York: Onyx, 1991.

———. *Zodiac*. New York: St. Martin's/Marek, 1986.

Greenman, Catherine. "A Well-Equipped Patrol Officer: Gun, Flashlight, Computer." *New York Times*, Thursday, January 21,1999.

Griffiths, Curt T., Brian Whitelaw, and Rick Parent. *Canadian Police Work*. Toronto: ITP Nelson, 1999.

Grolier Academic Encyclopedia, 1991. s.v. "murder."

Gugliotta, Guy, and Jeff Leen. *Kings of Cocaine: An Astonishing True Story of Murder, Money, and Corruption*. New York: Harper Paperbacks, 1989.

Gwynne, S. C. "Why So Many Want to Save Her." *Time* 151, no. 2 (January 19 1998): 56.

Haden-Guest, Anthony. "Crispo's Shadowy World." *New York* 18, no. 25 (June 24, 1985): 30–41.

Hall, Angus, ed. *The Crime Busters: The FBI, Scotland Yard, Interpol—The Story of Criminal Detection*. London: Verdict Press, 1976.

Hall, Neal. *The Deaths of Cindy James*. Toronto: McClelland & Stewart, 1991.

Hallifax, Jackie. "FBI Lab an Issue in Trepal Appeal in High Court." *naplesnews.com*, Thursday, August 29, 2002. www.bonitabanner.com/02/08/florida/d820146a.htm (accessed February 13, 2003).

———. "SCOFLA: Justices Hear Appeal in Chandler Case." *naplesnews.com*, Thursday, November 7, 2002. www.naplesnews.com/02/11/florida/d854274a.htm (accessed February 23, 2003).

Halliwell's Film Guide. Revised and updated edition. New York: Harper-Perennial, 1995.

Harrington, Joseph, and Robert Burger. *Justice Denied: The Ng Case, the Most Infamous and Expensive Murder Case in History*. New York: Plenum Trade, 1999.

Hawley, D. A., et al. "Identification of a Red 'Fiber': Chironomid Larvae." *Journal of Forensic Sciences* 34, no. 3 (May 1989): 617–21.

Hawley's Condensed Chemical Dictionary. 12th ed. New York: Van Nostrand Reinhold, 1993.

Helmer, William, and Rick Mattix. *Public Enemies: America's Criminal Past, 1919–1940*. New York: Facts on File, 1998.

Helpern, Milton, and Bernard Knight. *Autopsy: The Memoirs of Milton Helpern, the World's Greatest Medical Detective.* New York: St. Martin's Press, 1977.

Henderson, Bruce. *Trace Evidence: The Hunt for an Elusive Serial Killer.* New York: Scribner, 1998.

Herzog, Arthur. *The Woodchipper Murder.* New York: Zebra Books, 1990.

Hetzel, Richard L. "Luminol As an Investigative Tool." *Detective* (Fall 1990): 16–17.

Hewitt, Bill, and Meg Grant. "Mensa's George Trepal Was a Clever Plotter of Imaginary Murders, but His 'Perfect Crime' Was Fatally Flawed." *People Weekly* 35, no. 9 (March 11, 1991): 105–6, 108, 110, and 112.

Hiaasen, Carl, and Al Messerschmidt. "The Cocaine Wars." *Rolling Stone* (September 20, 1979): 82–85.

Hirschfeld, Neal. *Homicide Cop: The True Story of Carolann Natale.* New York: Berkley Books, 1982.

Hoffman, Andy. *Love Kills: The Stalking of Diane Newton King.* New York: Avon Books, 1994.

Hoffman, Martin. *The Gay World: Male Homosexuality and the Social Creation of Evil.* New York: Basic Books, 1968.

Hoffman, William, and Lake Headley. *Contract Killer: The Explosive Story of the Mafia's Most Notorious Hit Man Donald "Tony the Greek" Frankos.* New York: Thunder's Mouth Press, 1992.

Hogan, Steve, and Lee Hudson. *Completely Queer: The Gay and Lesbian Encyclopedia.* New York: Henry Holt and Company, 1998.

Holden, Ian G. "Homicidal Poisoning." *Medicine, Science, and the Law* 6, no. 1 (January 1966): 22–24.

Holmes, Ronald M., and Stephen T. Holmes. "Understanding Mass Murder: A Starting Point." *Federal Probation* 56, no. 1 (March 1992): 53–61.

"Homicide Investigation." *Mega Links in Criminal Justice.* November 17, 1999. www.faculty.ncwc.educ/toconnor/315/315lec10.htm (accessed November 19, 2000).

Hoppe, Christy. "Tucker Executed after Apologizing, Expressing Love." *Dallas Morning News*, Wednesday, February 4, 1998.

Hornyak, Tim. "Forensic Firm Aims to Be No. 1 with a Bullet." (Toronto, Ontario) *Globe and Mail*, Thursday, July 29, 1999.

Houde, John. *Crime Lab: A Guide for Nonscientists.* Ventura, Calif.: Calico Press, 1999.

Howard, Clark. *Zebra.* New York: Berkley Books, 1979.

Hughes, Joe. "Van Dam Investigators Seek Links to Past Crimes." *SignOnSanDiego.com.* February 20, 2002. http://oas.uniontrib.com/news/metro/danielle/20020220-9999_1mi20girl.html (accessed September 27, 2002).

"The Hunter Homicides." *Investigative Reports.* A&E Television, Tuesday, June 20, 2000.

Huntley, Sarah, et al. "Tragic, Violent Day." *Tampa Bay Online.* www.tampabayonline.net/reports/shooting/carrday1.htm (accessed September 18, 1998).

"Informational Hotline." *National Crime Information Center Newsletter* 24 (August 1991): 9.

Iserson, Kenneth V. *Death to Dust: What Happens to Dead Bodies?* Tucson, Ariz.: Galen Press, 1994.

Isikoff, Michael, Eleanor Clift, and Suzanne Smalley. "The Battle over Chandra." *Newsweek* 138, no. 4 (July 23, 2001): 20–24.

Jackman, Tom, and Troy Cole. *Rites of Burial.* New York: Pinnacle Books, 1992.

Jaffe, Frederick A. *A Guide to Pathological Evidence for Lawyers and Police Officers.* 3rd ed. Scarborough, Canada: Thomson Professional Publishing Canada, 1991.

James, Earl. *Catching Serial Killers.* Lansing, Mich.: International Forensic Services, 1991.

"Jane Doe #29." *L. A. Detectives.* A&E Television, Friday, June 23, 2000.

Joey, and, Dave Fisher. *Killer: Autobiography of a Mafia Hit Man.* Markham, Canada: Pocket Books, 1974.

Johnson, Donald E. "Forensic Anthropology." *Law and Order* 38, no. 10 (October 1990): 54–56.

Johnston, David. "Forensic Sleuth Probes '69 Case: Exhumed Remains of Cop to Be Examined Today." (Montreal) *Gazette*, final edition, Tuesday, August 27, 1996.

Jonas, George, and Barbara Amiel. *By Persons Unknown: The Strange Death of Christine Demeter.* Toronto: MacMillan of Canada, 1977.

Jones, Frank. *Paid to Kill: True Stories of Today's Contract Killers.* London: Headline, 1995.

Jonnes, Jill. *Hep-Cats, Narcs, and Pipe Dreams: A History of America's Romance with Illegal Drugs.* New York: Scribner, 1996.

"Judge Sentences van Dam Killer to Death." *CNN.com/Law Center*, Tuesday, January 7, 2003. www.cnn.com/2003/LAW/01/03/westerfield.sentencing (accessed February 14, 2003).

Junod, Tom. "One Too Many." *Esquire* 129, no. 6 (June 1998): 126–31 and 162–63.

Kane, Joseph Nathan, Steven Anzovin, and Janet Podell. *Famous First Facts.* 5th ed. New York: H. W. Wilson Company, 1997.

Katel, Peter. "The Trouble with Informants." *Newsweek* 125, no. 5 (January 30, 1995): 48.

Katz, Samuel M. "Felon Busters." *Popular Mechanics* 174, no. 5 (May 1997): 56–61.

KCPD Homicide Cold Cases. 1996–1998. www.kcpd.org/coldcase/index.htm (accessed March 25, 1999).

Keeney, Belea T., and Kathleen M. Heide. "The Latest on Serial Murderers." *Violence Update* 4, no. 3 (November 1993): 1–2, 4, and 10.

Kelleher, Michael D., and C. L. Kelleher. *Murder Most Rare: The Female Serial Killer*. Westport, Conn.: Praeger, 1998.

Keppel, Robert D., and William J. Birnes. *Signature Killers*. New York: Pocket Books, 1997.

Keppel, Robert D., and Joseph G. Weis. "Improving the Investigation of Violent Crime: The Homicide Investigation and Tracking System." *National Institute of Justice Research in Brief*. August 1993. NCJ141761.

Kessler, William F., and Paul B. Weston. *The Detection of Murder*. New York: Greenberg, 1953.

Kilian, Michael. "The Murdering Mind." *Chicago Tribune*, Friday, April 19, 1991.

"Kill Thy Neighbor." *American Justice*. A&E Television, Wednesday, June 21, 2000.

"The Killer's Trail." *Nova Online Television*. www.pbs.org/wqbh/nova/transcripts/2613sheppard.html (accessed March 4, 2001).

Kind, Stuart, and Michael Overman. *Science against Crime*. London: Aldus Books, 1972.

Kines, Lindsay. "Behind the Scenes with a Celebrity Cop: Mapping Evil: More Accepted by a Mystery Writer Than Some Vancouver Police Colleagues, Serial-Killer Profiler Kim Rossmo Has a Lot to Prove." *Vancouver* (B.C.) *Sun*, final edition, Saturday, June 19, 1999.

King, Gary C. *The Texas 7: A True Story of Murder and a Daring Escape*. New York: St. Martin's Paperbacks, 2001.

Koch, John. "Serial Killer Aileen Wuornos Executed." *upi.com*, Wednesday, October 9, 2002. www.upi.com/view.cfm?StoryID=20021009-104131-9199r (accessed February 22, 2003).

Kuncl, Tom. *Femmes Fatales: True Stories of the Most Vicious Women on Death Row*. London: True Crime, 1995.

Kunen, James S., and Stephen Sawicki. "Homicide No. 119." *People Weekly* 35, no. 1 (January 14, 1991): 42–47.

Kurland, Michael. *A Gallery of Rogues: Portraits in True Crime*. New York: Prentice-Hall General Reference, 1994.

———. *How to Solve a Murder: The Forensic Handbook*. New York: Macmillan, 1995.

Laird, Cheryl. "Stalking." *Houston Chronicle*, Sunday, May 17, 1992.

Landre, Rick, Mike Miller, and Dee Porter. *Gangs: A Handbook for Community Awareness*. New York: Facts on File, 1997.

Lane, Brian. *The Encyclopedia of Forensic Science*. London: Headline Book Publishing, 1992.

Lange, Tom, Philip Vannatter, and Dan E. Moldea. *Evidence Dismissed: The Inside Story of the Police Investigation of O.J. Simpson*. New York: Pocket Books, 1997.

Lardner, James. *Crusader: The Hell-Raising Police Career of Detective David Durk*. New York: Random House, 1996.

Larson, Erik. *Lethal Passage: How the Travels of a Single Handgun Expose the Roots of America's Gun Crisis*. New York: Crown, 1994.

Lasseter, Don. *Going Postal*. New York: Pinnacle Books, 1997.

Law Enforcement Equipment Company. 1998. www.leeco.com/page057.html (accessed May 26, 1999).

Lawrence, Neil, et al. *Tribute: A Day on the Beat with America's Finest*. New York: n.p., 1989.

Leo, John. "The Coming Shootout over Guns." *U. S. News and World Report* 114, no. 3 (January 25, 1993): 27.

Levesque, Nicolas. "CPIC Renewal Project to Modernize Police Information." *Blue Line Magazine* 12, no. 4 (April 2000): 14.

Levin, Jack, and James Alan Fox. *Mass Murder: America's Growing Menace*. New York: Berkley Books, 1991.

Levin, Jack, and Jack McDevitt. *Hate Crimes: The Rising Tide of Bigotry and Bloodshed*. New York: Plenum Press, 1993.

Levine, Lowell J. "Bite Mark Evidence." *Dental Clinics of North America* 21, no. 1 (January 1977): 145–58.

"Levy Suspect's Friends Questioned." *Calgary* (Alberta) *Herald*, final edition, Friday, October 4, 2002.

"Life Sentence for Parrott's Rapist-Killer."(Hamilton, Ontario) *Spectator*, final edition, April 14, 1999.

"Life Sentence without Parole for Chinatown Massacre Gunman." *NWCN.com*.www.nwcn.com/topstory/NW_042902WABmak.3a51f621.html (accessed February 14, 2003).

Linedecker, Clifford L. *O. J. A to Z: The Complete Handbook to the Trial of the Century*. New York: St. Martin's Griffin, 1995.

Lloyd, Joan E., and Edwin B. Herman. *Lights and Siren*. New York: Ivy Books, 1996.

Lowry, Beverly. *Crossed Over: The True Story of the Houston Pickax Murders*. New York: Warner Books, 1992.

———. "The Good Bad Girl." *New Yorker* 73, no. 46 (February 9, 1998): 60–69.

Ludes, B., et al. "Continuous River Monitoring of the Diatoms in the Diagnosis of Drowning." *Journal of Forensic Sciences* 41, no. 3 (May 1996): 425–28.

"Luminol." *ScienceWeb: The Science of Law and Order*. www.scienceweb.org (accessed July 22, 1998).

Luntz, Lester L., and Phyllis Luntz. "A Case in Forensic Odontology: A Bite-Mark in a Multiple Homicide." *Oral Surgery, Oral Medicine, Oral Pathology* 36, no. 1 (July 1973): 72–78.

Lyford, George, and Udy Wood, Jr. "National Crime Information Center: Your Silent Partner." *FBI Law Enforcement Bulletin* 52, no. 3 (March 1983): 10–15.

Lytle, L. T., and D. C. Hedgecock. "Chemiluminescence in the Visualization of Forensic Bloodstains." *Journal of Forensic Sciences* 23, no. 3 (July 1978): 550–62.

Maas, Peter. *Serpico*. New York: The Viking Press, 1973.

———. *Underboss: Sammy the Bull Gravano's Story of Life in the Mafia*. New York: HarperPaperbacks, 1997.

———. *The Valachi Papers*. New York: G. P. Putnam's Sons, 1968.

MacDonell, Herbert Leon, and Brian A. Brooks. "Detection and Significance of Blood in Firearms." *Legal Medicine Annual* (1977): 185–99.

Macko, Steve. "Man Kills Three Police Officers near Tampa." *EmergencyNet News Service*. May 20, 1998. www.emergency.com/flcopsht.htm (accessed January 26, 2000).

Mallion, Lou. "Crime-Scene Photography." *S.W.A.T.* 12, no. 7 (November 1993): 68–73.

Maple, Jack, and Chris Mitchell. *The Crime Fighter: Putting the Bad Guys out of Business*. New York: Doubleday, 1999.

Marriner, Brian. *On Death's Bloody Trail: Murder and the Art of Forensic Science*. New York: St. Martin's Press, 1991.

Martz, Larry, et al. "A Tide of Drug Killing." *Newsweek* 113, no. 3 (January 16, 1989): 44–45.

Mason, J. K. *Forensic Medicine for Lawyers*. 2nd ed. London: Butterworths, 1983.

McArdle, Phil, and Karen McArdle. *Fatal Fascination: Where Fact Meets Fiction in Police Work*. Boston: Houghton Mifflin, 1988.

McCormick, Anita Louise. *Shortwave Radio Listening for Beginners*. Blue Ridge Summit, Pa.: TAB Books, 1993.

McKenna, Thomas, and William Harrington. *Manhattan North Homicide*. New York: St. Martin's Paperbacks, 1996.

McKeown, Pat. "Bugs and Bodies or the Entomological Sleuth." *Rotunda* 23, no. 4 (Spring 1991): 12–19.

McLay, W. D. S. *Clinical Forensic Medicine*. London: Pinter Publications, 1990.

McQuillan, Alice. *They Call Them Grifters: The True Story of Sante and Kenneth Kimes*. New York: Onyx, 2000.

McQuillan, Blair. "Cadaver Dogs." *Blue Line Magazine* 10, no. 8 (October 1998): 14–15.

Medland, Mary. "Dentist Takes a Bite out of Murder." *Baltimore Business Journal* 8, no. 40 (March 11–17, 1991): 1 and 23.

Melanson, Philip. H. *The Robert F. Kennedy Assassination: New Revelations on the Conspiracy and Cover-Up, 1968–1991*. New York: Shapolsky Publishers, 1991.

"Menendez Brothers Get Life without Parole." *CNN Interactive U.S. News*. July 2, 1996. www.cnn.com/US/9607/02/menendez (accessed April 18, 2002).

Methvin, Eugene H. "The Face of Evil." *National Review* 47, no. 1 (January 23, 1995): 34, 36, 38, 40, and 42–44.

Michaud, Stephen D., and Roy Hazelwood. *The Evil That Men Do: FBI Profiler Roy Hazelwood's Journey into the Minds of Sexual Predators*. New York: St. Martin's Press, 1998.

Middleton, Michael L. *Cop: A True Story*. Chicago: Contemporary Books, 1994.

Miletich, John J. *Police, Firefighter, and Paramedic Stress: An Annotated Bibliography*. New York: Greenwood Press, 1990.

Millea, Holly. "Voyeurs, Guns, and Money." *Premiere* 12, no. 7 (March 1999): 62–69 and 100.

Miller, Brian, and Laud Humphreys. "Lifestyles and Violence: Homosexual Victims of Assault and Murder." *Qualitative Sociology* 3, no. 3 (Fall 1980): 169–85.

Miller, Hugh. *What the Corpse Revealed: Murder and the Science of Forensic Detection*. New York: St. Martin's Press, 1998.

Mims, Cedric. *When We Die*. London: Robinson Publishing, 1998.

"Missed Opportunities in the Bernardo Case." *National Magazine*. CBC Television, Thursday, July 11, 1996.

"Mobile Evidence Drying Station (MEDS)." Delta Latent Products, Inc. www.deltalatentproducts.com/evidence-handling.html#anchor 15812 (accessed February 7, 2001).

Monaco, Richard, and Lionel Bascom. *Rubouts: Mob Murders in America*. New York: Avon Books, 1991.

Moyer, Frank A. *Special Forces Foreign Weapons Handbook*. Boulder, Colo.: Paladin Press, 1983.

Muha, Laura. "She Finds What Killers Leave Behind." *Redbook* 190, no. 3 (January 1998): 94–99.

Mulgrew, Ian. *Who Killed Cindy James?* Toronto: McClelland-Bantam, 1991.

Murano, Vincent, and William Hoffer. *Cop Hunter*. New York: Pocket Books, 1990.

Murder and Mayhem: More Than 75 Case Histories of Heinous Crime. Lincolnwood, Ill.: Publications International, 1991.

"Murder in a College Town." *American Justice*. A&E Television, Wednesday, August 30, 2000.

"Murder or Suicide?" *Canada A.M.* CTV Television, Thursday, August 29, 1996.

"Murders and Attempted Murders—New York." In *New York Times Index 1972*. New York: The New York Times Company, 1973, 1351.

Murphy, James K. "The Polygraph Technique: Past and Present." *FBI Law Enforcement Bulletin* 49, no. 6 (June 1980): 1–5.

Murphy, Patrick V., and Thomas Plate. *Commissioner: A View from the Top of American Law Enforcement*. New York: Simon and Schuster, 1977.

Myers, Jim. "Notes on the Murder of Thirty of My Neighbors." *Atlantic Monthly* 285, no. 3 (March 2000): 72–76, 78–80, 82–84, and 86.

Napolis, Diana. "March 1991, *State Missouri v. Theron Reed Roland*, Court of Appeals of Missouri, Western District, No. WD 40883, 808, S.W. 2nd 885, State of Missouri, Respondent, First Degree Murder Conviction Affirmed." *Satanism and Ritual Abuse Archive*. 2000. www.newsmakingnews.com/karencuriojonesarchive.htm (accessed February 20, 2003).

"Narcotics Identification Kit (NIK)." Chief Supply. 1999–2001. www.chief-supply.com/narcoticstest.phtml#id (accessed February 8, 2001).

Nash, Jay Robert. *Murder, America: Homicide in the United States from the Revolution to the Present*. New York: Simon and Schuster, 1980.

"National Crime Information Center 2000 (NCIC 2000)." Press release, FBI Press Room. July 15, 1999. www.fbi.gov/pressrm/pressrel/pressrel99/ncic2000.htm (accessed February 6, 2001).

"NCIC Celebrates Twentieth Anniversary." *National Crime Information Center Newsletter* 87, no. 1: 1 and 4–5.

"NCIC Information." *National Crime Information Center Newsletter* 24 (August 1991): 7.

Ness, Eliot, and Oscar Fraley. *The Untouchables*. New York: Julian Messner, 1957.

"New Database Helps Crack a Murder Case." *Canada A.M.* CTV Television, Friday, August 2, 1996.

New Encyclopedia Britannica Micropaedia, 1997. s.v. "circumstantial evidence," "evidence."

New York Times Index, Annual Cumulative Volume, La-Z. New York: New York Times, 1938. Reprint ed., New York: R. R. Bowker, 1964.

New York Times Index 1972, vol. 60. New York: New York Times, 1973.

New York Times Index 1993, vol. 81. New York: New York Times, 1994.

Newland, Nancy A. "Line-of-Duty Death Policies: Preparing for the Worst." *FBI Law Enforcement Bulletin* 62, no. 11 (November 1993): 7–9.

Newton, Michael. *Armed and Dangerous: A Writer's Guide to Weapons*. Cincinnati, Ohio: Writer's Digest Books, 1990.

———. "Randy Steven Kraft." *CrimeLibrary.com*. www.crimelibrary.com/serial_killers/predators/kraft/1.html (accessed February 19, 2003).

———. *Rope: The Twisted Life and Crimes of Harvey Glatman*. New York: Pocket Books, 1998.

Nice, Richard, ed. *Dictionary of Criminology*. New York: Philosophical Library, 1965.

Nickel, Steven. *Torso: Eliot Ness and the Hunt for the Mad Butcher of Kingsbury Run. A True Story*. New York: Avon Books, 1990.

Nickell, Joe, and John F. Fischer. *Crime Science: Methods of Forensic Detection*. Lexington: University Press of Kentucky, 1999.

Noguchi, Thomas T., and Joseph DiMona. *Coroner*. New York: Pocket Books, 1983.

———. *Coroner at Large*. New York: Pocket Books, 1985.

Norris, D. O., and J. H. Block. "Use of Fecal Material to Associate a Suspect with a Crime Scene: Report of Two Cases." *Journal of Forensic Sciences* 45, no. 1 (January 2000): 184–87.

O'Connor, T. "Investigation of the Violent Crime Exemplar." *MegaLinks in Criminal Justice*. 2002. http://faculty.ncwc.edu/toconnor/315/315lect10.htm (accessed February 23, 2003).

O'Halloran, Ronald L., and Park Elliott Dietz. "My Dear John Deere." *Harper's Magazine* 287, no. 1721 (October 1993): 25–26.

O'Hara, Charles E., and Gregory L. O'Hara. *Fundamentals of Criminal Investigation.* 6th ed. Springfield, Ill.: Charles C. Thomas, 1994.

O'Maley, Thomas M. *General Investigative Techniques.* Minneapolis, Minn.: West Publishing, 1994.

"One Clean Cop." *Fifth Estate.* CBC Television. January 16, 1996.

Orth, Maureen. *Vulgar Favors: Andrew Cunanan, Gianni Versace, and the Largest Failed Manhunt in U.S. History.* New York: Delacorte Press, 1999.

Owen, David. *Hidden Evidence: Forty True Crimes and How Forensic Science Helped Solve Them.* Buffalo, N.Y.: Firefly Books, 2000.

Owen, Irvin K. "What About Dumdums?" *FBI Law Enforcement Bulletin* 44, no. 4 (April 1975): 3–6.

Papa, Juliet. *Ladykiller.* New York: St. Martin's Paperbacks, 1995.

Parks, Bernard C., and Michele Kim. "Investigating Vehicular Homicide." *Police Chief* 57, no. 4 (April 2000): 184 and 186.

Paulson, Al. "Modern Silenced 22s . . . Legally Possible for Most of Us." *Gun Digest* 47 (1993): 46–55.

Pedersen, Daniel. "Praying for Time." *Newsweek* 131, no. 5 (February 2, 1998): 66–67.

Pence, Irene. *Triangle.* New York: Pinnacle Books, 1998.

Perper, Joshua A., and Cyril H. Wecht, eds. *Microscopic Diagnosis in Forensic Pathology.* Springfield, Ill.: Charles C. Thomas, 1980.

Peters, Warren. "Are 22 Pocket Pistols Practical?" *Gun Digest* 53 (1999): 146–49.

Petraco, Nicholas. "Trace Evidence: The Invisible Witness." *Journal of Forensic Sciences* 31, no. 1 (January 1986): 321–28.

Philbin, Tom. *Cop Speak: The Lingo of Law Enforcement and Crime.* New York: John Wiley and Sons, 1996.

Phillips, Steven. *No Heroes No Villains: The Story of a Murder Trial.* New York: Random House, 1977.

"Picture Gallery: Barry George." *BBC News.* July 2, 2001. http://news.bbc.co.uk/english/UK/newsid 1419000/1419278.stm (accessed April 22, 2002).

Pileggi, Nicholas. *Casino: Love and Honor in Las Vegas.* New York: Simon and Schuster, 1995.

Pistone, Joseph D., and Richard Woodley. *Donnie Brasco: My Undercover Life in the Mafia.* New York: New American Library, 1987.

Police Jargon Glossary. www.fc.peachnet.edu/ci/IDIS1100/jargon.htm (accessed July 9, 2000).

"Police Meet to Discuss Protection from AIDS." *Police Stress* 8 (Winter 1987): 22.

Polson, Cyril John, D. J. Gee, and Bernard Knight. *The Essentials of Forensic Medicine.* 4th ed. Oxford: Pergamon Press, 1985.

"Polygraph Flawed in Chandra Levy Probe?" *CNN.com/U.S.* September 29, 2002, www.cnn.com/2002/US/South/09/29/levy.investigation.reut/index.html (accessed September 29, 2002).

Pooley, Eric. "Getting Away with Murder." *New York* 25, no. 38 (September 28, 1992): 26–33.

Posner, Gerald. "Who Is the Real Boston Strangler?" *Talk* 2, no. 2 (October 2000): 112–19, and 160–63.

Poss, Joe, and Henry R. Schlesinger. *Brooklyn Bounce: The True-Life Adventures of a Good Cop in a Bad Precinct.* New York: Avon Books, 1994.

Potter, Jerry Allen, and Fred Bost. *Fatal Justice: Reinvestigating the MacDonald Murders.* New York: W. W. Norton & Company, 1995.

Pron, Nick. "'Murder Inc.' Arrest Rate 92 Per Cent: Lessons to be Learned from Crack OPP Squad's Operations." *Toronto Star,* first edition, Wednesday, December 15, 1999.

Rachlin, Harvey. *The Making of a Cop.* New York: Pocket Books, 1991.

———. *The Making of a Detective.* New York: W. W. Norton and Company, 1995.

Ragle, Larry. *Crime Scene.* New York. Avon Books, 1995.

Ramsay, Laura. "Cyber Path to Psychopaths: Clue-Finding Computer Bloodhound Is the Policeman's New Best Friend." (Toronto, Ontario) *Financial Post,* weekly edition, Saturday, July 5, 1997.

Randall, Brad. *Death Investigation: The Basics.* Tucson, Ariz.: Galen Press, 1997.

Rappleye, Charles, and Ed Becker. *All-American Mafioso: The Johnny Roselli Story.* New York: Doubleday, 1991.

Reavill, Gil. "Drugfellas." *Maxim* 4 (July 2000): 104–8, 110, and 113–14.

Redmond, Jimm. "Sudden Death." *Outdoor Life* 202, no. 1 (August 1998): 58–62, and 64.

Redsicker, David R., and John J. O'Connor. *Practical Fire and Arson Investigation.* 2nd ed. Boca Raton, Fla.: CRC Press, 1997.

Redsicker, David R., et al. *The Practical Methodology of Forensic Photography.* Boca Raton, Fla.: CRC Press, 1994.

Regini, Charles L. "The Cold Case Concept." *FBI Law Enforcement Bulletin* 66, no. 8 (August 1997): 1–6.

Ressler, Robert K. "The Violent Criminal Apprehension Program: A Progress Report." *Detective* (Spring–Summer 1986): 17–19.

Ressler, Robert K., and Tom Shachtman. *Whoever Fights Monsters.* New York: St. Martin's Paperbacks, 1992.

Rho, Yong-Myun. "Murder or Suicide?" *New York State Journal of Medicine* 78, no. 6 (May 1978): 965–67.

Richardson, Leo. "Notification of Death." *FBI Law Enforcement Bulletin* 44 no. 5 (May 1975): 14–15.

Roemer, William F., Jr. *The Enforcer: Spilotro, The Chicago Mob's Man over Las Vegas.* New York: Donald I. Fine, 1994.

Rosenthal, A. M. *Thirty-Eight Witnesses: The Kitty Genovese Case*. New York: McGraw-Hill, 1964.

Royte, Elizabeth. "'Let the Bones Talk' Is the Watchword for Scientist-Sleuths." *Smithsonian* 27, no. 2 (May 1996): 82–90.

Rubin, Sabrina. "Murder, He Sculpted." *Reader's Digest* (Canada) 152, no. 913 (May 1998): 62–67.

Rule, Ann. *The Stranger beside Me*. New York: W. W. Norton and Company, 1980.

Russell, Diana E. H. *Dangerous Relationships: Pornography, Misogyny, and Rape*. Thousand Oaks, Calif.: Sage Publications, 1998.

Ryan, Harriet. "Westerfield Convicted, Will Face Death." *COURTTV.com*. September 27, 2002, www.courttv.com/trials/westerfield/convict_ctv.html (accessed September 27, 2002).

Ryan, Patrick J. *Organized Crime: A Reference Handbook*. Santa Barbara, Calif.: ABC-CLIO, 1995.

Ryzuk, Mary S. *The Gainesville Ripper: A Summer's Madness, Five Young Victims—The Investigation, the Arrest, and the Trial*. New York: Donald I. Fine, 1994.

Sabbag, Robert. *Too Tough to Die: Down and Dangerous with the U. S. Marshals*. New York: Simon and Schuster, 1992.

Sabljak, Mark, and Martin H. Greenberg. *A Bloody Legacy: Chronicles of American Murder*. New York: Gramercy Books, 1992.

Sachs, Jessica Snyder. "Fake Smell of Death: Teaching Dogs to Sniff Out Corpses or Drugs or Bombs Has Traditionally Been More Craft Than Science." *Discover* 17, no. 3 (March 1996): 86–92, and 94.

Sachs, Steven L. *Street Gang Awareness: A Resource Guide for Parents and Professionals*. Minneapolis, Minn.: Fairview Press, 1997.

Saferstein, Richard. *Criminalistics: An Introduction to Forensic Science*. 7th ed. Upper Saddle River, N.J.: Prentice Hall, 2001.

Salholz, Eloise et al. "A Grisly Murder Mystery." *Newsweek* 121, no. 5 (February 1, 1993): 57.

Salottolo, A. Lawrence. *Modern Police Service Encyclopedia*. Rev. ed. New York: Arco Publishing, 1970.

Sanders, Ed. *The Family: The Story of Charles Manson's Dune Buggy Attack Battalion*. New York: Dutton, 1971.

Sasser, Charles. W. *At Large: The Life and Crimes of Randolph Franklin Dial*. New York: St. Martin's Paperbacks, 1998.

———. *Homicide!* New York: Pocket Books, 1990.

Sbranti, J. N. "Search Is on for Woman from Valley." *modbee.com*. May 11, 2001, www.modbee.com/reports/levy/story/1947121p-2098769c.html (accessed September 19, 2002).

Sbranti, J. N., and Michael Doyle. "Condit Still Has Valley's Trust." *modbee.com*. May 20, 2001, www.modbee.com/reports/levy/story/1947142p-2098780c.html (accessed September 19, 2002).

Scanlon, Robert A., ed. *Law Enforcement Bible*. South Hackensack, N.J.: Stoeger Publishing, 1978.

Schaffter, S. R. *LAPD Codes*. December 31, 1996.

———. *LAPD Crime Descriptors*. December 31, 1996.

———. *LAPD Unit Call Signs*. December 31, 1996.

Scheck, Barry, Peter Neufeld, and Jim Dwyer. *Actual Innocence: When Justice Goes Wrong and How to Make It Right*. New York: Signet, 2001.

Schultz, Donald O. *Criminal Investigation Techniques*. Houston: Gulf Publishing, 1978.

Schutze, Jim. *By Two and Two: The Scandalous Story of Twin Sisters Accused of a Shocking Crime of Passion*. New York: William Morrow, 1995.

Scott, Gini Graham. *Homicide: 100 Years of Murder in America*. Los Angeles: Lowell House, 1998.

Scroggie, Robert J. "Firearm Silencers." *FBI Law Enforcement Bulletin* 46, no. 5 (May 1977): 16–24.

Seedman, Albert A., and Peter Hellman. *Chief!* New York: Arthur Fields Books, 1974.

Seligmann, Jean, et al. "Slashes, Stabs, and Bruises." *Newsweek* 125, no. 22 (May 29, 1995): 70–71.

"Separatists Take Quebec but Might Go Slowly." *International* (Paris) *Herald Tribune*, Wednesday, September 14, 1994.

Sewell, James D. "The Stress of Homicide Investigations." *Death Studies* 18, no. 6 (November–December 1994): 565–82.

Shawcross, Tim. *The War against the Mafia*. New York: HarperPaperbacks, 1994.

Sherrill, Robert. *The Saturday Night Special*. New York: Charterhouse, 1973.

Shillington, Patty. "The Mind of the Stalker, the Terror of the Stalked." *Miami Herald*, Sunday, July 4, 1993.

Sifakis, Carl. *The Mafia Encyclopedia*. New York: Facts on File, 1987.

Sigma. "Sigma Product Information Sheet for Sigma Product Number A8511-Luminol." www.sial.com/sigma/proddata/a8511.htm (accessed September 15, 1998).

Sikes, Gini. *8-Ball Chicks: A Year in the Violent World of Girl Gangsters*. New York: Anchor Books, 1997.

Simon, David. *Homicide: A Year on the Killing Streets*. New York: Ivy Books, 1991.

Simpson, Keith, and Bernard Knight. *Forensic Medicine*. 9th ed. London: Edward Arnold, 1985.

Singular, Stephen. *Talked to Death: The Life and Murder of Alan Berg*. New York: Beech Tree Books, 1987.

"Skakel Lawyers File Appeal." *CBSNews.com*, September 18, 2002. www.cbsnews.com/stories/2002/05/31/national/main510652.shtml (accessed February 7, 2003).

"Skeletal Remains in Rock Creek Park Identified As Chandra Levy." *Metropolitan Police District of Columbia News Room.* May 22, 2002, www.mpdc. org/blue/news.asp?sid=1529 (accessed September 27, 2002).

Slack, Charles. "Vial Meets Vile: Trail of Bugs Solves Puzzles of Death." *Richmond* (Va.) *Times-Dispatch,* Sunday, March 29, 1992.

Smalley, Suzanne, Mark Hosenball, and Karen Breslau. "You've Just Got Bones." *Newsweek* 139, no. 22 (June 3, 2002): 28–29.

Smith, Carlton. *Killing Season: The Unsolved Case of New England's Deadliest Serial Killer.* New York: Onyx, 1994.

———. *Seeds of Evil.* New York: St. Martin's Paperbacks, 1997.

Smith & Wesson. www.smith-wesson.com (accessed August 23, 2000).

Smock, W. S. "Recognition of Pattern Injuries in Domestic Violence Victims." In *Encyclopedia of Forensic Sciences,* vol. 1, edited by Jay A. Siegel, Pekka J. Saukko, and Geoffrey C. Knupfer, 384–91. San Diego, Calif.: Academic Press, 2000.

Snyder, LeMoyne. *Homicide Investigation: Practical Information for Coroners, Police Officers, and Other Investigators.* Revised and expanded 9th printing. Springfield, Ill.: Charles C. Thomas, 1959.

"Software Puts a New 'Face' on Crime Fighting." *Blue Line Magazine* 12, no. 5 (May 2000): 22.

Staggs, Steven. *Crime Scene and Evidence Photographer's Guide.* Temecula, Calif.: Staggs Publishing, 1997.

Stedman's Medical Dictionary. 26th ed. Baltimore, Md.: Williams and Wilkins, 1995.

Stengal, Richard, Bernard Diederich, and Bruce van Voorst. "Weapon of Choice: Hoodlums Love the Mighty MAC." *Time* (Canada) 126, no. 10 (September 9, 1985): 40–41.

Stern, Chester. *Dr. Iain West's Casebook.* London: Little, Brown and Company, 1996.

Stewart, James B. "Death of a Partner." *New Yorker* 69, no. 18 (June 21, 1993): 54–62 and 64–71.

Stine, Scott Aaron. "The Snuff Film: The Making of an Urban Legend." *Skeptical Inquirer* 23, no. 3 (May–June 1999): 29–33.

Stone, Michael. "East Side Story." *New York* 19, no. 44 (November 10, 1986): 42–53.

Stratton, John G. "Police Stress and the Criminal Investigator." *Police Chief* 46, no. 2 (February 1979): 22–26.

Stroud, Carsten. *Close Pursuit: A Week in the Life of an NYPD Homicide Cop.* Markham, Ont., Canada: Viking, 1987.

Sullivan, Gerard, and Harvey Aronson. *High Hopes: The Amityville Murders.* New York: Coward, McCann and Geoghegan, 1981.

"Suspected Kidnapper of Adam Walsh in 81 Dies in Florida Prison." *Minneapolis Star Tribune,* September 25, 1996. http://ask.elibrary.com/login.

asp?c=&host=ask&2Eelibrary%2Ecom%script=%Fgetdoc%Easp&query=
p... (accessed February 7, 2003).

Svoray, Yaron, and Thomas Hughes. *Gods of Death: Around the World, Behind Closed Doors, Operates an Ultra-Secret Business of Sex and Death. One Man Hunts the Truth about Snuff Films.* New York: Simon and Schuster, 1997.

Sweetman, Timothy, and Adele Sweetman. *Investigating a Homicide.* Incline Village, Nev.: Copperhouse Publishing, 1997.

Symonds, William C., Lorraine Woellert, and Susan Garland. "No Surrender from Mr. Saturday Night Special." *Business Week*, no. 3642 (August 16, 1999): 67.

Tanner, Hans, ed. *Guns of the World.* New York: Bonanza Books, 1977.

"Technology Unlocks the Architecture of a Crime." *American City and County* 111, no. 9 (August 1996); 58.

Tedeschi, C. G., William G. Eckert, and Luke G. Tedeschi, eds. *Forensic Medicine: A Study in Trauma and Environmental Hazards*, vol. 2, *Physical Trauma.* Philadelphia: W. B. Saunders Company, 1977.

"They Finally Got Me." *Newsweek* 87, no. 24 (June 14, 1976): 83–84.

"This Street Vendor Had High-Caliber Goods." *Edmonton* (Alberta) *Journal*, Sunday, July 23, 2000.

Toobin, Jeffrey, and Arlene Croce. "Ganging Up on the Gangs." *New Yorker* 70, no. 32 (October 10, 1994): 43–44.

"The Trial of David Westerfield." *SignOnSanDiego.com.* September 27, 2002. www.signonsandiego.com/news/metro/danielle/index.html (accessed September. 27, 2002).

"The Trial of Peter Demeter." *Time* (Canada) 104, no. 25 (December 16, 1974): 9–10.

Tuck, Simon. "Inspector Gadgets." (Toronto, Ontario) *Globe and Mail*, Thursday, June 10, 1999.

"20 Years Later, Adam Walsh Still a Symbol for Missing Children." *naplesnews.com*, Monday, July 23, 2001. www.naplesnews.com/01/07/florida/d584691a.htm (accessed February 7, 2003).

Ubelaker, Douglas H. "Hyoid Fracture and Strangulation." *Journal of Forensic Sciences* 37, no. 5 (September 1992): 1216–22.

United States Department of Justice, Federal Bureau of Investigation. *Managing Death Investigation.* Washington, D.C.: U.S. Department of Justice, Federal Bureau of Investigation, 1997.

United States Department of Justice, Federal Bureau of Investigation, National Crime Information Center. *National Crime Information Center: The Investigative Tool: A Guide to the Use and Benefits of NCIC.* Washington, D.C.: U.S. Department of Justice, Federal Bureau of Investigation, National Crime Information Center, 1984.

United States Department of Justice, Office of Justice Programs, Bureau of Justice Statistics. *Implementing the National Incident-Based Reporting System:*

A Project Status Report. Washington, D.C.: U.S. Department of Justice, Office of Justice Programs, Bureau of Justice Statistics, 1997. NCJ165581.

"United States—Gun Culture." *Canada and the World Backgrounder* (September 1996): 23–25.

"Unlucky 13." *Time* (Canada) 121, no. 9 (February 28, 1983): 23.

Unsolved Homicide Files. www.unsolvedcrimes.com/files/ (accessed September 21, 2000).

Van Nostrand's Scientific Encyclopedia, 8th ed., 1995. s.v. "sulfuric acid."

Vanderbosch, Charles G. *Criminal Investigation.* Washington, D.C.: International Association of Chiefs of Police, 1968.

Vanezis, Peter, and Anthony Busuttil, eds. *Suspicious Death Scene Investigation.* London: Arnold, 1996.

Vorpagel, Russell, and Joseph Harrington. *Profiles in Murder: An FBI Legend Dissects Killers and Their Crimes.* New York: Plenum Trade, 1998.

Waddell, Bill. *The Black Museum: New Scotland Yard.* London: Little, Brown and Company, 1993.

Wagner, James, and Patrick Picciarelli. *Jimmy the Wags: Street Stories of a Private Eye.* New York: William Morrow, 1999.

Walker, Tom. *Fort Apache.* New York: Thomas Y. Crowell, 1976.

Wallance, Gregory. *Papa's Game.* New York: Rawson, Wade Publishers, 1981.

Walsh, F. M., et al. "Autoerotic Asphyxial Deaths: A Medicolegal Analysis of Forty-Three Cases." *Legal Medicine Annual* (1977): 157–82.

Walsh, John, and Susan Schindehette. *Tears of Rage.* New York: Pocket Books, 1997.

Webster, Jack, and Rosemary Aubert. *Copper Jack.* Toronto: Dundurn Press, 1991.

Wecht, Cyril, and Charles Bosworth, Jr. *Who Killed JonBenet Ramsey?* New York: Onyx, 1998.

Wecht, Cyril, Mark Curriden, and Benjamin Wecht. *Cause of Death.* New York: Onyx. 1993.

Wells, Gary L. *Eyewitness Identification: A System Handbook.* Toronto: Carswell, 1988.

Weston, Paul B., Charles Lushbaugh, and Kenneth M. Wells. *Criminal Investigation: Basic Perspectives.* 8th ed. Upper Saddle River, N.J.: Prentice Hall, 2000.

"White Supremacist Guilty of Assaulting Three FBI Agents." *New York Times,* Friday, February 22, 1985.

Wick, Steve. *Bad Company: Drugs, Hollywood, and the Cotton Club Murder.* New York: St. Martin's Paperbacks, 1990.

Wilkinson, Frederick. *The Illustrated Book of Pistols.* London: Optimum Books, 1979.

Williams, Dennis A., Andrew Jaffe, and Anthony Marro. "A Swim in the Bay." *Newsweek* 88, no. 8 (August 23, 1976): 38.

Williams, John A. "Death and Decomposition." Course Notes. September 1997, www.und.nodak.educ/instruct/moore/FORENSIC.htm (accessed June 14, 1999).

Williams, Stephen. *Invisible Darkness: The Horrifying Case of Paul Bernardo and Karla Homolka.* Toronto: Little, Brown and Company (Canada), 1996.

Williams, Willie L., and Bruce B. Henderson. *Taking Back Our Streets: Fighting Crime in America.* New York: Scribner, 1996.

Willing, Richard. "Phoenix Cleans Up Crime Scenes." *Detroit News,* Tuesday, November 2, 1999.

―――. "Increasing DNA Exonerations Contradict Predictions." *USA Today.* January 18, 2002, www.usatoday.com/news/healthscience/health/2002-01-18-dna.htm (accessed April 19, 2002).

Witkin, Gordon. "The Debate about Invisible Detectives." *U.S. News & World Report* 121, no. 11 (September 16, 1996): 58–59.

Witkin, Gordon, Linda L. Creighton, and Monika Guttman. "More Murder Mysteries." *U.S. News and World Report* 116, no. 14 (April 11, 1994): 28, and 30–34.

Wolfe, Linda. *Wasted: The Preppie Murder.* New York: Simon and Schuster, 1989.

Wolfgang, Marvin E., ed. *Studies in Homicide.* New York: Harper and Row, 1967.

World Book Encyclopedia, 1996. s.v. "diatom," "evidence."

World Book Encyclopedia, 1997. s.v. "medical examiner," "murder."

World Book Encyclopedia, 1998. s.v. "dynamite."

Wylie, Max. "And Have Not Love, I Am Nothing." *Ladies' Home Journal* 81, no. 2 (March 1964): 76–77, 104–7, and 110–13.

Zawitz, Marianne W. "Firearms, Crime, and Criminal Justice: Guns Used in Crime." *Bureau of Justice Statistics Bulletin* (July 1995): 1–7.

Zonderman, Jon. *Beyond the Crime Lab: The New Science of Investigation.* New York: Wiley Science Editions, 1990.

Index

About the Author

JOHN J. MILETICH, former librarian at the University of Alberta, is the author of reference publications in the social and health sciences. He is also the author of *Police, Firefighter, and Paramedic Stress: An Annotated Bibliography*. He is a graduate of the University of Alberta and the University of Western Ontario.